PROGRESSIVE FOREIGN POLICY

for the UK 2008

Centre for the Study of Global Governance
and ippr's International Programme

This book represents a collaboration between the Centre for the Study of Global Governance at the London School of Economics (LSE), and the Institute for Public Policy Research (ippr). Following on from an ippr/LSE conference held in July 2006 on the question of future foreign policy directions for the UK, this publication aims to generate some innovative thinking on the major foreign policy challenges facing the UK over the next ten years, to articulate a distinctively progressive view of foreign policy, and to outline some new policy ideas in specific areas.

The Centre for the Study of Global Governance is a leading international institution dedicated to research, analysis and dissemination about global governance. Based at the London School of Economics, the Centre aims to increase understanding and knowledge of global issues, to encourage interaction between academics, policy-makers, journalists and activists, and to propose solutions to critical global problems.

The Institute for Public Policy Research (ippr) is the UK's leading progressive think tank, producing cutting edge research and innovative policy ideas for a just, democratic and sustainable world. ippr's International Programme was created in July 2002. Its aim is to apply ippr's core values to some of the most pressing global issues and to formulate practical policy responses to them. The programme seeks to make a policy contribution in four broad areas: global security, poverty reduction and sustainable development, human rights, and national and global governance.

The Centre for the Study of Global Governance and ippr commissioned a number of chapters for this book and would like to thank all the authors for their contributions. The editors wish to acknowledge the financial support of the LSE Miliband Programme which made the conference and this book possible. They would also like to thank Alex Glennie (ippr) and Kevin Young (LSE) for their editorial and research assistance.

PROGRESSIVE FOREIGN POLICY

New Directions for the UK

Edited by

DAVID HELD and DAVID MEPHAM

polity

First published in 2007 by Polity Press
Reprinted 2008

Polity Press
65 Bridge Street
Cambridge CB2 1UR, UK

Polity Press
350 Main Street
Malden, MA 02148, USA

ISBN-13: 978-07456-4114-0
ISBN-13: 978-07456-4115-7 (pb)

A catalogue record for this book is available from the British Library.

The publisher has used its best endeavours to ensure that the URLs for external websites referred to in this book are correct and active at the time of going to press. However, the publisher has no responsibility for the websites and can make no guarantee that a site will remain live or that the content is or will remain appropriate.

Typeset in 10.5 on 12 pt Sabon
by Servis Filmsetting Ltd, Manchester
Printed and bound in Great Britain
by MPG Books Ltd, Bodmin, Cornwall

For further information on Polity, visit our website: www.polity.co.uk

Contents

Notes on Contributors

Michael Clarke is Professor of Defence Studies at King's College London. He was the founding director of the Centre for Defence Studies and then the International Policy Institute at KCL, and is now the Director of Research Development for the college. He has been a specialist adviser to the House of Commons Defence Committee since 1997 and serves on the UN Secretary General's Advisory Board on Disarmament Matters.

Andrew Gamble is Professor of Politics at the University of Cambridge and author of *Between Europe and America: the future of British politics* (2004). He was previously Professor of Politics at the University of Sheffield, where he also served as Dean of the Faculty of Social Sciences, and Pro Vice-Chancellor.

Charles Grant is the co-founder and Director of the Centre for European Reform, an independent think tank that is dedicated to promoting a reform agenda within the European Union, after working for *The Economist* since 1986. He has published extensively on Russia, European foreign and defence policy, transatlantic relations and the Future of Europe debate.

David Held is Graham Wallas Professor of Political Science at the London School of Economics and Political Science (LSE). Among his books are *Democracy and the Global Order* (1995), *Global Covenant* (2004) and *Models of Democracy* (3rd edition 2006). He is the co-author of *Global Transformations* (1999) and *Globalization/*

Anti-Globalization (2002); and editor or co-editor of *Taming Globalization* (2003), *Global Governance and Public Accountability* (2005) and *The Global Inequality* (2007).

Mary Kaldor is Professor of Global Governance and Co-Director of the Centre for the Study of Global Governance at LSE. She is also co-founder and editor in chief of the *Global Civil Society Yearbook*. She has written widely on security issues and on democracy and civil society. Most recently she co-edited *A Human Security Doctrine for Europe: project, principles, practicalities* (2003). Other recent books include *Global Civil Society: an answer to war* (2003) and *New and Old Wars: organized violence in a global era* (1999).

Ian Kearns is Deputy Director of the Institute for Public Policy Research and Deputy Chair of the ippr Commission on National Security. Previously he was Director of the Graduate Programme in International Studies and Lecturer in Politics at the University of Sheffield. He has published on many issues, including conflict in the former Yugoslavia, the expansion of the European Union, digital technology and centre-left values, and the politics of conflict and security in Northern Ireland.

Nick Mabey is Chief Executive and a founder director of E3G (Third Generation Environmentalism), a non-profit organisation based in London and Berlin dedicated to accelerating the transition to sustainable development. He leads E3G's work on Europe's external role, energy and security. Before joining E3G he was a senior adviser in the UK Prime Minister's Strategy Unit. He has previously worked for the UK Foreign and Commonwealth Office and as Head of Economics for WWF UK.

David Mepham is an Associate Director and Head of the International Programme at the Institute for Public Policy Research (ippr). He is also a Visiting Fellow at the Centre for the Study of Global Governance at the London School of Economics. From 1998 to 2002, David was Special Advisor within the UK's Department for International Development. His most recent publications include *Changing States: a progressive agenda for political reform in the Middle East* (2006) and *Darfur: the responsibility to protect* (2006).

Steve Tsang is Louis Cha Fellow, Reader in Politics and Director of the Pluscarden Programme for the Study of Global Terrorism and Intelligence at St Antony's College, Oxford University, where he previously served as Director of the Asian Studies Centre and Dean of the College. He has published extensively on the history, politics and international relations of China, Taiwan and Hong Kong, and his most recent book is *Governing Hong Kong* (2007).

Kevin Watkins is the Director of the Human Development Report Office of the United Nations Development Programme (UNDP). Before joining UNDP, he served for thirteen years with Oxfam UK, most recently as Head of Research. He is also a Senior Research Fellow at Oxford University's Global Economic Governance Programme, and has written extensively on education, international trade and other development issues.

Leni Wild is a Research Fellow at the Institute for Public Policy Research. Since 2003, she has worked as part of the International Programme at ippr, and she is the author or co-author of three ippr reports. Previously she worked as a researcher at the NATO Parliamentary Assembly in Brussels. She has also worked for the late Robin Cook, then Leader of the House of Commons.

Paul D. Williams is an associate professor at the University of Warwick and visiting associate professor in the Elliott School of International Affairs, George Washington University, USA. He is author of *British Foreign Policy under New Labour, 1997–2005* (2005), co-author of *Understanding Peacekeeping* (2004) and co-editor of *Africa in International Politics* (2004).

Ngaire Woods is Director of the Global Economic Governance Programme and Dean of Graduates at University College, Oxford. Her most recent book is *The Globalizers: the IMF, the World Bank and their borrowers* (2006). She has previously authored or co-authored *The Political Economy of Globalization* (2000) and *Inequality, Globalization and World Politics* (1999). She has also written numerous articles on international institutions, globalization and governance.

Foreword

This book brings together some of the leading thinkers on international policy issues active in the UK. Between them, they tackle subjects as diverse and challenging as the rise of China, the relationship between security, justice and human rights, the prospects for democracy, Europe's global role, climate change, instability in the Middle East, and reforms to global governance. Without doubt, these are the issues that will determine the international landscape in the years to come.

The book focuses specifically on future international policy options for the UK. Clearly, many in Europe and other parts of the world are interested to see how UK foreign policy will develop and what ideas are emerging with respect to possible new policy initiatives. The UK is a major player in the world and has many assets at its disposal, starting with its membership of the European Union. Other elements that underpin the UK's global aspirations include its role in the G8, NATO, the UN Security Council and the Commonwealth, its close ties with the United States, and the work of the BBC, the British Council, companies, NGOs and academia. Many of the ideas and specific proposals set out in this book could enhance the UK's contribution to global peace, stability and justice.

As the editors argue persuasively in their introductory chapter, a progressive foreign policy should be rooted in a commitment to universal values like promoting human rights and demonstrating compassion with those who suffer. But it should be realistic about the practical constraints that often circumscribe foreign policy choices. As they say, the 'world does not change for the better simply because we wish it would'. To make a difference, values need to be complemented by well-thought-through policies, a good understanding of local contexts, and a significant degree of humility.

This book contains trenchant analysis and a series of imaginative but practical policy recommendations. It will be of interest to experts and the interested public alike. The book deserves a wide readership, not just in the UK or across Europe but around the world.

Javier Solana, Secretary General of the Council of
the European Union and High Representative for
the Common Foreign and Security Policy

Acronyms and Abbreviations

ACP	African, Caribbean and Pacific
ACWL	Advisory Centre on WTO Law
AIDS	Acquired Immune Deficiency Syndrome
ANC	African National Congress
APEC	Asia-Pacific Economic Cooperation
ARF	ASEAN Regional Forum
ASEAN	Association of South East Asian Nations
AU	African Union
BBC	British Broadcasting Corporation
CAP	Common Agricultural Policy
CCS	carbon capture and storage
CFSP	Common Foreign and Security Policy
CPIA	Country Performance and Institutional Assessment
DAC	Development Assistance Committee
DEFRA	Department for Environment, Food and Rural Affairs
DFID	Department for International Development
DRC	Democratic Republic of the Congo
DTI	Department of Trade and Industry
EEC	European Economic Community
EITI	Extractive Industry Transparency Initiative
ENP	European Neighbourhood Policy
EPAs	Economic Partnership Agreements
ESDP	European Security and Defence Policy
ETS	emissions trading scheme
EU	European Union

FATF	Financial Action Task Force
FCO	Foreign and Commonwealth Office
FDI	foreign direct investment
FTI	Fast-Track Initiative
G7	Group of Seven (leading industrial nations): Canada, France, Germany, Italy, Japan, UK, USA
G8	Group of Eight: G7 plus Russia
G20	Group of Twenty: G7 plus countries regarded as 'emerging markets' (Argentina, Australia, Brazil, China, India, Indonesia, Korea, Mexico, Russia, Saudi Arabia, South Africa, Turkey) plus the European Union
GATT	General Agreement on Tariffs and Trade
GDP	gross domestic product
GEF	Global Environment Facility
GNP	gross national product
HIV	Human Immunodeficiency Virus
HIPC	Heavily Indebted Poor Countries
IASB	International Accounting Standards Board
ICC	International Criminal Court
ICJ	International Court of Justice
ICCPR	International Covenant on Civil and Political Rights
ICESCR	International Covenant on Economic, Social and Cultural Rights
ICSED	International Centre for the Settlement of Environmental Disputes
IDA	International Development Association
IEA	International Energy Agency
IEAs	international environmental agreements
IFF	International Finance Facility
IFI	international financial institution
IGC	intergovernmental conference
IGO	intergovernmental organization
IMF	International Monetary Fund
INTERFET	International Force for East Timor
IOSCO	International Organization of Security Commissions
IPCC	Intergovernmental Panel on Climate Change
ippr	Institute for Public Policy Research
IPR	intellectual property rights
LSE	London School of Economics
MDGs	Millennium Development Goals
MEA	Millennium Ecosystem Assessment
MOD	Ministry of Defence

NAFTA	North American Free Trade Agreement
NATO	North Atlantic Treaty Organization
NGO	non-governmental organization
NPT	Nuclear Non-Proliferation Treaty
OECD	Organization for Economic Cooperation and Development
OPEC	Organization of Petroleum Exporting Countries
PBEC	Pacific Basin Economic Council
PPP	purchasing power parity
PRSPs	Poverty Reduction Strategy Papers
RAF	Royal Air Force
SDR	Strategic Defence Review
SFO	Serious Fraud Office
TRIPS	Agreement on Trade-Related Aspects of Intellectual Property Rights
UDHR	Universal Declaration on Human Rights
UN	United Nations
UNAIDS	Joint UN Programme on HIV/AIDS
UNCAT	UN Convention against Torture
UNDP	UN Development Programme
UNEP	UN Environment Programme
UNESCO	UN Educational, Scientific and Cultural Organization
UNFICYP	UN Peacekeeping Force in Cyprus
UNICEF	UN Children's Fund
UNMIK	UN Mission in Kosovo
WEO	World Environment Organization
WMD	weapons of mass destruction
WTO	World Trade Organization

Introduction

David Held and David Mepham

This book is concerned with the future direction of UK foreign policy in the post-Blair era. While most of the contributors reflect on Tony Blair's record during his ten years as Prime Minister, and while many, including the editors, are critical of aspects of his international policy, the book is not a history or a detailed audit of New Labour's foreign policy. Rather, the book is forward looking, addressing the major foreign policy challenges facing the UK over the next decade and suggesting how the UK government can and should respond to them more effectively.

The book has four interrelated objectives. First, it aims to define and develop a distinctively progressive perspective on UK foreign policy. Secondly, it identifies how the global context for UK foreign policy is changing, by analysing new global trends in areas like security, the environment, trade and finance. Thirdly, the book generates a range of new policy options for the UK: measures that could be taken to better advance the UK's foreign policy goals, both on particular issues like security, global justice, environmental sustainability, human rights and democratization, and towards particular regions of the world – the US, Europe, the Middle East and China. It also contains bold proposals for reforming global governance and making multilateralism work better. Fourthly, the book considers how UK foreign policy making needs to change to formulate and deliver more effective and progressive international policy outcomes. Some of the key analytical insights and policy ideas from individual contributors are highlighted in the summary at the end of this chapter.

Progressive foreign policy

What is meant by a progressive approach to foreign policy? While this is a question addressed throughout the book, we offer a preliminary definition here. Progressives can be thought of as those committed to human rights, social justice, sustainability, democracy, the international rule of law and multilateralism (Held 2004). In contrast with cultural relativists and narrow nationalists, progressives strongly defend the idea that there are some basic universal values.

Progressives argue that the world should be considered as a single moral realm in which every person – regardless of their nationality, class, race or gender – is equally worthy of respect and consideration (Beitz 1994; Pogge 1994). This notion has been referred to as the principle of egalitarian individualism. To think of people in these terms is not to deny the significance of cultural diversity or community or the reality of states. Rather, it is to affirm that all individuals have the capacity for reason and moral choice, and that this should be safeguarded everywhere by upholding some basic rights (Nussbaum 1996, pp. 42–3).

These considerations are not just abstract. They find direct expression in significant legal and institutional developments since the end of the Second World War. The United Nations (UN) Declaration of Human Rights in 1948 and subsequent international human rights treaties and covenants established the principle of egalitarian individualism as a universal reference point, with individuals now recognized as subjects of international law in a way that was not the case before 1945 (Crawford and Marks 1998). In many societies around the world, individuals have adopted the concept and language of rights to assert their claim to fair treatment, decent living conditions and greater justice. These universal values are also reflected in a wide range of global initiatives, regimes, institutions and networks established to tackle global problems (Held 2002).

As a result of these legal and normative developments, states are no longer regarded as wholly discrete or autonomous entities, in legal or political terms. The European Union, for example, has created a new set of institutions and multiple layers of law and governance that undermine traditional notions of national sovereignty. Within the wider international community, global rules drawn from universal principles are having an impact on state behaviour, albeit one that varies across countries, in areas like the conduct of war, human rights and the management of the natural environment. In this sense, the boundaries between states, nations and societies no longer claim the deep legal and moral significance they once had. This has been described as an 'unbundling' of the relationship between sovereignty, territoriality and political outcomes (see Ruggie 2003).

A progressive approach to foreign policy should help to build on these developments and strengthen the global commitment to these universal values. It should also be defined by a strong commitment to the idea of global justice. Despite growing prosperity for many people across the globe, we live in a world that is characterized by grotesque levels of poverty and deprivation. More than a billion people lack access to clean drinking water and 2.6 billion have no access to safe sanitation, while more than 10 million children die each year before their fifth birthday, as a result of malnutrition and infectious disease. A further 850 million people are chronically malnourished and 500,000 women die each year of pregnancy-related causes, with over 95 per cent of these cases occurring in the developing world (United Nations Development Programme 2005: 24). The existence of such poverty is an affront to any notion of universal values and human dignity, and a major potential source of global instability.

While most political philosophers today would argue that people in rich countries have obligations towards people living elsewhere in the world, few assert that these obligations are the same as those we owe to members of our 'own' society. A particularly clear example of this is the work of the late John Rawls. His most famous book, *A Theory of Justice*, makes no mention whatsoever of wealth inequalities between different societies (Rawls 1971). Issues of transnational justice are addressed, albeit selectively, in Rawls' later work *The Law of Peoples*, where he argues that 'well ordered peoples have a duty to assist burdened societies' (Rawls 1999). But he is less than specific about the extent of those duties and he rejects any notion of global distributive justice. For Rawls, obligations towards 'insiders' take clear priority over obligations to 'outsiders'.

Philosophers like Michael Walzer and David Miller agree with Rawls that it is not necessarily unjust to give greater attention to the interests and needs of one's co-nationals (Walzer 1983; Miller 2000). Their view is based on the advantages that are seen to result from stable, liberal and self-governing political communities. But they have gone further than Rawls in specifying the moral obligations on wealthy countries to promote justice beyond their national borders. Miller, for instance, identifies three such duties. First, he suggests that there is an obligation 'to respect the basic human rights of people everywhere'. Secondly, he argues that wealthier individuals and societies should 'refrain from exploiting those who are vulnerable to their actions'. Thirdly, he asserts that all political communities should 'have the opportunity to determine their own future and practise justice among their members' (Miller 2000). These three principles have potentially far-reaching implications for resource and power distribution and they provide a strong foundation for a progressive conception of global justice. But in some respects Miller's position understates the degree of global interdependence and the extent to which this should shape our notion of moral obligation towards people in other countries. If many of 'our' actions impact on others beyond our shores, including on the distribution of income, power and opportunity within and between countries, it is hard to argue, as Miller does, that issues of distributive justice should apply nationally but not globally (Mepham 2005).

This can be illustrated well by reference to the environment. Current patterns of production and consumption are imposing huge strains on the global environment, not least in respect of climate change (Stern et al. 2006) It is developed countries that are making the biggest contribution to these global environmental problems, but it is poor countries and people that will suffer most adversely from them. If all the world's six billion people were to consume at the level of the richest, the consequences would be ecologically catastrophic. On what moral basis, therefore, do the world's richest people defend a lifestyle for themselves that it would be impossible to extend to others and which imposes huge costs on people elsewhere? Without downplaying the political obstacles in getting from here to there (governments are answerable to national electorates), a progressive response to this question must surely involve a commitment to shift to more sustainable patterns of production and consumption nationally and globally, and support for a more equitable distribution of global wealth.

This commitment to values in foreign policy does not require a rejection of the idea of interests. But it does demand new thinking about the concept of the national interest in what is a radically changed global context. Traditionally, the national interest was framed largely in strategic terms, as the measures necessary to defend the state against threats posed by other states, with security policies oriented to deal 'only with threats deliberately directed by a human hand' (Ikenberry and Slaughter 2006: 12). But this is no longer true. In a world that is ever more interdependent, countries face major new threats like climate change, the spread of infectious disease and the risks of nuclear accidents. 'Danger now emanates from weakness as well as strength; distant lands can have a mighty reach, even if they lack modern technology. Failed and failing states can give rise to catastrophic terrorism, the proliferation of weapons of mass destruction

(WMD), regional aggression, global instability, massive human rights abuses, AIDS, drug trafficking and countless other evils' (ibid.). This is also true in respect of economics. The prosperity of national economies is now acutely dependent on economic developments in other parts of the world and on the overall health of the global economy. The traditional narrow interpretation of the national economic interest as a zero sum game is therefore increasingly obsolete.

This analysis suggests that a progressive UK foreign policy should continue to help achieve UK interests, but that these interests should be defined more expansively than has been the case previously. No country – but especially one as globally integrated as the UK – can pretend that events beyond our borders do not impact profoundly on our national prospects. 'Our' interests – 'our' prosperity and security, for example – are now likely to be dependent on achieving greater prosperity and security for others, on greater global justice and on enhanced international cooperation to manage common global problems.

A commitment to values in foreign policy should not be misconstrued as naivety about the ease with which those values can be advanced or realized in particular contexts around the world. After all, liberalism and democracy in the West took centuries to evolve and remain fragile achievements. In many parts of the world, human rights and democracy remain deeply contested concepts. Progressives are well aware that the world does not change for the better simply because we wish it would. To have a chance of making a difference, values need to be complemented by well-thought-through policies. Those policies must be realistic: that is to say, they must recognize the extent to which the actions of individual governments, international institutions and others are constrained and shaped by existing inequalities of wealth and power, by culture and by the pressures and limits of time. They also need to be rooted in a sophisticated understanding and analysis of the social, political, economic, cultural and historical context in particular societies, and underpinned by a significant degree of humility, a commitment to sustained dialogue and mutual respect. In this sense, a progressive foreign policy is one defined by values but grounded in a realistic understanding of the diverse world that it operates within.

A progressive foreign policy can be further defined by differentiating it from two other dominant approaches to contemporary international relations. First, a progressive approach is very different from a traditional conservative approach to foreign policy. The latter approach has much in common with the 'realist' perspective in international relations theory. The traditional conservative stance suggests that foreign policy is essentially about interests not values, it defines national interests very narrowly, it focuses almost exclusively on rela-tions between governments and downplays the role of non-state actors, and it is sceptical of the idea that values like human rights or democracy have universal relevance or application.

In terms of the debate about political reform in the Middle East, for example, traditional conservatives would tend to argue that many of the countries of the region are not well suited to more liberal and democratic governance and that the attempt to promote these con-cepts there is counterproductive, naïve and dangerous. The traditional conservative position gives top priority to stability and order. Moreover, unless there are clear and direct threats to the national interest, the dominant sentiment of traditional conservatives is that we should avoid meddling in other people's conflicts and recognize the practical limits of our influence over events beyond our borders.

By contrast, for the reasons already given, progressives believe that a narrow conception of the national interest is no longer morally or practically defensible. Nor do progressives accept that interests and values are necessarily in conflict. For example, a progressive UK foreign policy should protect and promote human rights not only because it is morally right to do so, but because it is an international legal obligation and because the spread of human rights and the rule of law will bring economic and commercial benefits to the UK. It should also do so because human rights and justice are the best long-term defence against insecurity, violence and extremism, including terrorism. Gross injustices, linked to a sense of hopelessness, feed anger and hostility. Defeating terrorism depends on convincing people that there is a legal and peaceful way of addressing their griev-ances.

Progressives argue, in addition, that the traditional conservative position on democracy and human rights is patronizing. While we do need to think through extremely carefully how we go about support-ing human rights or political reform in other people's societies, it is misleading to suggest that certain groups of people are not yet ready for human rights. To paraphrase (and adapt) Bruce Ackerman, there is no Islamic nation without a woman who insists on equal liberties, no Confucian society without a man who denies the need for defer-ence, and no developing country without a person who yearns for a predictable pattern of meals to help sustain his or her life projects (see Ackerman 1994: 382–3).

Secondly, a progressive approach is quite distinct from the neocon-servative foreign policy agenda that has been pursued by the Bush administration in the US. Progressives and neoconservatives both believe in values and are both advocates of active international engagement, but there the similarity ends. Neoconservatives believe in American 'exceptionalism' and assert that the US should use its military predominance to establish 'benevolent hegemony' over strategically important parts of the world (Fukuyama 2006). By contrast, progressives want the US to be a constructive player in global affairs and they recognize that there will be little progress on certain key issues without its engagement and cooperation. But progressives are clear that, too often, particularly in recent years, the US has been a hugely divisive and destructive actor in global politics.

The favoured *modus operandi* of the neoconservatives is unilateral action. The consistent preference of progressives is for multilateral responses. The neoconservatives disdain global institutions and the international rule of law; progressives champion both. As David Held and Ngaire Woods argue powerfully in separate chapters in this book, effective global institutions and a reformed system of global governance are not merely desirable but absolutely indispensable for tackling a wide range of global problems.

The neoconservatives have a highly militarized notion of security policy, while progressives believe that security threats and the underlying causes of instability need to be addressed through a multidimensional set of policy responses (Ikenberry and Slaughter 2006). In the case of terrorism, for example, the neoconservatives appear to believe that this is a phenomenon that lacks any kind of historical or political context, and that the attempt to understand the context is tantamount to excusing the violence itself. Progressives believe that we need to better understand and respond to those factors that are fuelling the rise of political and religious extremism, including anti-western Islamic terrorism. That involves dealing, as a matter of priority, with issues of political and economic injustice – subjects on which the neoconservatives have almost nothing to say.

Unlike neoconservatives, progressives believe in the importance of 'soft power': the capacity to effect or facilitate change through persuasion or the desire to emulate, as opposed to change brought about by various forms of coercion. That means thinking more intelligently about the use of development assistance and diplomacy, but also about ways in which the spread of ideas, knowledge and information can help change attitudes and behaviour.

Lastly, progressives reject the tendency of neoconservatives to view the world in Manichean terms, where the choices are presented as being between good and evil. Progressives recognize that the real world is messier and much more complex than the neoconservative approach suggests, and that good foreign policy depends less on evangelical zeal than on good analysis and sound judgement, consistent with a commitment to universal values, the international rule of law and a strengthened multilateral framework.

New Labour's record

Defined in these terms, how does the Blair government's international policy match up to the concept of a progressive foreign policy? While that record is often demonized by Blair's detractors and lauded by his supporters, a dispassionate assessment would suggest a more mixed picture.

Over the last decade, there are certainly many aspects of New Labour's international policy that have been progressive. This is particularly true of the government's work on global development issues. Since 1997, the government has strengthened significantly the UK's efforts to combat poverty and promote development across the developing world, particularly in Africa. The aid budget has tripled over the decade and 90 per cent of those resources are now focused in the world's poorest countries (Benn 2006). The government has also led international efforts to write off debts owed by the poorest, most indebted countries to bilateral creditors and multilateral institutions. And it has pressed for reforms to the global rules of trade that would bring benefits to poorer countries. The government has linked its international development strategy closely to the achievement of the Millennium Development Goals (MDGs), a set of targets for poverty reduction and development agreed by 147 governments at the UN Millennium Assembly in 2000. And it used the UK's presidency of the European Union and the G8 in 2005 to assert the case for a fairer global deal for Africa (Commission for Africa 2005).

Over the last decade, the UK's Department for International Development (DFID) and the Foreign and Commonwealth Office have also been very active in supporting human rights through reforms to legal systems, prisons, police and security forces, in working internationally to oppose the death penalty, in backing action to address human trafficking and bonded labour, in furthering women's rights and the rights of children, and in supporting freedom of expression. The government has banned anti-personnel landmines, backed reforms to the United Nations, supported the establishment and operation of the International Criminal Court and pressed for an International Arms Trade Treaty, setting common standards governing the transfer of arms and military equipment internationally. These policies are wholly consistent with a progressive approach to foreign policy. On top of this, Blair's governments have helped lead the way on many aspects of the climate change debate and on some of the policies necessary to combat its consequences.

But there have been other aspects of New Labour's foreign policy that have owed more to neoconservatism than to progressive politics. The clearest example of this is Tony Blair's ill-judged support for the war in Iraq and for George Bush's intellectually flawed and badly executed 'war on terror'.

The Iraq war has been a disaster for Iraq and the wider region, but it has also been a foreign policy disaster for the UK. As a result, the UK has lost an enormous amount of moral credibility globally, particularly but not exclusively in the Middle East and the wider Islamic world. Iraq has also seriously undermined the UK's ability to be an advocate for human rights, the United Nations and the international rule of law.

No less a figure than Kofi Annan described the war with Iraq, without a second UN resolution, as illegal. Although the US and the UK argued that military action should be taken because of Iraq's weapons of mass destruction, no weapons or even weapons programmes have been found since the start of the occupation. There has been some formal constitutional progress. However, violence, much of it sectarian, has reached appalling levels. While Iraq under Saddam was a truly brutal dictatorship, the form of US and UK military intervention has turned Iraq into a failed state, with human rights abuses and political killings amongst the highest in the world. The war has also served to radicalize Islamist opinion in the UK and internationally.

Although there have been differences of emphasis, Tony Blair's government was hugely supportive of President Bush's self-declared 'war on terror'. In this context, the UK has been extremely muted when it comes to the human rights violations perpetrated by its American ally, including the abuses committed at Guantanamo and the illegal detention of 100,000 people, mainly in Afghanistan and Iraq (Rogers 2006). The Blair government was also pusillanimous in its response to the US policy of extraordinary rendition (the process of detaining and transferring terrorist suspects to third countries, beyond the reach of normal legal processes and safeguards, for the purposes of interrogation).

These New Labour policies are inconsistent with the concept of a progressive foreign policy articulated here. They are also hard, if not impossible, to square with the foreign policy principles that the government set for itself following its election victory in 1997. In May of that year, the then Foreign Secretary Robin Cook set out a new mission statement for the Foreign Office and for the incoming government. Amongst other objectives, the mission statement asserted that the UK would 'work through international forums and bilateral relationships to spread the values of human rights, civil liberties and democracy' (Cook 1997). In introducing the new statement, Robin Cook famously said that UK foreign policy should have 'an ethical dimension' and that the Labour government would 'put human rights at the heart of foreign policy' (ibid.). In the first years of office, the government also promised to play a stronger role in Europe and to work for a more effective UN. But some of the central features of New Labour's foreign policy, particularly since 2001, have fallen woefully short of these declared goals.

Despite these failings, however, the UK still remains a significant player in international politics. As a permanent and extremely active member of the UN Security Council, a leading player in the European Union, the North Atlantic Treaty Organization (NATO) and the Commonwealth, and through the work of the British Broadcasting Corporation (BBC) and the British Council, the UK continues to exert real influence internationally. The challenge and opportunity facing a post-Blair UK government is to jettison the worst features of Blair's foreign policy, to build on the substantive achievements of the last decade and to develop new thinking and progressive policy responses to meet the international policy challenges of the next decade and beyond. The contributions to this book suggest how this might be done.

The structure of the book

The first five chapters in this volume address thematic issues. In chapter 1, Michael Clarke considers the changing nature of global security and power, and the implications of this for future UK security policy. He notes that progressives have sought to redefine the concept of security, to encompass any direct threats to the physical well-being of ordinary people (human security) and to rethink the resilience of societies in responding to different types of threat (biopolitics). While he does not suggest that these conceptual frameworks are beyond criticism, he uses them to expose the limitations of traditional highly militarized approaches to security and to advocate the need for the UK to adopt a more multidimensional security policy, involving legal instruments, diplomacy and development cooperation as well as military force, where unavoidable. Clarke attaches huge importance to strengthening the international non-proliferation regime and, in this context, he questions whether it is right for the UK to replace Trident with a new nuclear system. He also calls on the UK government to provide more funding for the International Atomic Energy Authority, allowing it to increase the number and quality of its inspections.

In chapter 2, Mary Kaldor draws a distinction between formal and substantive democracy, and argues that progressives should be committed to the latter, defined as helping to make it possible for ordinary people in different parts of the world to influence meaningfully the decisions that affect their lives. She notes that there has been a tension in recent UK policy between those advocating a muscular and 'top-down' approach to democracy promotion and others who see democracy as a more 'bottom-up' process. Kaldor suggests that the second of these offers the best prospect for securing further democratic progress globally and she highlights three ways in which a progressive UK government might support this. First, she calls for UK policy to be guided to a greater extent by ideas and information coming from the societies in which democratic change is occurring. Secondly, she observes that resources for democracy promotion might be allocated better by independent agencies than by government: for example, by the Westminster Foundation for Democracy or by a new European Democracy Foundation. Thirdly, she argues that policy-makers need to respond more imaginatively to the role of global civil society, which made such a critical contribution in supporting democratic transitions in Latin America and central and eastern Europe.

In the third chapter David Mepham reaffirms the importance of universal human rights to a progressive conception of foreign policy. He rejects the idea that human rights are a barrier to effective action against terrorism, suggesting that the UK government should be extremely cautious before jettisoning hard-won freedoms or taking punitive measures that antagonize the very communities whose cooperation is needed to prevent further acts of violence. He argues that the misconceived 'war on terror' should be replaced by an enhanced law enforcement strategy, where terrorist crimes are categorized less as acts of war and more as crimes against humanity, dealt with, wherever possible, through national and international institutions of justice. He suggests that support for human rights can help to counter the forces of political or religious radicalization. Mepham also calls for a new approach to the question of international military intervention to protect human rights. While he justifies this in exceptional cases like Darfur, he suggests that a progressive UK government needs to give much more attention to the 'how' of intervention, making sure that decent motives are not then tarnished by inappropriate means.

In chapter 4, Kevin Watkins acknowledges the UK's achievements on development issues over the last decade. But he calls for an enhanced UK effort to tackle global poverty, inequality and economic injustice. As he puts it, 'a progressive politics worth its name cannot focus on improving the human condition at home while turning a blind eye to mass poverty overseas, or to the obscene inequalities that divide rich and poor nations . . . Moreover, action to combat poverty and to promote equitable development can also reinforce other progressive foreign policy goals, including the achievement of greater common security.' His chapter focuses specifically on the issues of aid and trade. On aid, he suggests that a progressive UK government should work for increased levels of aid, helping poorer countries to make greater progress in areas like access to education, clean water and safe sanitation, and action against HIV/AIDS, malaria and tuberculosis. On trade, Watkins identifies the massive potential benefits that poorer countries could gain from a fairer global trading system: for example, through reforms to agricultural subsidies, a less dogmatic approach to trade liberalization and changes to existing rules on intellectual property. Such reforms cannot substitute for the actions that need to be taken by developing countries and people themselves, but they can help, he suggests, to create a more enabling global environment for development.

In the fifth chapter, Nick Mabey argues that a commitment to global sustainability and the equitable management of natural resources should be brought into the very heart of UK foreign policy making. The threat posed by climate change is the most obvious and dramatic example of why this is necessary. The impacts of global climate change are already being felt, but they are likely to become much more serious very quickly. Sir Nicholas Stern's influential report has suggested that unless immediate action is taken to reduce global emissions, the overall costs of climate change could amount to a permanent reduction in annual global gross domestic product (GDP) of 20 per cent by 2100. Many other global environmental conditions – from water scarcity to biodiversity – are also deteriorating rapidly. The UK will suffer seriously from these developments, but progressives should be concerned that it is the world's poorest people who will suffer most. Mabey suggests three areas for priority action by the UK. First, he calls for strong action by the UK to improve its own environmental performance. Secondly, he argues that the UK should enhance Europe's global role on environmental issues. Thirdly, he calls for greater international cooperation on the environment and better environmental governance at the global level, including the creation of a World Environment Organization.

The next four chapters of the book address UK policy towards particular countries or regions of the world. In chapter 6, Andrew Gamble and Ian Kearns assess the so-called 'special relationship' – the UK's relations with the US. While arguing that any UK government would want to retain good relations with America, they suggest that the interest of a progressive UK government is not in US dominance or unilateralism, but rather in the US embedding itself within a multilateral regime of rules and institutions. They observe that UK interests have been ill-served in recent years by the closeness of the relationship with the Bush administration, and they call on a future UK government to be bolder in criticizing US policy when it is damaging to UK interests or progressive values. They suggest that a revised relationship with the US should be based on a comprehensive assessment of the UK's security interests. Gamble and Kearns also argue that an over-reliance on the US relationship has weakened the UK's relations with its EU partners. They assert that a progressive UK government should give greater attention to its near neighbours and that a stronger and more effective Europe would provide additional foreign policy options for the UK and could help to persuade the US to act more multilaterally in global affairs.

Europe's global role is the focus of chapter 7 by Charles Grant. He acknowledges that over the last decade the UK has adopted a generally constructive attitude to the EU. However, he also argues that Blair did not fulfil his potential as a European leader, identifying the Iraq war and the decision not to hold a referendum on membership of the euro as particularly damaging to the UK's standing in Europe. But Grant remains optimistic about the UK's capacity to help shape Europe's global role. On climate change, he argues that the UK should be pressing for reform of the EU's emissions trading scheme and large binding targets for reductions in greenhouse gases during the international negotiations on a framework to replace the Kyoto protocol. He suggests that the UK should seek to strengthen the EU's Common Foreign and Security Policy (CFSP), particularly towards the Middle East and Russia. He sees potential for an enhanced European defence role, particularly if the UK can work more closely with France. And he suggests that a progressive UK government should remain a firm advocate of European Union (EU) enlargement, as a stimulus to economic and political reform in aspirant member countries. To achieve some of these goals, however, he suggests that it may be necessary to revive some of the foreign policy provisions of the ill-fated EU constitutional treaty.

In chapter 8 David Mepham addresses UK policy towards the Middle East. He argues that in the last few years the UK has paid a heavy price, in terms of regional influence and credibility, for its support for the Iraq war, and for its closeness to other US policies in the region. There is no area of UK foreign policy, he suggests, where a new approach is more urgently required. On Iraq, in line with the proposals of the Iraq Study Group, he calls for a new international strategy, involving key regional states, to help stabilize Iraq and encourage a reconciliation process within the country. He suggests that there is no guarantee that this new approach will work, but that it represents Iraq's best and last hope. On Iran, he warns against the UK supporting military action by the US or Israel in an attempt to thwart Iran's acquisition of a nuclear capability. He suggests that such a policy would have disastrous consequences, and that progressives should back a renewed diplomatic and political effort to help resolve this issue. On Israel/Palestine, he argues that a progressive UK government should work with its European partners and the Americans to play a more active and even-handed role in trying to secure a settlement to this seemingly intractable dispute, based on Israel's withdrawal from the occupied territories, the establishment of a viable Palestinian state and mutual security guarantees. Across the Middle East as a whole, Mepham asserts that a progressive UK government should strengthen its support for political and economic reform processes.

Chapter 9 by Steve Tsang looks at UK policy towards China. He argues that China's phenomenal economic expansion is very heavily dependent on, and vulnerable to, external developments. It is important that UK and other international policy-makers appreciate this, as well as seeing current developments within China in their broader historical context. He suggests that the way to deal with China is not through adopting a confrontational approach or by hectoring, but rather by encouraging the Chinese to adhere to the standards they have declared for themselves in their official policy statements, as well as international standards to which the Chinese are signatories. Tsang suggests that a progressive UK policy should work with others to encourage a more constructive Chinese role in respect of three crisis situations: North Korea, Iran and Darfur, where Beijing has particular influence.

Chapters 10 and 11 of the volume address the critical issue of global governance. In his chapter, David Held argues that a progressive UK government should champion effective multilateralism and a strengthened framework of global governance. He notes that it is currently far from clear which global public issues – such as global warming or the loss of biodiversity – are the responsibilities of which international agencies and that existing global governance arrangements are ill-equipped to address these multidimensional challenges. He criticizes the Washington security doctrine and the Washington economic consensus. In their place he advocates the development of a comprehensive human security agenda that is based on the rule of law, revitalized global institutions and support for global justice. Although he acknowledges the risks and dangers of the current moment, Held believes that this is an opportune time to rethink foreign policy goals and objectives, and that the wisdom embedded in the universal principles and institutional advances of the post-1945 era can and should be safeguarded, nurtured and advanced for future generations.

In chapter 11, Ngaire Woods argues for far-reaching reforms to the institutions of global economic governance, equipping them to tackle a wide range of global economic problems. She focuses specifically on reforms to the World Trade Organization (WTO), the International Monetary Fund (IMF) and the World Bank. On the WTO, she suggests that progressives should advocate trade rules that take greater account of countries' different starting points and levels of development, and that permit these countries to use the kinds of policy that rich countries used to develop in the past. On the IMF, Woods calls for every decision to command a 'double majority' – a majority of votes from the most powerful shareholders and a majority of countries. This would create a powerful incentive for rich countries to consult large groups of smaller and poorer countries. On the World Bank, she also suggests institutional reform, with the presidency of the Bank opened up to international competition and with this appointment made on merit.

In the final chapter, Leni Wild and Paul Williams consider the implications of the analysis advanced throughout this volume for the design and practical management and implementation of foreign policy. They suggest that progressive foreign policies have six defining characteristics: they derive from a broad conception of the national interest; have domestic legitimacy; are devised through accountable and transparent institutions; are in conformity with international law; are consistent and coherent; and are designed on the basis of a realistic appraisal of the available resources. Wild and Williams highlight the importance of the UK Parliament being given a bigger role on foreign policy issues: for example, over decisions to deploy troops or in overseeing the work of the intelligence agencies. They call for a shake-up of the structures of the civil service, so that government departments work better together, and they advocate making more use of expertise from outside government and other official channels. As they rightly conclude, 'Policy implementation should be brought in from the cold and placed at the heart of discussions about UK foreign policy.'

The quality of analysis contained in these chapters demonstrates that there is a wealth of expertise on foreign policy issues that exists outside of the formal corridors of government. If the UK is to improve the efficacy of its foreign policy making over the next decade, it will be important to draw on this expertise on a more sustained and systematic basis. This is not to denigrate the efforts of existing UK officials, but it is to argue that the global challenges facing the UK are today too diverse and multidimensional to be addressed exclusively in-house. To make the most of this outside knowledge and experience, we suggest that the UK establish a new Council of Foreign Policy Advisers. This body would consist of eight to ten international policy specialists, meeting regularly and chaired by the Foreign Secretary or another senior minister. The council would be tasked to provide additional strategic advice to the government in responding to a range of contemporary global challenges, and it could act as a useful sounding board for emerging ideas from ministers and senior officials.

References

Ackerman, B. (1994) 'Political liberalisms', *Journal of Political Philosophy*, 91, pp. 354–86.

Beitz, C. (1994) 'Cosmopolitan liberalism and the states system', in C. Brown (ed.), *Political Restructuring in Europe: ethical perspectives*, London: Routledge.

Commission for Africa (2005) *Our Common Interest: report of the Commission for Africa*, March.

Cook, R. (1997) *Mission Statement*, 12 May, Foreign and Commonwealth Office; available at www.fco.gov.uk.

Crawford, J. and Marks, S. (1998) 'The global democracy deficit: an essay on international law and its limits', in D. Archibugi, D. Held and M. Köhler (eds), *Re-imagining Political Community: studies in cosmopolitan democracy*, Cambridge: Polity.

Fukuyama, F. (2006) *After the Neocons: America at the crossroads*, London: Profile Books.

Held, D. (2002) 'Law of states, law of peoples: three models of sovereignty', *Legal Theory*, 8(1), pp. 1–44.

Held, D. (2004) *Global Covenant: the social democratic alternative to the Washington Consensus*, Cambridge: Polity.

Ikenberry, J. and Slaughter, A.-M. (2006) *Forging a World of Liberty Under Law: US national security in the 21st century*, Princeton: Princeton University Press.

Mepham, D. (2005) 'Social justice in a shrinking world', in N. Peace and W. Paxton (eds), *Social Justice: building a fairer Britain*, London: Politico's.

Miller, D. (2000) *Citizenship and National Identity*, Cambridge: Polity.

Nussbaum, M. (1996) 'Kant and cosmopolitanism', in J. Bohman and M. Lutz-Bachman (eds), *Perpetual Peace: essays on Kant's cosmopolitan ideal*, Cambridge, Mass.: MIT Press.

Pogge, T. (1994) 'Cosmopolitanism and sovereignty', in C. Brown (ed.), *Political Restructuring in Europe: ethical perspectives*, London: Routledge.

Rawls, J. (1971) *A Theory of Justice*, Oxford: Oxford University Press.

Rawls, J. (1999) *The Law of Peoples*, Cambridge, Mass.: Harvard University Press.

Rogers, P. (2006) 'The war on terror: past, present and future', openDemocracy.net; available at www.opendemocracy.net/media/article.

Ruggie, J. (2003) 'Taking embedded liberalism global: the corporate connection', in D. Held and M. Koenig-Archibugi (eds), *Taming Globalization*, Cambridge: Polity.

Stern, N. et al. (2006) *The Economics of Climate Change: the Stern Review*, London: HM Treasury.

United Nations Development Programme (2005) *International Cooperation at a Crossroads: aid, trade and security in an unequal world*, Oxford: Oxford University Press.

Walzer, M. (1983) *Spheres of Justice*, London: Martin Robinson.

1

Rethinking Security and Power

Michael Clarke

The profound changes in the global security environment of recent years have far-reaching implications for the UK's approach to defence and security policy. But the magnitude of these changes has not yet been fully appreciated by UK policy-makers. It is not an exaggeration to say that we are living in a new era in world politics. The pursuit of a progressive and effective UK security policy in this new environment therefore raises important intellectual and practical challenges for policy-makers.

The twentieth century played to the natural strengths of the United Kingdom and bolstered its international position for the best part of seventy years, even as its relative power and capacity in the world declined. The UK played key roles in the world wars and greatly influenced the peace-making and economic arrangements that followed. The country's imperial and post-colonial status, its unique relationship with the US and its maritime advantages in a world of burgeoning international trade gave the UK a central role as one of the pillars of international security and world order throughout the century. When the Cold War was in its more hostile phases (for example, in the late 1940s, the 1958–63 period and again in the early 1980s), UK influence with both the United States and the Soviet Union was increased. Global security scares played to the UK's natural strengths; as an effective military ally, an interlocutor, an offshore base in Europe and a diplomatic voice of experience. No wonder that it was a common, and accurate, perception that the UK habitually 'punched above its weight' in world politics, particularly in matters of security. The twentieth century may have been full of global conflict, human trauma, fear and upheaval, but it allowed the UK to maximize its strengths and disguise many of its weaknesses, to exert power beyond its capacity and to maintain a role through to the 1990s as one of the architects of the international security system.

The twenty-first century, however, does not magnify these traditional strengths in the same way. In fact, the opposite is the case. The military power that fought world wars, was prepared to mobilize the nation to help defend western Europe and linked the US so directly to the UK's own security is now employed in messy interventions and open-ended nation-building operations that stretch the capacity of the country's forces to operate and the willingness of the public to support them.

The same is broadly true in the international economic arena, which is so intimately linked to the politics of security (Strange 1988: 29–31). The UK's role remains prominent in the twenty-first century but has been transformed in some crucial ways over the last generation. Economic considerations are high on the agendas of the world's major states. The United Kingdom is one of the seven largest economies in the world, with a fairly consistent 2–2.5 per cent gross domestic product (GDP) growth. With the exception of Canada, it is also the most open economy among the Group of Seven (G7) countries, highly dependent on foreign direct investment, service industries and earnings from the City (World Market Research Centre 2003). The UK therefore has both more to gain and more to lose from the performance of a globalized world economy that is less and less constrained by political structures (Bryant 1994). In conditions of globalization, the wealth of service economies can rise and fall more quickly than that of manufacturing economies. Technological innovation is a great leveller in matters of economic prosperity, as well as security, and is ever less dependent on past infrastructures of power and production. Adaptation is the key to survival for developed as well as developing societies.

The United Kingdom remains a significant player in all these fields: in security politics, in the western economies, in technological innovation and its application to modern society. But while the UK contributes much in these areas, it can determine or command very little. The key security and economic structures of the twenty-first century now rest on different pillars. The UK is no longer one of them, but rather a player among them. In these circumstances, a progressive approach to policy is significant beyond its intrinsic value. The failure to respond and adapt to underlying changes in the security environment is particularly hazardous for any power so closely identified with the structures of a previous era, and risks policy failure on a grand scale. The problem is that there is no consensus on exactly what 'progressive' means in the current security environment.

It is a commonplace observation that international security cannot be satisfactorily understood only in terms of relations between states, however carefully some of the classic modern analysts such as Hedley Bull (1977) or Kenneth Waltz (1979) define the complications and extensions of inter-state relations. In a world where even the United States is discovering the limitations of military power in producing the security it wants for its people, it is evident that the concept of 'security', no less than that of 'progressive', has to be redefined.

Approaches to redefining security

Attempts at the redefinition of both concepts revolve around the notion of 'human security' as a progressive principle for action and as a potent device to analyse global security. A stark human security agenda can be stated easily: it is any threat to the physical well-being of ordinary people. In addition to the direct effects of violent conflict, it therefore encompasses other threats such as forced migration, environmental degradation, crime and terrorism, and even natural disasters. Lloyd Axworthy is an eminent exponent of this view, writing in 2003 that 'all people have a right to feel secure against war, violence, disease, disaster and terror' (Axworthy 2003: 24). This approach maintains that military conceptions of security are either largely irrelevant or simply misleading in understanding what really drives insecurity for most people (Ullman, in Brown 2003: 311).

Fragile states, human mobility and the communications revolution have produced various symptoms of globalization that have exacerbated misery as well as prosperity, and have thrown up challenges to human well-being that appear to be only indirectly connected to traditional notions of 'international' security: that is, between one state and another. For example, HIV/AIDS is already believed to be responsible for the same number of deaths (around 25 million) since 1983 as warfare has been since 1945, and the proportion is set to rise steeply on the basis of current infection rates. Conflict is currently responsible for around 100,000 deaths in Africa annually, but AIDS now kills 2.5 million Africans every year – some 6,000 people each day (Heinecken 2001: 8; Elbe 2003).

Faced with the sudden death of 230,000 people in the 2004 Indian Ocean tsunami disaster, or the distinct possibility that global warming will result in the inundation of coastal lowland China, where

500 million people and 65 per cent of its industrial output are located, it is not surprising that the idea of 'human security' should seem more urgent and relevant than traditional 'international security'. Thus, 'if people perceive an issue to threaten their lives in some way *and respond politically to this*, then that issue should be deemed to be a security issue' (Hough 2004: 9). And if the definition is drawn as widely as this, as Axworthy points out, 'the tools with which we have to respond to security threats are primitive in light of the demands placed upon them' (Axworthy 2004: 20). Nothing less than a fundamental rethink will be required, in which military power should be regarded as only one of the policy tools available to address such problems, and certainly not the most pre-eminent of them (Commission on Human Security 2003).

An extension of this approach is encapsulated in the discussion of security in terms of 'biopolitics' – a concept that displaces the rediscovered fashion for 'geopolitics' in the United States – by referring to the self-reliance and resilience of populations rather than states, and the ways in which *societies* can be bolstered against the threats their members naturally face (Dillon, 2004). If the Cold War overemphasized the security of state structures in traditional terms, biopolitics tries to redress the balance by accounting for the lesser role of the state in many aspects of modern and postmodern global society, and stressing the importance of human and social resilience as a key building block to more sustainable twenty-first century states. Geopolitics and biopolitics are not mutually exclusive. Cold War international politics were dominated by alliances designed to compete between uniquely centralized systems throughout the world. But those alliances have either broken down completely, like the Warsaw Pact, or changed out of all recognition, like the North Atlantic Treaty Organization (NATO) through its involvement in nation building in Afghanistan. The insecurities of the Cold War were driven by the competition between powerful states and their ability to mobilize societies behind their interests; but the insecurities of the present era are created mainly by the weaknesses of states and the volatility of the societies they encompass (Freedman 2004: 256).

Current security problems such as terrorism, criminality, the existence of weapons of mass destruction (WMD) and the ripple effects of social collapse elsewhere are all symptomatic of an ongoing structural change brought about by the globalization of world politics. In contrast to the Cold War period, the present era is characterized by floating coalitions, decentralized threats, shadow economies, transborder flows of all kinds, and regional and global insurgent networks that threaten the fabric of international security in several places at once

(Collier 2003). Both for good and bad, effective states today interact with, and intervene in, less effective states to try to make themselves more secure. Powerful societies, in other words, dominate less powerful ones in a constant, and not overly successful, attempt to create more stable conditions for themselves in a fragmented world.

This is not new. Biopolitics is a modern refinement of some older, colonial-era understandings of security in a world that was not at that time all parcelled out into modern nation states. It represents a renewed attempt to unite the evident needs of a global security agenda with those of development agendas in a form that recognizes a strong interdependence between them. An acceptance of this interdependence produces many pragmatic advantages that further advance human well-being, but also imperialistic behaviour that does little to bolster the resilience of societies and their populations (Cooper 2004: 24–6).

What unites these approaches is an understanding that the global security environment in this century is clearly a hybrid of different elements (Picciotto et al. 2006: 11–20). A variety of international actors, not all of them states, define the security agenda for the world by 'securitizing' some issues: classifying them to be important over and above other political objectives. Deeming something a security matter is never innocent or objective: security 'is a quality actors inject into issues by securitizing them' and thereby claim endorsement for emergency measures that go above and beyond the normal course of daily politics (Buzan et al. 1998: 5, 204). Actors perceive that if a 'securitized' issue is not tackled, then other more mundane political issues cannot be dealt with normally. This applies as much to those who promote a 'war on poverty' as to those who promote a 'war on terror'; a perception that unless these issues are resolved, other objectives simply cannot be achieved.

Robert Cooper's influential analysis of the international system argues that the major 'securitizing actors' – key states – are far from irrelevant, and must somehow create an overarching structure of security which allows other desirable political processes to develop. Different types of state ('premodern', 'modern' or 'postmodern') coexist in the current global system and will behave in different ways accordingly. Few of them wield decisive power, and all of them are struggling to understand the systemic workings of the global order. Even the United States is now unable to dictate which issues should and should not be securitized. Long-term US commitments in areas such as Asia, Africa and the Middle East will require the widest possible coalitions for the promotion of security and greater democracy. 'The task is becoming too big even for America' (Cooper 2004: 186).

The *Human Security Doctrine for Europe* report of 2004 reached similar conclusions. It suggested that there were five key human security threats to Europe: terrorism, WMD, regional conflicts, failing states and organized crime. The problem was to 'securitize' them, and the report, in effect, called for the European Union (EU) to be the chief actor in shaping the perceptions of which issues should be regarded as requiring extraordinary attention. But the EU still lacks essential credibility as a major security actor. In Europe, the nation state may be undergoing many transformations but it is not going out of business. The forces of interdependence and globalization have provoked as much a series of national as of international reactions to problems. Though we increasingly perceive the mainsprings of international security issues at the individual and societal level – the human security and the biopolitical perspectives – most of the solutions that appear within our grasp remain within national or regional political structures, albeit in some cases through foreign interventions (Buzan and Waever 2003).

Key states, and some important non-state actors, have a crucial role to play in creating the permissive conditions in international society for other desirable political processes to take place. Though countries like the UK may no longer be pillars of the system, they can still have an important role in defining how 'twenty-first century security' should be interpreted. The political realities remain that what the more powerful regard as important will, ipso facto, become so. The US reaction to the 9/11 attacks meant that Washington decided to 'take on' the terrorists, primarily as a war rather than a policing issue, and the rest of the world cannot avoid having part of its agenda shaped by that reaction. Policymakers normally understand the importance of recognizing power where it is seen to exist, but they should not be blind to the prospect of redefining and 'securitizing' a different set of priorities as a way of dealing with other human concerns.

The limits of progressive security policy

The social democratic left instinctively leans towards human security concerns, yet also recognizes the responsibility of the major states and institutions to create basic security frameworks in which these concerns can be addressed. On the face of it, the Labour government that came to power in 1997 made a credible attempt to inject these progressive ideas about human security into the UK's foreign, defence and security policies, but the effort has since been largely derailed by its close military relationship with the US.

The new emphasis was evident from the beginning: a declaration that the 'ethical dimensions' of policy would be given more weight; the creation of the Department for International Development (DFID) outside the Foreign and Commonwealth Office, with its own cabinet minister and a steep increase in the annual foreign aid budget; emphasis on the UN convention on controlling small arms and light weapons, more scrutiny of arms trade issues and an early commitment to support the Ottawa Convention on the abolition of anti-personnel landmines. The Ministry of Defence conducted its long-heralded Strategic Defence Review (SDR) in 1998, concluding that 'we must be prepared to go to the crisis, rather than have the crisis come to us' (Ministry of Defence 1998: 2). The review gave specific emphasis to the progressive internationalist view of security for which UK forces would henceforth be reorganized: '[T]here is today no direct military threat to the United Kingdom or Western Europe,' it said. Nevertheless, 'as well as defending our rights we should discharge our responsibilities in the world. We do not want to stand idly by and watch humanitarian disasters or the aggression of dictators go unchecked. We want to give a lead. We want to be a force for good.' To do this would require 'an integrated external policy . . . using all the instruments at our disposal, including diplomatic, developmental and military' (Ministry of Defence 1998: 4–5).

Such progressive credentials were followed up internally with the creation of an initiative for 'defence diplomacy' to maximize the use of the military for wider purposes, the establishment of two 'Conflict Prevention Pools' to target money more effectively to African and to global conflict prevention activities, and later the creation of a Security Sector Defence Advisory Team and then the Post Conflict Reconstruction Unit – all attempts to concentrate energy and resources on conflict prevention and the amelioration of suffering arising from global instability.

Externally, the government took on board the lessons of military operations in Bosnia and tried to promote more active and effective peacekeeping and peace support operations among its allies. The Prime Minister reversed previous policy on European defence in 1998 and launched a UK–French initiative at St Malo to push the European Union's defence capabilities decisively forward. This was complemented by an international policing initiative at the Sintra conference. The UK also broke ranks with the United States to support the Kyoto Treaty on climate change and the establishment of the International Criminal Court. There was no shortage of progressive international thinking, particularly in the first of the three Labour administrations.

Nevertheless, traditional elements of UK defence policy were not only maintained but explicitly strengthened, on the assumption that a

Labour government would show it could pursue them more effectively than its predecessor. The SDR made some cuts in defence spending but guaranteed a stable level of spending for the following three years. All major defence equipment projects were maintained, the nuclear programme was endorsed and the defence establishment and the armed forces were rationalized to create better capabilities for expeditionary operations. Instead of preparing for major war in Europe, the UK would gear up for smaller, combat-based operations in different parts of the world. Rather than build a full war-fighting capacity and then take forces from it to meet other military contingencies, the UK would now plan for a variety of smaller operations but maintain the ability to aggregate its forces if it confronted a major war scenario sometime in the future.

The Labour government believed strongly in NATO and in the UK continuing to play a disproportionate role in it, albeit with an average of 2.7 per cent of gross national product (GNP) spent on defence, around a third more than most of its European partners. Most significantly, the government wanted to strengthen its security relationship with the United States. Tony Blair worked hard to create a close personal friendship with Democratic President Bill Clinton, and then equally hard to get on good terms with Republican President George W. Bush (Kampfner 2003: 87–8). Personal relations were important, but the linkages went much further. The restructuring of UK armed forces was conducted on the basis that they should be more able to plug into the technical 'transformation' agenda being pursued by the Pentagon. UK forces had to be able to fit into a US battle plan and keep up with the US technologically, at least in some of the key combat areas. The US Air Force and the Royal Air Force (RAF) worked closely together to enforce the no-fly zones over Iraq. The UK aimed to be an effective and valued military partner of the US, not merely a political friend, and certainly not a token ally. A government paper expressed it with simple clarity as it outlined the UK's military ambitions: 'it is inconceivable that the most demanding of operations could be conducted without the involvement of the United States' (Ministry of Defence 2004: 2).

This pragmatic balance of traditional security concerns and a desire to act as a 'force for good' was reasonably successful for the first five years. The Blair government was at least as ambitious as its predecessors to act as a transatlantic bridge between European and North American security policy. Tony Blair threw himself into the St Malo process to increase European defence capabilities, precisely because he was confident he could present this positively to the US. He would not choose between an EU and a NATO defence orientation; instead he would simultaneously strengthen them both and enhance the value of the UK as a critical security actor. The Kosovo crisis in 1999 appeared to bear out this approach. A United Nations (UN) resolution to authorize a military intervention was not possible, and the US and UK drove NATO into a commitment to action under its own political authority. It was controversial but ultimately effective in routing Serbian forces from Kosovo and undermining the authority of Slobodan Milosevic. The following year UK forces conducted a textbook operation in Sierra Leone – using impressive combat power to break the hold of vicious guerrilla forces that threatened the legitimate government of the country, and setting up a big post-conflict programme – with the support of both the US and the UN.

However, the balancing act was decisively upset by the 9/11 attacks and America's pursuit of the 'war on terror' in response to them. The war played directly into the preferred agenda of the 'neoconservatives' in Washington, and in both substance and style quickly became controversial among America's allies as much as its adversaries. President Bush declared that all nations now had to 'choose' where their loyalties lay (Frum 2003: 224–45). This was a more tangible problem for the UK than for most. US policy, already swinging towards greater unilateralism after 1998, now turned firmly in favour of a traditional, geopolitical and state-centred approach to international security. The US was being threatened by rogue leaderships, located or sponsored by states, and would apply military power to the problem of 'super-terrorism', exactly as it would have applied it to any traditional military adversary – it would disrupt, deny, destroy and deter the enemy, fighting as far from the homeland as possible, and acting pre-emptively if necessary (White House 2002). For the UK, this turn of the wheel in Washington was attractive as well as dangerous. It emphasized the unique security cooperation between the UK and the world's greatest superpower: the use of UK special forces in Afghanistan, the human intelligence that the UK could provide from the Middle East, information sharing, the ability of UK forces to gear up for big operations, and so on. But the forceful US approach also posed a major political challenge to the highly nuanced way the UK government had conceived of international security up until then.

After meeting with George Bush in April 2002, Tony Blair was convinced that US military action against Iraq was now inevitable (Cook 2004: 135–6). His critics have accused Blair of 'going along' with a war plan in 'poodle fashion' (Kettell 2006: 65). But in reality he was still trying to achieve a pragmatic balance, being drawn into ever more ambitious diplomatic designs in order to do so. He intended to play the ultimate manager's role – delivering to Washington the support of other Europeans for united military action, and delivering to Europe a US acceptance of United Nations authority, where tough resolutions would build a head of pressure on Saddam Hussein, and possibly avoid an outright war altogether. Diplomatic unity could avoid war, and Blair would be its architect.

The reality, of course, was very different, as everyone involved in the crisis overplayed their hands, and UK diplomacy failed on almost every front (Clarke 2004). The build-up to the war seriously damaged the credibility of the government, as did the failure to justify it in terms of WMD, as much as the failure to create any stability in the aftermath of the invasion. Four years on, the whole operation has been generally acknowledged as a strategic blunder and a military quagmire. For different reasons, the same outcome is in danger of being realized in the UK-led NATO operations in Afghanistan.

Unlike the Europeans, the US interprets the terrorist problem it faces essentially as a foreign war that it, and its allies, must fight. Yet this is a war in which the US, as coalition leader, is distinctly lacking in competence in everything save traditional war fighting itself. As its avowedly 'most loyal ally', this constantly corrodes the careful balance and the moral authority that the UK has sought to build in security affairs. The immediate results have been that UK forces are overstretched by operations in deteriorating conditions and are struggling to meet the ambitious nation-building targets they have been set, let alone any new ones that might arise (Ministry of Defence 2006b: paras 62–68). NATO, one of the backbones of UK security policy for so long, is struggling to maintain credibility; and the transatlantic relationship, notwithstanding some rethinking in Washington as the post-Bush era begins to take shape, is now too diverse for the UK to act as an effective 'bridge'.

It may be regarded as simply unfortunate, or somehow a temporary setback, that the UK was forced to choose between the elements it was seeking to balance, and that it chose the United States at a time when the US had retreated back into a geopolitical and militaristic interpretation of international security. On this view, the pragmatic balance between traditional security structures – US policy, NATO, war fighting and intervention – and newer elements of human security – the development and security interface, multi-agency support to nation building, conflict prevention measures, the promotion of social resilience – can be re-established when President Bush has gone, or perhaps when America's war on terror is scaled back.

But the real problem for a progressive security policy is not that the balance was upset, but rather that the UK was increasingly trying to balance the wrong things. The US is the world's only military superpower, a fact that must be respected, but it has been increasingly unable to build the political coalitions it needs to achieve its objectives. It cannot command a convincing consensus for its interpretation of what should be 'securitized', nor how that should be pursued (Freedman 2006: 26). Similarly, NATO and EU summit communiqués are replete with references to democratization, developmental objectives, environmentalism, and transnational and social threats to societies across the whole Euro-Asian land mass. But while both organizations have an impressive record in helping Europe through its post-Cold War transition, neither has been able to address these issues in a convincing way outside their own memberships. They have also failed to build an effective consensus on what should be 'securitized', and are only pillars of a twenty-first century security order in a very narrow sense.

Nor does the problem rest only with institutions. The optimism of a decade ago that the powerful in the world could be a force for good in Bosnia, East Timor, Sierra Leone, Kosovo, Macedonia, Somalia, the Solomon Islands, Albania, even in the Great Lakes region of Africa, has been replaced by a nervousness that similar commitments are now best avoided. The emerging wisdom appears to be that powerful states can do nothing really effective for Darfur or Liberia, for Somalia or Afghanistan, for Lebanon or in Gaza. There is little influence that they can wield in relation to destabilizing developments in Ukraine or Georgia; not much they can do to prevent the spread of WMD, the consequences of global warming or the burgeoning of international crime. Increasingly, the insecurities that affect most people, most often, are instinctively regarded as too difficult to be worth the time and money to address them more than peripherally. Partly as a consequence of this pessimism, the trends towards conflict prevention, reform of the security sectors and integrated instruments to promote greater human security have all lost political momentum in the UK and in many of its partners.

Elements of a new progressive security policy

If the existing model of a progressive UK security policy is not sustainable, and not only because of the mishandling of the 'war on terror', the problem of creating a more effective approach becomes pressing. There is no longer an accepted security structure, or an acceptable leadership, that can create a powerful consensus. The cautious optimism of the 1990s has more or less evaporated. We are not likely to see the establishment of a conscious, new global security order to rival the creations of 1815, 1945 or even 1919. George Bush Sr spoke earnestly of a 'new world order' in 1991, but it faded before it was even a blueprint. The diffusion of power and the diversity of actors in global politics make this virtually impossible. The authority of the UN will not be quickly increased and the major regional organizations around the world (such as the African Union) no less than the functional ones (such as the World Trade Organization) have a patchy record at best.

So, on the one hand, the UK is physically very safe. Its territorial integrity is hardly under threat. The only credible traditional state-based challenge to the UK might arise from a resurgent and hostile Russia aiming for coercive regional influence in central Asia or eastern Europe. But it is difficult to see how this would translate into a significant challenge to the UK's existence, or involve the UK standing against Russia alone. On the other hand, the UK faces immediate policy challenges that do not directly threaten its existence. Such immediate challenges include energy availability, international crime, terrorism, particularly if linked with the technologies of WMD, the threat to UK interests posed by chaos and breakdown across the Middle East – or even in East Asia where centres of production are concentrated – financial instability and perhaps, over the long term, problems of food security.

These challenges are underpinned and reinforced by a second level of changing global structures outlined clearly in the government's own statements, particularly *The Future Strategic Context for Defence* (Ministry of Defence 2001) and *Strategic Trends* (Ministry of Defence 2003) reports. Demographic trends will increase urbanization and produce volatile mega-cities, populated predominantly by young people in societies that may not be able to employ them. Globalized economic growth is likely to be powerful but inequitable, and will favour the knowledge hotspots, even in poorer countries, over the manufacturing concentrations. Environmental stress will disproportionately increase the pressures on poorer societies and make them less resilient. Social diversity will grow, even as economic homogeneity increases. Meanwhile, science and technology will continue to empower individuals, groups and organizations more than it will empower the state. The technologies of WMD will continue to develop and disperse.

The intractability of both these levels of challenge, however, can be seen to stem from the deeper structural deficiencies outlined earlier: the lack of confidence and effective process in contemporary global politics. In effect, there is no consensus among the powerful over what could be achieved to make the world more structurally stable and simultaneously to promote greater physical well-being for its citizens. Crises and dislocations increasingly happen because there is not enough being done to prevent them. There is less shoring-up against minor problems becoming major tragedies. This applies as much in the natural or environmental fields as in the political.

For the UK a progressive security policy should begin from this point and work upwards to address the other levels of challenge. The UK has a big stake in the codification of international norms and values when they are under attack from so many quarters (Tickell 2004). As an open society with an open economy, no longer able to affect the structure of world politics dramatically, but with an erstwhile sense of internationalism and responsibility, the UK has much to lose in the present hiatus. But it also has much to gain in addressing some of its most immediate security preoccupations if it can be identified as an influential player in a new international consensus on security.

The threat of jihadi-style terrorist attacks in the UK may still be statistically very small, but we should not underestimate the profound impact that further attacks would have on the fabric of our society. The UK's counter-terrorism strategy has always stressed the primacy of the rule-of-law and the importance of building stronger international legal norms against terrorism. But this stance is undermined in the eyes of much international and domestic opinion by the questionable legality of the UK's war on Iraq, its apparent condoning of the US's extraordinary rendition procedures and its lack of apparent influence in Washington over the detention facility at Guantanamo Bay. The lack of an effective international consensus on terrorism is directly damaging to the UK's internal security. That moral ambiguity which leads 13–15 per cent of the UK's Muslim population to sympathize with the 9/11 bombers, and 7 per cent of them with the 7/7 bombers, is a major problem for the police and security services as they try to reinforce the social fabric against 'home-grown terrorists' (You Gov poll, 23 July 2005; Populus poll, 4 July 2006; Populus poll in association with You Gov, 7 February 2006; Pew Global Attitude Project, *Guardian*, 23 June 2006; 1990 Trust, 2006).

The UK's counter-terrorism policy is soundly based in legal principle, but would be on much firmer political ground if it also contributed to a stronger international consensus on security against terrorism (Cordesman 2006). That consensus would be greatly enhanced by rationalizing UK involvements in Iraq and Afghanistan, drawing down rapidly in Iraq and pressing harder for a greater international nation-building effort in Afghanistan, at least in the relatively stable areas of the north and west and in Kabul. If this is not forthcoming during 2007 then continuing NATO operations will be pointless and should be concluded. Chasing a mixed bag of jihadis, Taliban and local tribesmen in Helmand and Kandahar is not addressing the international problem of terrorism unless it creates space for powerful, international nation building. At home, the domestic consensus against terrorism would be stronger if it concentrated not on what jihadi terrorists do – since they will always claim some moral equivalence in Iraq, Afghanistan, Gaza or Lebanon – but on what they stand for; their vision of how they would forcibly change the current fabric of UK society and its politics. The values of an open democracy are its own best defence, but in a globalized world they have to be pursued with more consistency abroad if they are to have sufficient influence on a multinational society at home.

The need to promote a new international consensus is even stronger in the case of WMD. Far from the nightmare of a nuclear attack during the Cold War, UK security services now fear that the country is more vulnerable than most to a terrorist attack involving WMD. This would be less devastating than a nuclear attack of thirty years ago, but would probably have irreversible effects on society and its normal functioning. The UK depends on the international nuclear non-proliferation regime and on effective international police coordination to meet this challenge. But the non-proliferation regime is currently in deep trouble after thirty years of reasonable success, with a crisis created by the nuclear ambitions of North Korea and Iran. US scepticism over the efficacy of the non-proliferation treaty becomes a self-fulfilling prophecy. US counter-proliferation policies, with their emphasis on assertive unilateral action against potential proliferators, are not pursued consistently but nevertheless severely damage attempts to maintain the non-proliferation regime. There is very little security from nuclear terrorism in all this for Britain. A fragmented international system where nuclear weapons are so much the objects of prestige is one where nuclear terrorism against countries like the UK is both more feasible and more likely.

The progressive answer to the problem is for the UK to rededicate itself to the nuclear non-proliferation regime and to work with other European and developed world powers to deepen the consensus on making an international regime approach work effectively. As with the 'war on terror', pragmatism is not always wise when it wins out over consistency. The government should seriously consider whether its decision in 2006 to replace the UK's nuclear deterrent strengthens or further weakens the nuclear non-proliferation regime. A replacement for Trident has been justified on the grounds that it might be relevant to Britain's nuclear security in forty years' time (Ministry of Defence 2006a: 6–7). But if the decision is another blow to the non-proliferation regime at the present critical time, then its impact will be to make the UK less secure against the terrorist nuclear threat that MI5 has already identified as real and immediate (*Washington Post*, 11 November 2006: A15).

The wider issues of international security identified in *Strategic Trends* – the problems of failed states, global sources of instability and all the stresses that environmental, technical and economic drivers will further put upon them – are impossible to address outside an international consensus, even for the US. The present consensus on how to tackle such issues is weak, diverse and infused with a weary pessimism after more than a decade of disappointing initiatives. Nevertheless, if the UK plays to its natural strengths, then it still has a lot to offer a progressive international agenda. The UK was involuntarily associated with a Cold War international order that is now neither effective nor accepted. Its controversial support for the US-led 'war on terror' has exaggerated this association and diminished its claim to exert useful influence on American policy.

But if the UK is seen to rededicate itself in some explicit way to consensus building in international security, it could make the most of its natural diplomatic advantages to help 'securitize' a different combination of issues on the international scene and inject some optimism into thinking about human security. The UK has the basis of more joined-up approaches to policy implementation than many of its partners and a good international reputation for internal coherence in its external policy. It has a fairly centralized decision-making process and a robust party-political mechanism to build a domestic consensus behind any shift in the direction of policy. Not least, the UK has some long-term leverage on the development and codification of international law and in applying standards of domestic law at the international level.

The UK has well-honed military instruments that it should continue to use. It is likely that the armed forces will be employed in operations that serve the cause of international stability – peacekeeping and peace support operations – rather than the defence of the UK directly. The armed forces are an important component of a progressive approach to security policy, but military force should be used only where nothing else will do, as was the case in Bosnia in 1995 and Sierra Leone in 2000. There is a natural tendency among leaders to turn to the armed forces as the one policy instrument they can manipulate incisively. However, military force is sometimes too attractive – even glamorous – an option to be used prudently.

Moreover, when military force is required for operations short of war, it should be assumed that humanitarian operations will not merely follow the forces into the theatre of operations but be an intrinsic part of their planning (Fry 2005). The humanitarian response must be as agile and effective as that of the military (Richmond 2006: 291–2). The 'revolution in military affairs' needs to be accompanied by an interlocking and interdependent 'revolution in humanitarian affairs'. Non-military instruments are normally far more suited to addressing the structural challenges of stability cost-effectively than the military, but they can only do so, and be sustained, on the basis of a solid domestic and international consensus that they should be used. The result, otherwise, is that the international response to instability rapidly becomes part of the problem itself.

This also raises the possibility of a restructuring of resources devoted to security and external relations away from some military systems and towards other investments in international stability. A shift in resources would be effective only if it were part of a multinational initiative to redirect donor expenditures, but the UK could at least take a lead by being prepared to offer, say, a quadrupling of its expenditure on the International Atomic Energy Authority and its network of inspections, or on the resources devoted to international policing or on the role of gendarmeries and police training in unstable regions. Increases in expenditure of these magnitudes could enhance the effectiveness of such international initiatives in a dramatic way and are still a fraction of the costs attributed to 'big ticket' military platforms whose direct impact on UK security at the margin is necessarily limited.

None of this has to be posed as a stark alternative to active transatlanticism, or support for NATO or for an evolving EU defence policy. Those elements will still exist. But the maintenance of the institutional forms of these associations should not take precedence over the ability to form a wide consensus on threats to human well-being that matter most to the UK public.

The UK will still have to manage its relationship with the US, and the hope must be that this will be pursued in a more consistent way after the Bush administration leaves office. The US, nevertheless, is on a generally divergent course in the twenty-first century. If we are now in the Asian century, the US will have significantly different interests from its European allies as it becomes a 'Pacific first' rather than an 'Atlantic first' power. This is not a surprise. During the twentieth century the UK consistently saw itself as a bridge across the Atlantic – an image strengthened by Tony Blair as Prime Minister. For the future this will be much harder to sustain. The UK, rather, should see itself as a hub of developed world diplomacy; an influencer and consensus-builder among the progressive security actors in the world. These security actors will include states, global companies, international institutions and groups of influential individuals. There is no reason why – post-Iraq – the UK should not be in a good position to perform such a role. This way the UK would help draw a post-Bush US back towards more wholehearted and optimistic involvement in the web of multinational diplomacy created to deal with security problems that are too complex to deal with successfully in any other way.

References

Axworthy, L. (2003) *Navigating a New World: Canada's global future*, Toronto: Alfred A. Knopf.

Axworthy, L. (2004) 'Human security, threat and opportunity', in UNOG/DCAF, *State and Human Security in the Age of Terrorism*, Geneva.

Benn, H. (2006) 'Five thousand people lifted out of poverty every day', speech delivered to Labour Party Conference, 27 September.

Brown, M. E. (2003) *Grave New World: security challenges in the twenty-first century*, Washington, DC: Georgetown University Press.

Bryant, R. (1994) 'Global change: increasing economic integration and eroding political sovereignty', *Brookings Review*, 12, pp. 42–5.

Bull, H. (1977) *The Anarchical Society*, New York: Columbia University Press.

Buzan, B. and Waever, O. (2003) *Regions and Powers: the structure of international society*, Cambridge: Cambridge University Press.

Buzan, B., Waever, O. and de Wilde, J. (1998) *Security: a new framework for analysis*, London: Lynne Rienner.

Clarke, M. (2004) 'The diplomacy that led to war in Iraq', in P. Cornish (ed.), *The War in Iraq, 2003*, London: Macmillan.

Collier, P. (2003) *Breaking the Conflict Trap: civil war and development policy*, Washington/Oxford: World Bank/Oxford University Press.

Commission on Human Security (2003) *Human Security Now*, New York: Commission on Human Security.

Cook, R. (2004) *The Point of Departure*, London: Simon and Schuster.

Cooper, R. (2004) *The Breaking of Nations: order and chaos in the twenty-first century*, London: Atlantic Books.

Cordesman, A. (2006) 'The lessons of international cooperation on terrorism', *Journal of the Royal United Services Institute*, 151(1), February, pp. 48–53.

Dillon, M. (2004) 'The security of governance', in W. Larner and W. Walters (eds), *Global Governmentality: governing international spaces*, New York: Routledge.

Duffield, M. (2005) 'Getting savages to fight barbarians: development, security and the colonial present', *Conflict, Security and Development*, 5(2), pp. 141–59.

Elbe, S. (2003) *Strategic Implications of HIV/AIDS*, Adelphi paper 357, London: International Institute for Strategic Studies.

Freedman, L. (2004) 'The new security equation', *Conflict, Security and Development*, 4(3), December, pp. 245–59.

Freedman, L. (2006) 'The transatlantic agenda: vision and counter-vision', *Survival*, 47(4), pp. 19–38.

Frum, D. (2003) *The Right Man: an inside account of the surprise presidency of George W. Bush*, London: Weidenfeld and Nicolson.

Fry, R. (2005) 'Expeditionary operations in the modern era', *Journal of the Royal United Services Institute*, 150(6), December, pp. 60–3.

Heinecken, L. (2001) 'Living in terror: the looming security threat to southern Africa', *African Security Review*, 10(4), pp. 7–17.

Hough, P. (2004) *Understanding Global Society*, London: Routledge.

Kampfner, J. (2003) *Blair's Wars*, London: The Free Press.

Kettell, S. (2006) *Dirty Politics? New Labour, British democracy and the invasion of Iraq*, London: Zed.

Ministry of Defence (1998) *Strategic Defence Review*, Cm 3999, London: The Stationery Office.

Ministry of Defence (2001) *The Future Strategic Context for Defence*, London: The Stationery Office.

Ministry of Defence (2003) *Strategic Trends*, Shrivenham: Joint Doctrine and Concepts Centre, March.

Ministry of Defence (2004) 'Government's response to the House of Commons Defence Select Committee's Report', HC 465-1, September.

Ministry of Defence (2006a) *The Future of the United Kingdom's Nuclear Deterrent*, Cm 6994, London: The Stationery Office.

Ministry of Defence (2006b) *Ministry of Defence Annual Report and Accounts 2005–06*, London: The Stationery Office.

1990 Trust (2006) *Survey, Muslim Views*, London: 1990 Trust, October.

Picciotto, R., Olonisakin, F. and Clarke, M. (2006) *Global Development and Human Security: towards a policy agenda*, Stockholm: Swedish Ministry of Foreign Affairs.

Strange, S. (1988) *States and Markets: an introduction to international political economy*, London: Pinter.

Tickell, C. (2004) 'The need for international rules', *Journal of the Royal United Services Institute*, 149(4), August, pp. 8–12.

Waltz, K. (1979) *Theory of International Politics*, Reading, Mass.: Addison-Wesley.

White House (2002) *The National Security Strategy of the United States of America*, Washington, DC: The White House.

World Markets Research Centre (WMRC) (2003) *G-Index of Globalization*, Foreign Policy Magazine, Globalization Index, Washington, DC.

2

Deepening Democracy

Mary Kaldor

Nowadays nearly everyone is in favour of 'democracy promotion'. Support for democracy has certainly been an important thrust of the policy of the UK Labour government since 1997. When Labour came to power, the then Foreign Secretary, Robin Cook, set out an agenda for promoting human rights and democracy in a new Mission Statement for the Foreign Office: 'The Labour government does not accept that political values can be left behind when we check in our passports to travel on diplomatic business. Our foreign policy must have an ethical dimension and must support the demands of other peoples for democratic rights on which we insist for ourselves' (Cook 1997).

But there has always been a tension within New Labour between the more muscular approach to foreign policy favoured by Tony Blair, which seems to echo Cold War rhetoric and aims to replicate regimes on the western model, and a more 'bottom-up' approach advanced by people like Robin Cook. The Prime Minister's position was laid out in his famous Chicago speech of 1999 where he linked democracy promotion to the UK's security interests, arguing that

> [the] spread of values makes us safer . . . No longer is our existence as states under threat. Now our actions are guided by a more subtle blend of mutual self-interest and moral purpose in defending the values we cherish. In the end, values and interests merge. If we can establish and spread the values of liberty, the rule of law, human rights and an open society then that is in our national interests too. (Blair 1999)

In keeping with this approach, various policies have been adopted to advance democratic goals, including war, as in Kosovo, Iraq and

Afghanistan, sanctions as in Serbia or Iraq, and large-scale expenditure on 'capacity building' in many other countries.

In this chapter, I argue that a progressive UK foreign policy should promote democracy in a substantive sense. That is to say, it should try to make it possible for ordinary people in different parts of the world to influence the decisions that affect their lives. Despite the spread of formal democracy, substantive democracy is under erosion everywhere, in the UK as well as other countries. I argue that this has something to do with globalization. If we are to renew the democratic process, then it is not just a matter of spreading the formal procedures of democracy, it also requires new fora that will provide access for ordinary people to all levels of governance (local, national, global) and a new responsiveness at all levels of governance to public debate and deliberation. In other words, it requires the possibility of negotiating a global social covenant.

Interestingly, most of the literature on democracy promotion and what is known as democratic transition focuses on the national level. Within the globalization literature, there is a lot of discussion of the global democratic deficit but this is rarely taken into account in the democratization literature. This is why the gap between formal and substantive democracy is usually explained in terms of the legacy of authoritarianism or the weakness of democratic culture, despite the fact that the gap characterizes older western democracies as well as newly democratic countries.

In developing this argument, I start by elaborating the distinction between formal and substantive democracy. I then discuss the spread of formal democracy and argue that this has to be understood primarily as a process of global integration: the way in which the practices and institutions needed to participate in the global market and in global decision making are constructed. The various techniques of democracy promotion determine the terms of integration. The more bottom-up the approach, the more the emphasis is on dialogue and communication, the more favourable the terms and the greater the possibilities for substantive democracy. In the last section, I will discuss the need for a global framework for democracy and some of the steps that a progressive UK government could take to advance substantive democracy at different levels.

Formal versus substantive democracy

A few years ago I undertook an evaluation of the European Union's democracy programmes in central and eastern Europe. This included organizing seminars in which participants were asked what they understood by the term 'democracy'. When a seminar was organized in Brussels, the majority of participants emphasized elections, as well as institutions like an independent judiciary, the separation of the legislature from the executive, or even an active civil society. When the seminars were organized inside the newly democratic central and east European countries, the answers were much more subjective. 'It means that bureaucrats are our servants, even if they do not realize it,' said a Polish woman. 'It means that we have to take individual responsibility for decisions and decide for ourselves what we think about political issues instead of following what we are told,' said one young Georgian. And a Romanian girl talked about the new opportunities to choose a life, to be able to travel and to follow one's own interests.

This difference between democracy as a set of procedures or institutions and democracy as the expression or framework for a more subjective notion of freedom has been widely discussed in the literature on political thought. There have always been varying usages and definitions of the term 'democracy'. As George Orwell pointed out: '[N]ot only is there no agreed definition but the attempt to make one is resisted from all sides . . . The defenders of any kind of regime claim that it is a democracy and fear they might have to stop using the word if it were tied down to any one meaning' (Orwell 1957: 149). For de Tocqueville, democracy had essentially two meanings: one was a political regime that was accountable to the people and defined in terms of a range of institutional and procedural mechanisms; the other was a condition of society characterized by its tendency towards equality. This societal democratic condition, the 'habits of the heart', could not be reduced to the formal institutional aspects of democracy. He travelled to America to observe this societal condition and was much impressed by what he called 'democratic expedients' such as lively newspapers, local government and, above all, the practice of association. According to De Tocqueville, 'if men are to remain civilized or to become so, the art of associating together must grow and improve in the same ratio as the equality of conditions is increased' (De Tocqueville 1945: 118).

By formal democracy, I mean the framework of rules and institutions that provide the necessary conditions in which members of a community can shape their own lives to the extent that this does not conflict with others (Held 1995). These institutions encompass an inclusive citizenship, the rule of law, the separation of powers (executive, legislature and judiciary) including an independent judiciary capable of upholding a constitution, elected power-holders, free and fair elections, freedom of expression and alternative sources of information, associational autonomy, and civilian control over the security forces (Kaldor and Vejvoda 1999). By substantive democracy, I mean a process, which has to be continually reproduced, for maximizing the opportunities for all individuals to shape their own lives and to participate in and influence debates about public decisions that affect them.

This contrast between procedural and substantive democracy is paralleled by two other distinctions often drawn in democratic theory. One is the distinction between popular or direct democracy and liberal or representative democracy. Athens is the paradigmatic example of direct democracy, while liberal representative models emerged at the end of the eighteenth century in western Europe and North America (Held 2006). Up until the twentieth century, democracy tended to be equated with direct democracy. For this reason, political theorists were sceptical of democracy because they feared that if every citizen participated directly in decision making, it would lead to what we now call populism: decisions based on fear and prejudice rather than the public use of reason. The liberal democratic model was supposed to resolve this problem by electing representatives who would engage in rational debates about key decisions. The representatives were not supposed to express particular positions or special interests; they were supposed to debate the public good. In his speech to the electors of Bristol on 3 November 1774, Edmund Burke pointed out that

> Parliament is not a *Congress* of Ambassadors from different and hostile interests; which interests each must maintain, as an Agent and Advocate, against other Agents and Advocates; but Parliament is a *deliberative* Assembly of *one* Nation, with *one* Interest, that of the whole; where, not local Purposes, not local Prejudices ought to guide, but the general Good, resulting from the general Reason of the whole. (Burke 1774)

Another distinction is drawn between democracy as a method and democracy as a goal. For Joseph Schumpeter, democracy was viewed as a relatively efficient method of choosing a government, which he likened to a steam engine or a disinfectant. He defined this method as 'that institutional arrangement for arriving at political decisions in which individuals acquire the power to decide by means of a competitive struggle for the people's vote' (Schumpeter 1961: 269). The idea that contestation is likely to produce the best outcome in terms of decision making is the political counterpart of the economic idea that competition in the marketplace will lead to economic efficiency. This Schumpeterian view of democracy contrasts with the idea that democracy is an end in itself, a process through which individuals can realize their aspirations.

Liberal representative models of democracy and the notion of democracy as a method of choosing a government tend to emphasize procedures and institutions both as defining characteristics of democracy and as safeguards against what Kant called 'democratic despotism'. But while it seems true that nothing better than the liberal representative model of democracy has been invented, and while procedures and institutions are the necessary condition for substantive democracy, these are not sufficient to ensure that individuals can influence the circumstances in which they live. Undoubtedly, attempts to represent the 'social condition' as the pre-eminent 'substantive value', as in the former Communist countries, led to tyranny in the twentieth century. However, formal procedures can easily be subverted or 'hollowed out' if an underlying normative commitment to democracy is not embedded in society.

The global spread of democracy

The last three decades of the twentieth century witnessed the global spread of democratic institutions. In 1974, when the Portuguese dictatorship was overthrown, only 39 out of a total of 145 countries were classified as democratic by Freedom House. By 1997 this had increased to 117 out of a total of 191 countries. In other words, whereas roughly a quarter of the countries in the world were classified as democracies in 1974, this had increased to over 60 per cent by 1997 (Diamond 1999). Democratization spread from southern Europe in the 1970s to Latin America and East Asia in the 1980s, and to central and eastern Europe and Africa from 1989 to the early 1990s. Although some of these countries have moved out of the democratic category, others have joined them, including many post-conflict countries in which elections are often held as an exit strategy for the international community. Samuel Huntington dubbed this recent spread of democracy as the 'third wave' of democratization (Huntington 1991).[1]

This global spread of democracy gave rise to great optimism in the 1990s, and ideas like Francis Fukuyama's 'end of history' thesis expressed the conviction that the world was finally discovering that liberal representative democracy combined with free markets constitutes the best possible system of governance. As Gia Nodia, a Georgian democracy specialist, put it: 'the most basic contention that lay at the basis of third-wave optimism was the notion that democracy is now the only "normal" political regime – the only game in the global village, if you will. At the end of the day, democracy is the only political regime that is fully compatible with modernity' (Carothers 2004: 193).

Yet despite the spread of democratic institutions, there remains a big gap between formal and substantive democracy. Many of the countries classified as democracies perform poorly on Freedom House's freedom scores, made up of a combination of political rights and civil liberties. In many countries, democratic procedures that have been specified in laws and constitutions are only partially implemented. Newly emerging democracies may therefore be characterized by varying combinations of a weak rule of law, the lack of an independent judiciary, limitations on freedom of speech and association, ethnic or religious exclusion, election fraud or presidential domination.

These procedural weaknesses are often associated with substantive weaknesses, which may include: the tendency for political parties to extend control over different spheres of social life in ways that limit political participation; government repression of the media and non-governmental organizations (NGOs); a politicized and clientilistic administration; various forms of racist or xenophobic sectarianism which may provide a basis for populism; and a widespread sense of personal insecurity that undermines the ability and readiness to debate public issues owing to inadequate law enforcement and an undeveloped judiciary. Political participation is also often low, as evidenced by low voter turnouts, low membership of political parties, and widespread apathy, disillusion and cynicism. Indeed, the introduction of democratic procedures such as elections may lead to conflict, state failure and/or elective dictatorship. Few countries in central and southern Europe or South America have escaped this fate.

In a widely quoted article entitled 'The end of the transition paradigm', Thomas Carothers suggests that most so-called transition countries have actually entered a 'political grey zone' characterized by two broad models – 'feckless pluralism' (Latin America) or 'dominant power politics' (post-Communist world, Africa and the Middle East) (Carothers 2004). A number of other terms have been used to describe these types of polity, including illiberal democracy, pseudo democracy, cosmetic democracy, façade democracy, semi-democracy and virtual democracy.

The gap between formal and substantive democracy is usually explained in terms of the legacy of authoritarianism, and this is an important factor. The anomie, submissiveness and passivity of individuals, the experience of patronage and clientelism, the suspicion of parties, politicians and bureaucrats, and the pervasiveness of exclusivist ideologies can all contribute to a profoundly distorted and traumatized 'societal condition'. But a number of authors point out that the gap, while larger in newly emerging democracies, can be found in older democracies as well. Thus Carothers talks about the 'syndrome of post-modern fatigue with democracy and perhaps politics itself' (Carothers 2004: 150).

Others point to the 'simultaneity' problem – the fact that the transition to democracy is taking place at the same time as the transition from a statist planned economy to a market system. The introduction of economic liberalization and privatization has often led to dramatic falls in income and deterioration in public services, as well as increased inequality. These all contribute to dissatisfaction with the political class (see Andras Bozoki in Kaldor and Vejvoda 1999; see also Elster et al. 1998).

But what is rarely discussed in the literature on 'transition' or newly emerging democracies is the global context. Those who write about democratization tend to analyse the process within a national or comparative framework. Yet the spread of democratization has coincided with the speeding up of the process known as globalization – growing interconnectedness in political, economic or cultural spheres. Theorists of globalization point to the global democratic deficit which results from the speeding up of globalization (see, for example, Archibugi and Held 1998; Rosenau 1997). In the context of globalization, democracy, in a substantive sense, is undermined. This is because, however perfect the formal institutions, so many important decisions that affect people's lives are no longer taken at the level of the state. Democracy assumes congruence between the state, the people, the economy and territory. Yet this congruence no longer exists. Increased migration means that the 'people' cross boundaries and live in multicultural global cities. The economy is increasingly shaped by the decisions of global companies, free-floating speculators and international financial institutions. States have to take into account a range of international agreements which constrain national choices.

This applies to all countries to a greater or lesser degree. What is the meaning of elections when, for example, decisions about the size of budgets or environmental regulations or war and peace are taken by the International Monetary Fund (IMF), the European Union (EU) or the United Nations (UN)? Is the gap between formal and substantive democracy that we observe in the newly emerging democracies not merely a symptom of globalization that affects all democracies at the national level?

It can be argued that the spread of democracy is both a cause and a consequence of globalization. The collapse of authoritarian states was precipitated by market pressures, increased communication (travel, radio and television, and more recently faxes and the Internet) and the extension of international law. In the 1970s and 1980s, the failure of the statist model of development, diminished levels of economic aid and the growth of indebtedness contributed to growing disaffection. This led to demands, often from outside donors, to introduce democratization measures that would legitimize painful economic reforms. In some countries, frustrated bureaucrats saw an opportunity to translate political positions into economic wealth. These impulses towards democratization from above were paralleled by pressure from below, as communication with the outside world and the adoption of human rights laws by non-democratic states helped to nurture nascent civil societies. But while economic, political, technological and legal interconnectedness may have contributed to democratization, the processes of political and economic liberalization have also further accelerated global integration.

Indeed, it can be argued that the spread of democratic procedures is essentially a form of global integration. It is a way in which the institutions and practices necessary to participate in the global system are established. These can range from regulations governing foreign investment and trade, to the political legitimacy required to be considered a serious actor in the various fora of global governance. The Foreign and Commonwealth Office (FCO) Human Rights Report for 2005 argues that the increased commitment to democracy promotion is driven by a twin logic: 'because it is the right thing to do and because we have a direct interest in building the conditions for sustainable global security and prosperity while fostering reliable and responsible international partners' (Foreign and Commonwealth Office 2005: 205).

Whether global integration also leads to substantive democracy, however, depends on whether individuals are able to influence the terms of global integration. In many cases, newly emerging democracies are offered standard recipes for transition, all of which are adopted by competing political parties. The language of transition is often reminiscent of the language of authoritarianism, as supposedly technical solutions are offered to social and economic problems and the pain of transition is considered the medicine needed to reach some promised utopia. The Communists called on people to tighten their belts and work harder so that they could attain socialism; nowadays people are told much the same things in the hopes of reaching the Nirvana of capitalism. Citizens come to experience their rulers as being as distant and manipulative as in former times. Moreover, the lack of choice in the new democracies often leads to an emphasis on religious and ethnic difference as a way of winning votes, in the absence of any progressive alternative to the standard transition recipe.

Of course, there are important differences among the newly emerging democracies. Some states, especially those in the Balkans and Africa, have disintegrated under the impact of liberalization. Ian Bremmer suggests that it is during the transition from authoritarianism to democracy that the risk of instability is greatest (Bremmer 2006). Yet other states, particularly in southern and central Europe, are considered relatively successful. The explanation for this contrast lies partly in the specific political experiences of each state, and partly in economic factors. But if we understand the spread of democratic institutions as a form of global integration, then these differences also relate to the extent to which newly emerging democracies are able to shape their position in the global system. And this, in turn, depends on the various instruments through which democracy is developed. The more that democratic institutions are introduced as a result of pressure from above, the less favourable are likely to be the terms. Conversely, the more that democracy is the outcome of the actions of individuals wanting to influence the conditions of their lives, the better the terms of global integration and the more substantive is democracy.

Techniques of democracy promotion

During the Cold War, the political left were generally suspicious of democracy promotion, seeing it as a guise for neocolonial interventionism. The general presumption during this period was one of non-interference in the internal affairs of other countries. In the 1970s and 1980s, however, peace and human rights groups became increasingly active in opposing dictatorships, especially the apartheid government in South Africa and the military dictatorships in Latin America. Those against the Cold War division of Europe began a strategy of 'détente from below', linking up with opposition groups in eastern Europe (Kaldor 2003a).

The typical approach of western activists was to provide moral and material support to local civil society groups such as the African National Congress (ANC) in South Africa, human rights groups in Latin America and groups like Solidarity or Charter 77 in central Europe, by helping with literature and campaign materials, publicizing their cause, protecting local dissidents through public disclosure, demonstrating or travelling to the region in solidarity. The debates with local groups led to the development of joint strategies, including pressure on western governments to use various instruments to oppose repression and dictatorship. Hence the sanctions on South Africa, the human rights legislation introduced in Congress in relation to Latin America, and the insistence on respect for the Helsinki Final Act in Europe. These were all examples of what Keck and Sikkink (1998) call the 'boomerang effect'.

Even before the 1989 revolutions in central and eastern Europe, western governments and international institutions joined the bandwagon. The democratization of much of the post-Communist world further reduced the international resistance to governmental involvement in democracy promotion. Since the concern of this book is foreign policy, it is worth outlining the various tools available to policy-makers in government to promote democracy. Broadly speaking, it is possible to distinguish three types of tool.

The first type of tool is *administrative*. Administrative tools consist of coercive pressure by governments on other governments; they are pressures 'from above'. They include efforts to bring about regime change (as in Afghanistan and Iraq), sanctions (as have been applied to South Africa, Iraq, Serbia and North Korea) as well as conditionalities attached to aid. The EU always attaches a democracy clause to agreements with third countries. During the 1990s, international financial institutions (IFIs) insisted on political and economic reforms as a condition for loans.

The second type of tool is *monetary*. It has been estimated that some $2 billion a year is spent on democracy assistance, mainly by the United States and Europe, although the true figure is probably much higher (Youngs 2006). Democracy assistance tends to cover such areas as: elections and election monitoring, security sector reform, judicial reform and transitional justice mechanisms, support for political parties and parliamentary institutions, public service reform and support for media and civil society. US assistance is both public and private – the Open Society Foundation (George Soros) is probably the biggest single funder of democracy programmes. After 9/11, the US increased official democracy assistance from US$800 million (in 2000) to $1.4 billion (in 2005) (Mathieson and Youngs 2006). European funding is primarily public.

The UK is one of the biggest donors in the democracy field. In 2005–6, the Department for International Development (DFID) committed €508 million (14 per cent of total aid) to the 'governance' budget. Under Clare Short, the emphasis was more on state capacity than democracy, but Hilary Benn has put more emphasis on policies aimed at increasing political freedom. In addition, the FCO has various democracy budgets. Particularly important is the Global Opportunities Fund, which allocated 60 per cent of its total funding (€87 million in 2005–6) to democracy, human rights and good governance initiatives.

Finally, the Westminster Foundation for Democracy, comprised of all the Westminster political parties as well as representatives from civil society, spends around €8 million per year.

The third type of tool is *communication and dialogue*. Essentially this means engaging both government and civil society in debates among themselves and with outsiders. This was primarily what the peace and human rights groups did in the 1970s and 1980s, and it is also often the job of diplomats. Chris Patten as the EU's External Affairs Commissioner put great emphasis on political dialogue within the EU framework.

The effectiveness of different democracy promotion techniques still needs to be systematically assessed. There are, however, many criticisms of current techniques. It is often argued that administrative and financial techniques are counterproductive because democracy cannot be imposed or bought from the outside. External military intervention can destroy regimes but it cannot build democracy – the consequence is more likely to be state failure, as in Iraq and Afghanistan. Sanctions weaken the state, but simultaneously allow the state to mask its weaknesses by enabling a mobilization of political support against the external enemies who impose sanctions. An influx of money may lead to the formation of artificial NGOs and the crowding out of genuine grass roots initiatives. It may foster corruption, or fund the training of individuals who then use their new skills to find jobs abroad.

A related criticism is that administrative tools and money are directed less at the democratic process and more at establishing pro-western governments. Thus the United States favoured its own expatriate allies in Iraq, but failed to respect the results of legitimate elections in Palestine in 2006 because they were won by Hamas, an organization it classified as 'terrorist'. The sanctions on Serbia and Iraq were not aimed at promoting democracy as such; rather they were related to foreign policy goals such as the elimination of weapons of mass destruction (WMD) in Iraq or the prevention of ethnic cleansing in Bosnia and Kosovo in the case of Serbia. The more muscular approach to democracy promotion often conflates pro-democracy with pro-western.

There is merit to these arguments, but they are not always accurate. Sometimes military intervention can help provide security and the conditions for a political process that can lead to democracy. The UK-led intervention in Sierra Leone in 1999–2000 is an example of this. Sanctions do seem to have worked in South Africa, and it is often said that targeted sanctions against Milosevic and his cronies were a major reason for his capitulation at the end of the North Atlantic Treaty Organization (NATO) bombing. Funding for independent radio in

Serbia or for young people's resistance movements like Otpor (Serbia) and Pora (Ukraine) helped to contribute to the colour-coded revolutions in these countries. Moreover, while Pora was pro-western, this was not true of Otpor. Meanwhile, it can be argued that the sanctions against South Africa were successful because they were a response to civil society pressure and could not be used by the South African government to mobilize public opinion against those who imposed the sanctions.

Ultimately, there are no blueprints for democracy promotion. While experiences and methods can be offered, what fits any particular situation will be a complex set of political compromises that result from an ongoing process, rather than externally provided standard recipes.

When the USA and the UK invaded Iraq in 2003, they assumed that they would be welcome. This perception was based on talks held with exiles and politicians in the relatively free Kurdish region in northern Iraq. But they had not talked to others inside Iraq who were offering alternative advice at that time. These included underground movements and parties such as the Al Da'wa Party (Shi'ite Islamist), the Communist Party, the General Union of Students (GUSIA) and the League of Iraqi Women. There were also artists who met and talked at the Hewar (dialogue) gallery established by a well-known artist who left the Ba'ath Party at the time of the invasion of Kuwait. A group known as the Wednesday Group, composed of current and ex-Ba'athists, met once a week to discuss political and intellectual issues, even after one of their members was arrested and executed (Said in Anheier et al. 2004). Among both Sunni and Shi'ite clerics, there were those who were trying to create more open space within the mosques in a strategy reminiscent of the Catholic Church in Poland.[2]

These underground groups were suggesting a strategy more like the opening up of eastern Europe. For example, they proposed that the UN should run the oil-for-food programme instead of allowing it to be channelled through the government, which had turned the programme into a device for the ruling clique to sustain their incomes. They also favoured the return of the weapons inspectors, not just because this would be more likely to bring the WMD programme under control, but because the presence of the inspectors made them feel safer. They pointed out that the 1991 cease-fire resolution did cover security issues like the elimination of WMD but that it also included commitments to human rights and political pluralism. They suggested that these commitments should receive more emphasis: for example, human rights monitors could have accompanied the weapons inspectors (Kaldor 2003b).

This is not to say that communication necessarily means taking local advice. Such advice is often conflicting and may involve special pleading. But communication and dialogue are both key to empowering civil society and shaping democracy strategies. Financial and administrative instruments can be useful where they are a response to bottom-up demands. But they are less likely to be effective where they are used to export particular models of democracy or support particular pro-western factions. Communication has to be sustained if 'opening up' is to lead to substantive democracy. It is not just a matter of limited engagement designed to bring about a regime change. The toppling of dictators is just one moment in the continuous process of constructing the practices and institutions needed for global integration.

Whether this makes things worse, for example through the spread of 'new wars' or transnational crime, or whether it makes things better, by leading to substantive democracy, will depend on the extent to which pressure from below is mobilized to influence the terms of global integration. For example, can civil society groups mobilize with counterparts in other countries on issues like debt repayment, trade agreements and the terms of membership in international organizations like the Council of Europe and NATO? In other words, communication has to cover broad global issues such as social justice, human rights and environmental responsibility, and not just the issue of formal democratic institutions.

The role of global civil society

The neoconservatives often point to Israel as the only democracy in the Middle East. One can quibble about the claim. There is a case to be made for counting Turkey and Lebanon as democracies, even if, as in the case of Lebanon, politics are organized on a consociational basis. Elections are held with some regularity in Iran, even though reformist candidates are often disqualified. All the same, there is no doubt that elections in Israel are freer and fairer than anywhere else in the Middle East, and debates in the Knesset or in Israeli civil society are as lively as anywhere else in the world. Palestinians often say that they have learned about democracy from watching Israeli television. Yet what does it mean to have a democracy based on an exclusive notion of community: that is to say, an exclusive Jewish state? A much more extreme example is South Africa under apartheid. Mamdani argues that during the colonial period in Africa, civil and political rights were reserved for the Europeans while a coercive tribal law was imposed on the 'natives' (Mamdani 1996). He considers that South Africa under apartheid represented the generic case of this type of dualism between citizen and subject. During the apartheid years, white South Africans held free elections and debated among themselves and claimed they were the only democracy in Africa, even though blacks were excluded and repressed.

These examples highlight a more general problem with democracy. Representative democracy is necessarily exclusive. It is territorially based and it excludes non-citizens: those who are not permanent residents. In a world where territorial boundaries matter less and where communities are no longer congruent with territory, the exclusive character of democracy helps to explain the limitations on substantive involvement in democracy. For example, should Iraqis not be able to vote in American elections? Should British citizens not be able to influence conditions in Pakistan, since so many minority groups in the UK come from that country?

In contrast to democracy, civil society is no longer territorially bounded. Like democracy, civil society is one of those terms that has very many definitions and the discussion about definitions is part of what civil society is about. I define civil society as the medium through which social contracts or bargains are negotiated between the individual and the centres of political and economic authority. Civil society is a process of management of society that is 'bottom-up' rather than 'top-down' and that involves the struggle for emancipatory goals. Civil society also includes reactionary groups – those struggling to preserve traditions or those who have exclusionary agendas – but it is the site where all these issues are debated and negotiated. Civil society makes possible governance based on consent, where consent is generated through politics. Substantive democracy is possible only where procedural democracy is accompanied by and indeed constructed by a strong and active civil society.

Up until 1989, the definition of civil society was much narrower. Moreover, civil society was considered to exist only in part of the world – primarily north-west Europe and North America. The reinvention of the concept of civil society in the 1970s and 1980s was linked to the wave of new social movements that developed after 1968 – the generation described by Ulrich Beck as 'freedom's children' (Beck 1998). These movements operated outside formal party politics and were concerned with new issues such as gender, the environment, peace and human rights. They were harbingers of more radical demands for democracy based on autonomy, participation and self-organization – but also of a growing global consciousness and the sense of a common humanity. They also made use of the emerging infrastructure of globalization – air travel and improved information and communications technology.

The language of civil society which expressed these aspirations was reinvented simultaneously in societies struggling against authoritarianism and militarism in Latin America and eastern Europe. In both cases, there was a similar emphasis on human dignity and on 'islands of engagement'. The intellectuals in both regions understood civil society as something that was distinct from the state, even anti-state, involving a rolling back of the state in everyday life. They linked this idea with transnational concerns – opposition to the Cold War and to national security doctrines that were prevalent in Latin America – and with the belief that the reinvented concept of civil society had global relevance. In both cases, these ideas expressed a practical reality: on the one hand, the growth of international legal instruments that could be used to criticize the state, and on the other hand, involvement in transnational networks of activists with North America and western Europe which helped to protect these islands of engagement, and through which these ideas were debated, refined and exported.

At a moment when democracy at a national level appears to be 'hollowing out', the informal political sphere is increasingly active through NGOs. This includes those operating at local levels and those with global brand names like Oxfam, Human Rights Watch and Greenpeace, as well as a new wave of global social movements like the Social Forums, the anti-war movement and Islamist and other national or religious movements.[3] Moreover, new types of informal policy making are being pioneered on big global issues like social justice, climate change and war. These problems are being tackled through consumer practices (fair trade or carbon miles) and through volunteering (delivering humanitarian aid or acting as civilian monitors).

The challenge for the promotion of substantive democracy is how to close the gap between the political class that is produced by a nationally based formal democracy, and global civil society. On the one hand, this would mean that efforts to establish democratic procedures at local and national levels should be the outcome of debates at local levels, even if external models, ideas and experiences are taken into account. A substantive democracy in this sense would be based on a social contract negotiated among those territorially defined individuals who are constructing a democracy, even though they are influenced by or have links with external actors. On the other hand, closing the gap would also mean that any agreements about democratic procedures reached at local and national levels should be supplemented by a process of negotiating a global social contract.

Substantive democracy is possible only if people live in a relatively secure environment in which they are able to make decisions without fear and without coercion, and where they have some control over the allocation of resources or are able to take preventive measures in the event of environmental risks. Essentially, citizens need to be directly involved in deliberation about the big global issues of our time – human security, social justice and climate change.

Implications for UK foreign policy

In light of this analysis, what should a progressive UK foreign policy look like when it comes to supporting democracy? As a preliminary observation, it should be noted that the distinction between foreign policy and domestic policy is eroded in a global era. If we are talking about human security, social justice or climate change, then the design of UK policy should not be the sole responsibility of the Foreign and Commonwealth Office, the Department for International Development and the Ministry of Defence. The Home Office, the Treasury and the Department for Environment, Food and Rural Affairs (DEFRA) need to be involved as well. Moreover, in so far as foreign policy deals with diplomatic relations between states, there would need to be a recasting of diplomacy. Diplomatic relations can no longer be merely relations among national elites. It is important for diplomats to open up communication and dialogue with all levels of society, to be 'bottom-up' as well as 'top-down'.

In terms of concrete policies, the implication of my argument is threefold. First, administrative tools and money need to be guided by debates at local, national and global levels. The aim of democracy promotion is to help create and protect political spaces where projects and procedures can be discussed and negotiated. Bureaucrats tend to favour 'capacity building' and measurable outcomes. Yet the most important role that outsiders can play is in facilitating discussions and meetings and responding to local agendas. This may mean less rather than more funding. But what it does require is more ambitious efforts to create channels through which ordinary people and the associations they form can have access to political authority at all levels.

At a global level, this means promoting new forms of accountability for multilateral institutions that will require organizations like the IMF, the World Bank and the UN to engage seriously with local opinions. At national levels, it means fostering interactions between governments, municipalities and civil society that will help to overcome taboos, bring factional groups together, stimulate a notion of public interest and empower organizations that are engaged in important public policy work around, for example, gender issues or human rights. Capacity-building assistance has been poured into Iraq and much has vanished through security costs and corruption. Yet what is really needed in Iraq is a broad dialogue, especially involving those groups like the Iraqi women's network and humanitarian organizations that are outside the current factional intrigues.

Secondly, governments may not be the best institutions for imposing administrative measures or spending money, since they are more likely to be guided by national self-interest and to favour particular factions, whatever Tony Blair may say about the merger of values and interests. Administrative measures should be adopted only within a multilateral framework and after civil society consultations. Money could be better spent at arm's length by independent public bodies. For example, much more UK democracy funding might be channelled through the Westminster Foundation, which is accountable to political parties and civil society. It might also be a good idea to establish a European or an International Democracy Foundation that would be relatively autonomous from national governments, the EU and international institutions, and which could include representatives of civil society from potential democracies as well as from donor countries in its decision-making processes.

Systematic evaluation of democracy promotion initiatives would be another mechanism for ensuring that assistance is guided by 'bottom-up' concerns. Instead of formal benchmarks, stakeholder meetings involving recipients and their peers could be used to assess the utility and effectiveness of democracy assistance. Such stakeholder meetings would also create opportunities to foster debate about democracy promotion in specific contexts.

Thirdly, and perhaps most importantly, democracy promotion means the provision of imaginative responses to demands from global civil society. The best form of empowerment is success, and the knowledge that engagement leads to meaningful outcomes. Action designed to fulfil an emerging global social contract or covenant – that is the consequence of numerous debates, campaigns and arguments taking place all over the world – offers a political project that can help to recast democracy at local and national levels. A good example of what is meant by this is the enlargement of the European Union. The EU can be understood as a new type of multilateral organization at a regional level, promoting, as it were, regional public goods. Membership of the EU for newly emerging democracies has become an appealing political project that does take democracy forward. In the same way, a global social covenant could offer a political project for 'civilizing' globalization and pressing for global public goods, such as resource redistribution or global action to tackle climate change, which represents an alternative to backward-looking sectarianism.

Democracy promotion efforts that attempt to improve political procedures are necessary to create democracy in a substantive sense. But the 'political grey zone' that has been created so far is unsustainable. The alternative to democracy in a substantial sense is not a return to authoritarianism; closed societies are no longer an option. This is the politics of fear based on various forms of populist exclusion, state weakness and, in the final instance, 'new wars' and terror. The London bombing illustrated what might be described as the 'perverse boomerang effect' when disaffected minorities make common cause with those with similar nihilistic political positions elsewhere. Reinvigorating democracy, both at home and abroad, means both a bottom-up process of communication and, at the same time, taking seriously an ambitious global agenda.

Notes

1 The first two waves, both of which were ended by a reverse wave, were 1828 to 1926 and 1943 to 1964.
2 Members of the Council of Sunni Clerics whom I met in May 2004 told me how they had come to the conclusion that they could never defeat Saddam Hussein through a coup; instead, from 1999 onwards they developed a strategy, together with their Shi'ite counterparts, of slow strangulation (see Kaldor and Said 2003).
3 For information and mapping of global civil society, see the annual yearbooks *Global Civil Society*.

References

Anheier, H., Glasius, M. and Kaldor, M. (eds) (2004) *Global Civil Society 2004/5*, London: Sage.

Archibugi, D. and Held, D. (eds) (1998) *Reimagining Political Community: studies in cosmopolitan democracy*, Cambridge: Polity.

Beck, U. (1998) *Democracy without Enemies*, Cambridge: Polity.

Blair, T. (1999) 'Doctrine of the international community', speech by the Prime Minister to the Economic Club of Chicago, Hilton Hotel, Chicago, US, 22 April; available at: www.number-10.gov.uk/output/Page1297.asp.

Bremmer, I. (2006) *The J Curve: a new way to understand why nations rise and fall*, New York: Simon and Schuster.

Burke, E. (1774) 'Speech to the electors of Bristol', 3 November, *Works*, vol. 1, pp. 446–8; available at: http://press-publ.uchicago.edu/founders/documents/v1ch13s7.html.

Carothers, T. (2004) *Critical Mission: essays on democracy promotion*, Washington, DC: Carnegie Endowment for International Peace.

Cook, R. (1997) *Foreign and Commonwealth Office Mission Statement*, 12 May; available at: www.guardian.co.uk/ethical/article/0,,192031,00.html.

De Toqueville, A. (1945) *Democracy in America*, New York: Vintage Books (originally published in 1835).

Diamond, L. (1999) *Developing Democracy: toward consolidation*, London: Johns Hopkins University Press.

Elster, J., Offe, C. and Preuss, U. K. (1998) *Institutional Design in Post-communist Societies: rebuilding the ship at sea*, Cambridge: Cambridge University Press.

Foreign and Commonwealth Office (2005) *Human Rights Annual Report*, London: FCO.

Held, D. (1995) *Democracy and the Global Order: from the modern state to cosmopolitan governance*, Cambridge: Polity.

Held, D. (2006) *Models of Democracy*, 3rd edition, Cambridge: Polity.

Held, D., McGrew, A., Goldblatt, D. and Perraton, J. (2003) *Global Transformations Reader*, Cambridge: Polity.

Huntington, S. (1991) *The Third Wave: democratization in the late twentieth century*, Norman, Okla.: University of Oklahoma Press.

Kaldor, M. (2003a) *Global Civil Society: an answer to war*, Cambridge: Polity.

Kaldor, M. (2003b) 'In place of war: open up Iraq', *OpenDemocracy*, 13 February.

Kaldor, M. and Said, Y. (2003) *Regime Change in Iraq*, Centre for the Study of Global Governance Discussion Paper 26, London: London School of Economics and Political Science, November.

Kaldor, M. and Vejvoda, I. (1999) *Democratisation in East and Central Europe*, London: Pinter.

Keck, M. and Sikkink, K. (1998) *Activists Beyond Borders: advocacy networks in international politics*, Ithaca, NY: Cornell University Press.

Mamdani, M. (1996) *Citizen and Subject: contemporary Africa and the legacy of late colonialism*, Princeton: Princeton University Press.

Mathieson, D. and Youngs, R. (2006) 'Democracy promotion and the European left: ambivalence confused?', FRIDE *Working Paper 29*, Madrid: Fundación para las Relaciones Internacionales y el Diálogo Exterior, December.

Orwell, G. (1957) *Selected Essays*, London: Penguin.

Rosenau, J. (1997) *Along the Domestic–Foreign Frontier: exploring governance in a turbulent world*, Cambridge: Cambridge University Press.

Schumpeter, J. A. (1961) *Capitalism, Socialism and Democracy*, London: George Allen and Unwin.

Youngs, R. (ed.) (2006) Survey of European Democracy Promotion Policies 2000–2006, Madrid: Fundación para las Relaciones Internacionales y el Diálogo Exterior (FRIDE).

3

Human Rights, Justice and Security

David Mepham

The purpose of this chapter is to reaffirm the importance of human rights to a progressive conception of foreign policy. It will argue that a UK foreign policy that aspires to be progressive should give enhanced priority to the protection and promotion of human rights globally. At the same time, the chapter suggests that the context for advancing human rights internationally has changed very dramatically in recent years, especially following the 11 September 2001 attacks in the US and the wars with Afghanistan and Iraq. While George Bush talks about the spread of freedom and democracy, the pursuit of these objectives has been hugely damaged by the manner in which the US administration has pursued its so-called 'war on terror'. This policy has been carried out in the name of security but it has been seriously counterproductive, with the world today more unstable, dangerous and divided than it was six years ago.

Tony Blair's staunch backing for Bush's strategy has also undermined the UK's standing on human rights issues in many parts of the world. If the UK government is to restore its global credibility on these issues, it will need to learn from the mistakes and failures of recent policy and think more imaginatively about how human rights can best be supported in different contexts around the world.

For the purposes of this chapter, human rights are defined as a set of basic entitlements – civil, cultural, economic, political and social – that should be available to all human beings regardless of race, creed, gender, age or any other social status. A set of entitlements or legitimate claims of this kind was first set out in the Universal Declaration on Human Rights (UDHR) in 1948. Subsequent international agreements – for example, the International Covenant on Civil and Political Rights (ICCPR) and the International Covenant on Economic, Social and Cultural Rights (ICESCR) – defined more clearly the scope of these entitlements. Although public discussion of human rights often focuses exclusively on civil and political rights, progressives should stress the equal importance of economic and social rights, and the extent to which the two sets of rights are inter-dependent and mutually reinforcing.

Structurally this chapter is organized into four parts. First, the chapter defends the idea of the universality of human rights against cul-tural relativists, communitarians and 'clash of civilizations' theorists. The second section addresses the highly charged and topical question of the relationship between human rights, security and counter-terrorism. Are human rights a luxury we can no longer afford or our best defence against religious and political extremism? Thirdly, it will be argued that human rights matter to progressive politics because they are a vital means for combating political and economic injustice, some-thing which is important in its own terms but also an essential precon-dition for greater common security. Fourthly, the chapter looks at the issue of intervention and human rights. It will address specifically the 'responsibility to protect': the emerging global norm that the interna-tional community has an obligation to act when faced with massive human rights abuses or war crimes. Throughout this chapter, we will look at examples of UK foreign policy over the last decade: those areas in which UK policy has been progressive, as well as other areas in which it has been less so, or where UK foreign policy has fallen seriously short of its declared human rights principles. The chapter will suggest some future directions and priorities for UK foreign policy.

In defence of universalism

A progressive UK foreign policy should strongly defend the idea that there are some basic universal values: that 'national, ethnic or gendered boundaries should not determine the limits of rights to or responsibil-ities for the satisfaction of basic human needs, and that all human beings require equal moral respect and concern' (Held, chapter 10 in this volume). These were the values that inspired the drafters of the United Nations (UN) Declaration of Human Rights in 1948 and that have contributed, over the last six decades, to the emergence of a com-prehensive international human rights framework, rooted in universal principles of human dignity and equal worth.

The immediate context for the drafters of the UDHR was the experience of European fascism and the Holocaust. Above all else, the enunciation of a set of universal human rights was seen as a way to prevent these horrors from being repeated ever again, to create what has been called 'firewalls against barbarism' (Ignatieff 2001). This remains a key defence of human rights today.

But despite the appeal of universal human rights values – and the efficacy of human rights over six decades as instruments of justice, empowerment and individual freedom (a subject addressed later in this chapter) – the concept is not without its critics. There are two challenges in particular that need to be contested. The first challenge comes from cultural relativists. They assert that the rights set out in the UDHR and in other international human rights agreements reflect western values and cultural norms that are inappropriate to different cultures in other parts of the world. In the 1980s and 1990s this argument was often made by reference to so-called 'Asian values'. Essentially, the argument is that western culture values individual freedom while 'Asian values' give priority to order and discipline. These arguments continue to be made in parts of east Asia, but similar arguments are made across the Islamic world. For example, some Muslims argue that universal human rights run counter to the basic precepts of Islamic teaching in respect of gender relations and freedom of expression.

There are several criticisms that can be made of the relativists' position. Most obviously, the fact that something is part of one's traditional culture does not mean that it is necessarily ethically right or should not be open to challenge. Societies would never develop if every change to existing practice were ruled ineligible by virtue of its novelty.

Cultural relativists also downplay the role of non-westerners in the development of international human rights agreements and their subsequent promotion. The drafters of the UDHR drew on the perspectives of people from many different countries and cultures. Far from its being the imposition of western values on non-western peoples, many of those involved in the formulation of this document were themselves from Asia, Africa, Latin America and the Middle East. Representatives from the developing world made the most significant contribution to the two international human rights covenants in the 1960s (Tharoor 2000).

Moreover, the core values embodied in the international human rights agreements are reflected, to a very large extent, in all of the world's philosophical, cultural and religious traditions. The West has no monopoly on the 'concepts of justice and law, the legitimacy of government, the dignity of the individual, or protection from oppressive or arbitrary rule' (ibid.).

But if universal human rights are fully consistent with, and an essential precondition for, cultural diversity and moral pluralism, they are not value-neutral. They are not, for instance, consistent with abusive forms of government or the coercion of the individual. The case for human rights is precisely that individuals should be allowed to make their own moral choices. Many of the strongest arguments for cultural relativism are made by powerful elites that wish to retain their power over others, and relativism is often an alibi for oppression and discrimination (invariably against women).

The one argument of the cultural relativists that carries particularly strong contemporary resonance is the claim that neocolonialism underpins the concept of universal human rights. The charge is misplaced but it is understandably popular. For example, the Iraq war and broader US policy in the Middle East have damaged the cause of human rights and democratic change in the region, not least by undermining the standing of some local human rights advocates (who are sometimes attacked as apologists for western policy). But the demand that Middle Eastern states comply with basic international human rights standards is not neocolonial. The criticism of Bush and Blair's strategy was not that they were wrong to want to see political reform in the Middle East but that their policies in the region have been so profoundly ill-conceived and poorly executed as to hinder rather than enhance this declared goal (Mepham 2006).

A second contemporary challenge to the idea of universal human rights comes from within western societies themselves. While the neo-conservatives in the US administration have been advocating the spread of democracy and freedom in regions like the Middle East, a growing number of high-profile European and North American academics have questioned the very viability of universal human rights. Some of these thinkers would describe themselves as communitarian, others as liberal, postmodernist or realist. This includes philosophers and political theorists like Amitai Etzioni, John Gray, Stuart Hampshire, Alasdair MacIntyre and John Rawls (Halliday 2000). Despite some profound differences between them, they cohere in their scepticism about the easy transferability of human rights principles to non-western societies. At root, they argue that rights only make sense in the context of a particular kind of society and that this type of society does not necessarily exist in other parts of the world.

However, this position can be challenged on several grounds. Local or national cultures in most part of the world are less distinct and discrete than this approach might suggest. As Fred Halliday has argued,

'The communities/nations we have today in fact grew out of the breakup of earlier, much larger entities, entailing the severing of transnational links. They are constituted by the appropriation of international ideas, currents, populations and technologies' (Halliday 2000: 25). Amongst communitarian thinkers there is also a commonly stated assumption that there is an 'essential' national culture in other people's societies that somehow needs to be discovered or interpreted (Sandel 1998). But it would be more accurate perhaps to view all national cultures as being diverse and subject to different interpretations. There is not one view of Shia Islam in Iran, for example, but many competing ones. In addition, by appearing to abstain from commenting on, or seeking to influence, social and political practices in other people's societies, western theorists may actually strengthen the forces of repression in those societies. One of the things that encourage human rights activists living under authoritarian governments is the knowledge that their efforts are supported by transnational networks of human solidarity.

In defending universal values, progressives should also critique the fashionable but flawed and dangerous notion that the world faces a 'clash of civilizations'. This much-discussed thesis is usually linked to Samuel Huntington's influential book of this name (Huntington 1996).

The thesis is flawed because it assumes that the world can be divided up neatly into 'little boxes of disparate civilizations', with the world's populations partitioned into 'those belonging to "the Western world", "the Hindu world", "the "Buddhist world" ' (Sen 2006: 11). This approach denies the plurality of individuals' identities, the extent of internal divisions within civilizational categories and 'the reach and influence of interactions . . . that go across the borders of so-called civilizations' (ibid.). Furthermore, Huntington's system of classification lacks internal logic. India, for example, is described as part of the 'Hindu civilization', though 145 million of its citizens are Muslim. Moreover, there is no basis for Huntington's claim that these civilizations must necessarily be in conflict with each other. In fact, conflicts are often within cultural and so-called civilizational categories rather than between them, and the causes of these conflicts are generally political or economic rather than cultural.

But Huntington's thesis is dangerous, too. It panders to the siren voices of western chauvinists and Islamic or Hindu fundamentalists. By invoking culture as the defining reference point of international politics, it downplays the importance of global humanitarian norms, the emergence of which has been one of the great advances of the last sixty years. Progressives should argue that human rights abuses are unacceptable regardless of who commits them and who the victims are. Giving priority to cultural or civilizational categories in inter-national relations suggests that 'their' human rights abuses matter more than 'ours', or that the nationality or religion of victims or perpetrators is a relevant factor in determining whether we support or condemn a particular act of violence.

George Bush's use of universalist language and his calls for the spread of democracy and freedom across the world have left many progressives feeling disorientated. But the response should not be to turn our backs on the idea of universal values or to concede ground to cultural relativists or theorists who suggest an inevitable conflict between civilizations. Tony Blair's closeness to the Bush administra-tion has greatly damaged UK standing on this issue. The future direc-tion, however, should be clear. A progressive UK government needs to restate its commitment to the consistent promotion of universal values, including international human rights and international humanitarian law, and to work with others in the international system to further these principles.

Human rights, security and terrorism

In the aftermath of the 11 September 2001 attacks on the US, President Bush declared a 'war on terror', in which the US and its allies would use all means necessary, not least military force, to combat what it regarded as a global threat posed by fanatical Islamists. Although there have been some important differences of emphasis in the UK's approach (including a greater commitment to existing international legal norms), Tony Blair has been extremely supportive of the broad thrust of US policy over this period. In a later section, we will consider the specific issue of military intervention and human rights, including the wars with Afghanistan and Iraq. However, the focus in this section is on other aspects of US and UK counter-terrorism policy and their implications for human rights.

The UK government under Blair has made strong commitments to human rights and has specifically rejected the claim that there is a trade-off between human rights and security. For example, the 2005 Human Rights Report of the UK Foreign Office says, 'The UK is con-vinced that respect for human rights is an essential element of an effec-tive counter-terrorism strategy' (Foreign and Commonwealth Office 2005: 15). But this commendable statement has not always been upheld in practice. Indeed, in contradiction to it, Tony Blair talked about the need to strike a new balance between security and human rights, with the obvious implication that we must give up some rights to gain more security. There are three specific criticisms that can be made of UK policy over this period.

First, the UK has said far too little about the human rights abuses perpetrated by its American ally in various parts of the world. Tony Blair once described the situation at Guantanano Bay as 'an anomaly'. It would be more accurate to describe it as a gross violation of human rights. For over five years, the US has held hundreds of 'terror suspects' without access to lawyers or the prospect of a fair trial, in flagrant disregard of international humanitarian law and the Geneva Conventions. Since 11 September 2001, some 100,000 people have been detained without trial, primarily but not exclusively in Afghanistan and Iraq (Rogers 2006).

The Bush administration has also created an environment within the US military in which torture and other forms of cruel and inhumane punishment have become widespread (Brody 2005). In late 2001, the Defense Secretary, Donald Rumsfeld, approved a series of coercive techniques for 'softening up' detainees for interrogation, 'including the use of guard dogs to induce fear in prisoners, hooding them, and removing their clothes' (2005: 147). While the Bush administration has sought to shift responsibility on to a few individuals, the much-publicized abuses in US prisons in Afghanistan and especially at Abu Ghraib in Iraq are better seen as an inevitable consequence of the 'anything goes' mentality that appears to characterize Bush administration policy towards terrorist suspects. An additional element of US policy has been the practice of 'extraordinary rendition', involving the transfer of terror suspects to third countries for the purposes of interrogation, often to countries such as Egypt or Syria that are known to practise torture.

In response to all these examples of human rights abuses by the US administration, the UK government's recent policy has been pusillanimous. By failing to criticize these US abuses more forcefully, UK credibility on human rights has been seriously undermined. It has also made it harder for the UK to criticize other governments around the world which are violating human rights, and now claim to do so in the name of anti-terrorism (Amnesty International 2007; Human Rights Watch 2006).

Secondly, the Blair government has itself pursued policies that damage human rights internationally. The UK's approach has been significantly different from that of the US. For example, there is no evidence that the UK government has directly supported or condoned torture or inhumane treatment. But the UK's obligations under the UN Convention against Torture (UNCAT) require more than passive non-cooperation in torture.

Take the case of extraordinary rendition. UK government ministers have repeatedly stated their belief that renditions to destinations where detainees might be tortured are not taking place through UK airports or airspace. But the UK government has refused to conduct any proper investigation into whether UK airports or airspace have been used for this purpose. This is despite considerable evidence that aircraft involved in previous renditions have passed through the UK, stopping for refuelling purposes en route, and then flown on to countries known to practise torture (Joint Committee on Human Rights 2006a; Amnesty International 2007). A progressive UK foreign policy should be calling for an immediate end to this inhumane practice.

The UK government has also introduced extensive new powers to question terrorist suspects for longer periods before they need to be charged or released, to broaden the definition of terrorism and to deport terrorist suspects to third countries, even where there are concerns about the use of torture in those countries. It has sought to justify the latter policy by linking these deportations to memorandums of understanding with the countries concerned. But undertakings not to use torture made by states known to use torture lack credibility and would appear to violate the UK's obligations under international law. These policies have been criticized strongly by, amongst others, the UN Special Rapporteur on Torture, the UN High Commissioner for Human Rights and the Commissioner for Human Rights of the Council of Europe – and with good reason. There is evidence, for example, that individuals deported from other western countries on the basis of diplomatic assurances have later been tortured (Amnesty International 2007).

Preventing acts of terrorism in the UK clearly requires effective legal, policing and intelligence policies. But such policies should safeguard basic human rights principles and avoid taking steps that antagonize the very communities whose cooperation is needed to prevent further acts of violence. This does not mean adopting a policy of 'human rights absolutism' – the idea that human rights can never be questioned. The argument here is that we should be extremely cautious before jettisoning hard-won freedoms, that the alleged trade-offs between security and human rights are greatly overstated, that to defeat political violence we need to win public support and cooperation and not just increase our punitive powers, and that constitutional safeguards tend to strengthen our security rather than weaken it. The UK's experience of tackling terrorism in Northern Ireland provides some salutary lessons. 'Repressive British government policies and actions in the 1970s and 1980s opened up a wellspring of support for violent terror groups such as the IRA and the INLA that may not have existed otherwise. This is a clear illustration of how legal coercion and police and military repression pushed moderates into the camp of the extremists' (Ashby Wilson 2006: 32).

The UK Parliament's Joint Committee on Human Rights has made a number of thoughtful suggestions for tackling terrorism while upholding human rights (Joint Committee on Human Rights 2006b). Specifically, the committee calls on the government to resort more frequently 'to the criminal law in the effort to counter terrorism', as opposed to lengthy pre-charge detention. The committee proposes that there is a need for new mechanisms of independent accountability and oversight of both the security and intelligence agencies and the government's claims based on intelligence information. It also suggests that there should be greater parliamentary oversight of anti-terrorism policies.

One other area in which UK policy has run counter to its declared commitments on human rights is that of arms transfers. The UK is licensing military equipment to a number of states that are listed as 'major areas of concern' in the annual report on human rights by the Foreign and Commonwealth Office (FCO). This includes China, Colombia, Indonesia, Israel, Russia and Saudi Arabia. Despite the passage of the Export Control Act (2002), the government has also failed to introduce adequate controls over UK arms brokers and traffickers. Many of the weapons feeding conflict and human rights abuses in the developing world are being supplied by arms brokers, including brokers from the UK; but UK controls will do little to curb the activity of UK nationals involved in this trade.

A progressive UK foreign policy should introduce much tighter controls over military transfers. This should include a presumption to deny arms export licences for countries that violate human rights, the introduction of stronger controls over UK arms brokers and traffickers, a strengthening of the European Union (EU) Code of Conduct on arms exports, and support for an International Arms Trade Treaty that sets high common standards governing weapons transfers internationally.

A third criticism of recent UK policy relates to the notion of the 'war on terror' itself. While the term was coined by George Bush, Tony Blair has been a strong supporter of this approach, in a way that has been damaging to the UK's global standing. Criticism of the 'war on terror' is more than an issue of semantics. The failings and flaws in US and UK policy over the last six years stem directly from this muddled and misconceived concept.

The threat of terrorist violence against western civilian targets is a very serious one. But action to address this threat is not a war in any conventional sense. For example, the terrorist bombings in London in July 2005 were carried out not by foreigners but by Muslims born and raised in the UK. Addressing this challenge means countering the sources of radicalization amongst a small section of the British Muslim community and those factors that are making them turn to extreme violence. There are issues here about education, multiculturalism and the role of radical preachers.

But there is a UK foreign policy dimension to this, too. It seems very clear, for example, that the war with Iraq has helped to fuel Muslim extremism in the UK (and internationally). A leaked letter from Michael Jay, the then Permanent Secretary at the Foreign Office, says that UK foreign policy has been a 'recurring theme' in the Muslim community, 'especially in the context of the Middle East peace process and Iraq'. The letter continues, 'this seems to be a key driver behind recruitment by extremist organisations' (quoted in Bright 2005). Similarly, a report by US intelligence agencies, released in September 2006, suggests that Iraq has become a 'cause celebre' for Islamic militants worldwide and helped to 'recruit supporters for the global jihadist movement' (*Christian Science Monitor* 2006).

More broadly, there is a lack of evidence that the counter-terrorism strategies of the US and the UK are working: on the contrary, in the period since 11 September 2001, hostility to the West has grown, extremist groups have gained new recruits and there has been an increase in terrorist incidents, with more terror attacks in the five years after 11 September than in the five years before (Rogers 2006). Al-Qaeda or like-minded individuals and groups have 'perpetrated at least thirty major attacks in that time: they include Karachi (three times), Islamabad, Bali (twice), Jakarta (twice), Istanbul (twice), London, Madrid, Sinai (three times), Riyadh, Tunis, Casablanca and Mombasa' (ibid.).

A further profound flaw in the concept of the 'war on terror' is the assumption that terrorist violence lacks any kind of political, social or historical context. But if terrorism is defined as the 'intentional or reckless killing of civilians in order to communicate a political message', then this is a tactic not an ideology, with a long history, and one that has been used as often by states as by non-state actors (Gearty 2006). Nor is it a tactic confined to the peoples of one continent or one religion.

To counter this kind of violence more effectively requires an enhanced law enforcement strategy, in place of the 'war on terror'. 'A justice model would mean categorizing terrorist crimes less as acts of war and more as crimes against humanity, and seeking, wherever possible, to deal with them using both national and international institutions of justice' (Ashby Wilson 2005: 30). Such an approach should be central to a progressive UK policy, involving stronger international cooperation between governments, multilateral institutions, and police, intelligence and law enforcement agencies.

Reducing the risks of violence, terrorism and global instability also requires a sustained effort to address the underlying causes or drivers of political and religious radicalization. The more effective protection and promotion of human rights is fundamental to this and is the focus of the next section.

Human rights and justice: tackling the roots of instability

Over the last six decades, human rights have become an important means by which oppressed and marginalized groups have sought to improve their political and civil status and their economic and social conditions. Most governments in the world have signed up to the international human rights treaties and covenants. Although many of these governments fail, to varying degrees, to fulfil their international obligations, the fact that they are signatories to these commitments can and has been used by oppressed and disenfranchised people to better assert their rights, by international advocacy organizations to lobby on their behalf, and by other governments to exert peer pressure for compliance with agreed standards. A progressive UK foreign policy should protect and promote human rights not only because it is morally right to do so, because it is an international legal obligation and because the spread of human rights and the rule of law will bring economic and commercial benefits to the UK (Mepham and Cooper 2004). It should also do so because human rights and justice are the best long-term defence against insecurity and violence, including terrorism. There are two particular dimensions to this.

First, progressives should help to tackle global poverty and promote sustainable development and economic justice. The Nobel Prize winner for economics, Amartya Sen, has argued convincingly that development is about freedom: the progressive enlargement of people's opportunities to make reasoned choices about their lives (Sen 1999). Human rights and human capabilities are absolutely crucial to this. Where individuals are exposed to systemic discrimination on the grounds of race, class or gender, and where they have no voice in the decision-making processes of their societies, they tend to suffer from poverty and acute economic disadvantage. Conversely, where their rights are strengthened and respected, individuals and groups are better able to demand and secure adequate levels of food and shelter, and access to health care, education and other essential services.

Of course, it is usually true that the individuals involved in organizing or carrying out terrorist attacks are not poor themselves (indeed, they may be relatively well off). But political and religious extremists are adept at taking advantage of conditions of poverty and economic grievances, particularly amongst the young.

There are important links, too, between poverty and civil war. World Bank research suggests that the risk of civil war is fifteen times higher in low-income countries than in wealthier countries (World Bank 2003). Such conflicts have devastating human and developmental consequences for people living in these countries and in surrounding states. But they have impacts on developed countries too. Developed countries will often be expected to provide substantial humanitarian assistance or even to intervene militarily in response to the crises brought on by violent conflict.

At its best, UK international policy over the last decade has reflected these insights and made a very positive contribution to economic justice in other parts of the world. The government has tripled aid resources. It has refocused these resources on the poorest countries, in addition to untying its aid and taking action on debt relief. It has also promoted policies to make the global trading system fairer for poorer countries, and championed the Millennium Development Goals internationally.

In recent years, the UK's Department for International Development (DFID) has rightly placed a stronger emphasis on improving structures of governance in partner countries and worked to strengthen the rights of the poor. These are central themes of the government's 2006 International Development White Paper: 'Making Governance Work for the Poor' (DFID 2006). Over the next decade, there is considerable scope for the UK to build on these achievements and strengthen its contribution to global development (see chapter 4 in this volume).

A second priority area for a progressive UK policy should be to help support the establishment of more effective, accountable and rights-upholding states. The importance of this can be illustrated with reference to the Middle East. The political stagnation that characterizes much of the region is failing millions of its people and contributing to huge social tensions. Widespread repression, a lack of political voice, a sense of alienation and disempowerment – these are the very conditions that are breeding anger, extremism and violence. This anger is directed mainly at local rulers, but it can also impact outside the region, including through anti-western Islamic terrorism. There is a powerful security argument, therefore, for trying to support political change in the Middle East (Mepham 2006).

Traditionally, human rights advocates have had an ambivalent attitude towards the state, focusing largely on the state as a violator of human rights. But while states continue to violate human rights on a very large scale, they are also needed to protect and promote them. This is as true of economic and social rights as it is of civil and political ones, which is why the traditional distinction between positive and negative liberty is increasingly redundant. Effective state institutions are required for the achievement of all of these rights.

This can be seen most dramatically in so-called failed or failing state situations, where the state is unable to exercise its authority over its territory (Rotberg 2003; Fukuyama 2004). Some of the world's worst human rights violations of recent years have occurred under these conditions, in places like Afghanistan, Liberia, the Democratic Republic of the Congo (DRC) and Somalia. Where the central state lacks the will or capacity to enforce its writ over the whole territory, power becomes divided up between regionally or ethnically based factions or warlords. In the case of the DRC, over 4 million people have died over the last decade from the lawlessness, killing and impoverishment that has resulted from the collapse of functioning state institutions.

Another clear tension between states and rights relates to the issue of national self-determination. Many states face pressure from secessionist groups to concede independent statehood. While the creation of new states can sometimes be justified, as the last resort in resolving intractable conflicts, it cannot be the answer in most cases. There are very few states that are genuinely homogeneous in national, ethnic or cultural terms, and the attempt to divide the world on such a basis would be a recipe for global instability and turmoil. Rather than splintering the international state system even further, a progressive response should seek, wherever possible, to find political and constitutional protections for the human rights of minorities within existing nation states.

The suggestion is sometimes made that the spread of democratization globally is the key to this. But that claim should be qualified. There is a global trend towards greater democracy and this is a very welcome and important development. But the relationship between democracy and human rights is not always a mutually reinforcing one. In Latin America, for example, the last two decades have witnessed a significant shift from autocracy to democracy, yet many countries in the region continue to have poor human rights records. Elsewhere, not least in the Balkans and Africa, transitions towards democracy have sometimes been associated with the emergence of 'winner-takes-all' political systems and the violation of the human rights of minority communities. This in turn has led to further violence and conflict. Regimes that come to power through elections but that have a poor record of upholding human rights have been described as either 'illiberal democracies' or 'semi-authoritarian regimes' (Ottaway 2003; Zakaria 2003).

In supporting political reform, therefore, progressives should give as much if not more emphasis to constitutionalism as to democracy (particularly where democracy is defined narrowly as the holding of periodic elections). In this context, constitutionalism means a balance of powers, including checks on the executive, a fair and independent legal process, and a free press and media. This emphatically does not mean that progressives should give up on elections, but they do need to think more intelligently about how external actors can best support moves towards democracy in specific contexts (see chapter 2 in this volume; Carothers 2007).

Over the last decade, DFID and the FCO have been very active in supporting human rights through reforms to legal systems, prisons, police and security forces, in working internationally to oppose the death penalty, in backing action to address human trafficking and bonded labour, in furthering women's rights and the rights of children, and in supporting freedom of expression. A wide range of policies and actions of these kinds are set out in the DFID White Paper and the FCO's annual human rights report – itself an important initiative to enhance the transparency of the UK government's policy making on human rights issues (Foreign and Commonwealth Office 2005).

In other areas, however, the UK's record has been far less impressive. This chapter has already addressed some aspects of UK anti-terrorism policy and policy on arms transfers. The next section will consider UK policy towards Iraq and Afghanistan. In addition, the UK has pursued a rather inconsistent policy towards rights-violating governments abroad. Where the country is small, or where there are no major trade or geopolitical interests at stake, the UK has been prepared to be quite tough on human rights issues. For example, the UK has taken a strong public stand in opposition to human rights violations in Burma and, in the last few years, in Zimbabwe. While responding to human rights violations in larger and more powerful states is obviously much more complex and difficult, the UK does not appear to have given adequate priority to human rights in its relations with key countries like Russia, China and Saudi Arabia (Mepham and Cooper 2004). In these cases, economic or geopolitical interests have consistently taken precedence over human rights issues.

Over the next decade, there is real scope for the UK to enhance its commitment to human rights internationally, including by building on the practical initiatives that DFID and the FCO already undertake. But the UK also needs to think more imaginatively about new ways of supporting human rights. There is potentially an important role here for the European Union. The EU made adherence to key human rights agreements a precondition of membership in central and eastern Europe and this has been a successful mechanism for effecting change in the human rights policies of aspirant member states. While EU membership for the Middle Eastern states is not on the agenda, the relationship between the EU and the Middle East could be much better used to create incentives for political reform and greater safeguards for human rights, including greater access for countries to the European single market. The new European Neighbourhood Policy (ENP) should be used in this way to further EU human rights objectives in the Middle East (Mepham 2006).

There is also scope for strengthening the UN's role in supporting human rights, particularly by enhancing the role of the UN High Commissioner for Human Rights, Special Rapporteurs, the Human Rights Treaty Bodies and Special Procedures (the bodies specifically mandated to investigate particular countries and concerns). The creation of a new UN Human Rights Council in place of the discredited Human Rights Commission is a further opportunity. A progressive UK government should press for the council to make good on its undertaking to review the human rights records of member states and to suspend from membership those countries that commit gross and systematic violations of human rights.

There is one additional area where the UK could make an innovative contribution to the global advancement of human rights over the next decade: this relates to the role of companies and human rights. While the UK government has viewed itself as something of an international leader when it comes to the promotion of voluntary codes of corporate social responsibility, it has been more cautious when it comes to the application of international human rights law to companies. But this approach is being undermined by new national and international legal precedents, not least new legal provisions relating to bribery overseas (Mepham and Cooper 2004). The UK should participate constructively in international debates on the corporate sector and human rights, particularly those under way in the UN (Misol 2006). This is not an argument for the introduction of heavy-handed 'command and control' regulation, but rather for the creation of a more transparent legal and regulatory framework for companies, where corporate rights are matched by a stronger sense of corporate responsibilities.

The responsibility to protect

Upholding human rights internationally also requires fresh thinking on the question of 'humanitarian intervention', particularly in the light of military interventions in Afghanistan and Iraq. Humanitarian intervention has been defined as 'the threat or use of force across state borders by a state (or group of states) aimed at preventing or ending widespread and grave violations of the fundamental human rights of individuals other than its own citizens, without the permission of the state within whose territory force is applied' (Keohane 2003: 1). The Blair government has been a strong supporter of military intervention, with the UK having intervened in Kosovo, Sierra Leone, Afghanistan and Iraq – and having used 'humanitarian' arguments, albeit inconsistently and to varying degrees, to justify these interventions.

The disastrous consequences of military action and occupation in Iraq raise huge issues for Iraq and the wider Middle East (see chapter 8 in this volume). But the Iraq experience also raises profound questions about the future of interventions for humanitarian protection purposes, even though human rights concerns were not a decisive factor in the decision to go to war in the Iraq case.

When is it right to intervene forcefully on human rights grounds, what kind of legal authority is required to legitimize intervention and what are the preconditions for interventions to be effective in human rights terms? The most serious attempt to answer these questions in recent years is *The Responsibility to Protect* (International Commission on Intervention and State Sovereignty 2001). The commission proposes a reconceptualization of state sovereignty – 'sovereignty as responsibility'. It asserts that 'sovereign states have the primary responsibility for the protection of their people from avoidable catastrophe – from mass murder, rape, starvation – but when they are unable or unwilling to do so, that responsibility must be borne by the wider community of states' (2001: viii).

The commission suggests that the responsibility to protect embraces three specific responsibilities: first, a 'responsibility to prevent' – to address both the root causes and direct causes of internal conflict and man-made crises putting populations at risk; secondly, 'the responsibility to react' – to respond to situations of compelling human need with appropriate measures, which may include coercive measures like sanctions and international prosecution, and in extreme cases, military intervention; thirdly, 'the responsibility to rebuild' – to provide, particularly after a military intervention, full assistance with recovery, reconstruction and reconciliation, addressing the causes of the humanitarian crisis that the intervention was designed to halt or avert. The commission was right to say that 'prevention is the single most important dimension of the responsibility to protect', that 'preventive options should always be exhausted before intervention is contemplated' and that 'more commitment and resources should be devoted to it' (2001: 19).

Many of the issues addressed in the last section of this chapter might be described as forms of structural prevention. But in addition to these measures, there is an important role for political or diplomatic pressure. Action to further human rights might also involve targeted sanctions. The UK should work with other governments and the UN to refine the sanctions instrument, so that it puts pressure on errant governments rather than harming innocent civilians. Targeted sanctions might include: arms embargoes, ending military cooperation and training programmes, financial sanctions against the foreign assets of a country and restrictions on travel. And there is a role for legal measures, including indicting individuals for war crimes or gross human rights abuses under the provisions of the International Criminal Court. Indeed, the threat of international prosecution is one of the more effective tools available to the international community to change the calculations of warring parties.

But it is the second of the commission's 'responsibilities' – the responsibility to react – which is the most contentious and the most challenging to implement. Progressives need to recognize that in extreme cases military action may be the only means left for preventing or ending massive human rights violations. One of the critical issues is how bad a situation has to be to warrant military action. The commission suggests that all of the relevant decision-making criteria for such a judgement can be summarized under the following six headings: 'right authority, just cause, right intention, last resort, proportional means and reasonable prospects' (2001: xii). In the light of Iraq and Afghanistan, and with massive human rights abuses still continuing in Darfur, it is worth addressing these criteria in turn (Mepham and Ramsbotham 2006)

Progressives should generally favour obtaining explicit authorization by the UN Security Council of forceful interventions for human protection purposes. One of the reasons that military action against Iraq was so unpopular internationally was precisely because the US and UK governments chose not to do this. However, the question of UN authority for interventions is not unproblematic. Should the legitimacy of intervention depend on the votes of countries like China that deny democratic elections to their own people?

In terms of just cause, the commission's proposed thresholds for military intervention are well judged. Action is justified in two broad sets of circumstances:

to halt or avert: (1) large scale loss of human life, actual or apprehended, with genocidal intent or not, which is the product either of deliberate state action, or state neglect or inability to act, or a failed state situation; or (2) large scale 'ethnic cleansing', actual or apprehended, whether carried out by killing, forced expulsion, acts of terror or rape. (International Commission on Intervention and State Soverignty 2001: 32)

The issue of right intention has acquired heightened significance in the light of the Iraq intervention. While governments have many and often mixed motives for foreign policy actions, humanitarian objectives should be the primary reason for intervention if that intervention is to have a reasonable chance of delivering a humanitarian outcome. An intervention carried out with right intentions is much more likely to involve the necessary prewar planning for the postwar period. Such planning was almost entirely absent in the case of Iraq. It was also poor in the case of Afghanistan.

In advance of military intervention, every reasonable diplomatic and non-military option for the resolution of the humanitarian crisis should have been explored – this is the criterion of last resort.

The fifth criterion – that of proportional means – has also assumed added importance in the light of interventions in Iraq and Afghanistan. The commission states that 'finding a consensus about intervention is not simply a matter of deciding who should authorise it and when it is legitimate to undertake. It is also a matter of deciding how to do it so that decent objectives are not tarnished by inappropriate means' (2001: 37).

Intervention for human protection purposes should involve extensive responsibility for ordinary people living in the country concerned, on whose behalf and in whose interests these interventions are supposedly being carried out. This kind of intervention should also involve taking much greater care to minimize both civilian casualties and injuries, as well as damage to the country's infrastructure (Mepham and Cooper 2004). Conservative estimates suggest that 50,000 civilians have been killed in Afghanistan and Iraq. It has also been estimated that as many as 100,000 people have suffered serious injuries, with many thousands of people maimed for life (Rogers 2006).

The sixth and final criterion is that of reasonable prospects. If there is less enthusiasm for international humanitarian interventions today than five years ago, it is because governments and opinion formers have witnessed how difficult these operations are to do in practice. This is not an argument against military intervention in all circumstances. In Rwanda in 1994, timely military intervention could have prevented genocide. In Kosovo in the late 1990s, military intervention did end Serbian aggression against the Kosovo Albanians, although it has been much harder to protect the human rights of the Serbian minority and to establish decent governance. In Sierra Leone, military intervention helped prevent that country from descending back into brutal civil war – a war in which 50,000 lost their lives.

These latter interventions were legitimate, though there are still criticisms of the way in which they were done. Some form of military action was justified in Afghanistan, following the attack on the US and the links between Al-Qaeda and the Taliban. But serious mistakes have been made in respect of this intervention, too. Despite the election of President Karzai, the warlords remain dominant in many parts of the country, human rights abuses are widespread, development progress has been extremely slow, and, far from being defeated, the Taliban constitute a serious threat again in the south of the country. While the international community should certainly not walk away from Afghanistan, progressives should be advocating a new approach – with a more sustained international effort to stabilize the country, particularly the south; increased investment in infrastructure and help with providing livelihood opportunities for ordinary Afghans; a greater effort to strengthen the rule of law and to build up government capacity; and an explicit focus on human rights issues in international discussions with the Afghan government. Progress here will require more international troops to be deployed to the south of the country, higher levels of development assistance that are used more effectively, and a tougher line with Pakistan, which is not doing nearly enough to rein in Taliban forces that operate brazenly from across the Pakistani border (Grono and Nathan 2006).

While each of the six criteria for intervention is important, therefore, the last two carry particular weight. Progressives should focus much more attention on the 'how' of intervention for human protection, locating it within a wider operational and political context. Operationally, a protection force needs an adequate mandate, decent equipment, and sufficient numbers of appropriately trained troops (Holt and Berkman 2006). It requires civilian monitors and police. Politically, any intervention needs to be linked to a process of mediation, conflict resolution and peace building. Military force can provide protection in the short term, but it requires appropriate political and constitutional structures to guarantee these things in the long term. Again, this massively reinforces the argument for investing heavily in longer-term structural prevention, helping to create political institutions, legal structures and economic conditions that can better safeguard human rights and security.

When considering the question of intervention, it is important then that progressives do not treat the above criteria as some kind of pro-forma checklist, whereby action is regarded as appropriate and legitimate 'only if we are able to put a tick into each box':

> Rather, what is required is a practically minded judgement taken in the round based on individual circumstances. Such a judgement will sometimes involve a tough-minded acknowledgement that there are wrongs that cannot be righted, but, equally, it will not allow the best to be the enemy of the good – what is required is a form of judgement that constitutes the creative interaction between the standard criteria and the full specifics of the particular case. (Brown 2003: 45)

Conclusion

Over the last ten years, the UK government has done much to advance the cause of human rights internationally. But it has undermined this positive contribution by the closeness of its relationship with a US administration that has ridden roughshod over some key international human rights principles. The UK's own record has also fallen short in a number of important areas, including some aspects of its anti-terrorism policy, arms exports and its support for the ill-judged war with Iraq.

Over the next decade, there are real opportunities for the UK, acting independently, through the EU and the UN, and in concert with other countries, to strengthen its contribution to human rights internationally. Progressives should be champions of a broader human security agenda that addresses the underlying causes of conflict, violence and extremism. Greater adherence to human rights internationally would be good for the UK, and is an essential precondition for the achievement of greater global security.

References

Amnesty International (2007) Submission to the House of Commons Foreign Affairs Committee, Human Rights Annual Report, January.

Ashby Wilson, R. (ed.) (2005) *Human Rights in the 'War on Terror'*, Cambridge: Cambridge University Press.

Bright, M. (2005) 'Leak shows Blair told of Iraq war terror link', *Guardian*, 28 August, available at: http://observer.guardian.co.uk/politics/strong/ 0,6903,1558066,00.html.

Brody, R. (2005) 'The road to Abu Ghraib: torture and impunity in US detention', in *Torture: does it make us safer, is it ever OK?*, London/New York: New Press/Human Rights Watch.

Brown, C. (2003) 'Selective humanitarianism: in defence of inconsistency', in D. K. Chatterjee and D. E. Scheid (eds), *Ethics and Foreign Intervention*, Cambridge: Cambridge University Press.

Carothers, T. (2007) 'How democracies emerge – the sequencing fallacy', *Journal of Democracy*, 18(1), pp. 12–27.

Christian Science Monitor (2006) www.csmonitor.com/2006/0925/dailyUpdate.html.

Department for International Development (2006) *Eliminating World Poverty: making governance work for the poor*, London: HMSO.

Foreign and Commonwealth Office (2005) *Human Rights Annual Report*, London: FCO.

Fukuyama, F. (2004) *State Building: governance and world order in the twenty-first century*, London: Profile Books.

Gearty, C. (2006) 'Human rights in an age of counter-terrorism', Oxford Amnesty Lecture, 23 February.

Grono, N. and Nathan, J. (2006) 'Not too late for Afghanistan', International Crisis Group, 17 August.

Halliday, F. (2000) *Nation and Religion in the Middle East*, London: Saqi Books.

Held, D. (2004) *Global Covenant: the social democratic alternative to the Washington Consensus*, Cambridge: Polity.

Holt, V. and Berkman, T. (2006) *The Impossible Mandate: military preparedness, the responsibility to protect and modern peace operations*, Washington, DC: The Henry L. Stimson Center.

Human Rights Watch (2006) *World Report 2006*, New York.

Huntington, S. (1996) *The Clash of Civilizations and the Remaking of the World Order*, New York: Simon and Schuster.

International Commission on Intervention and State Sovereignty (2001), *The Responsibility to Protect*, International Development Research Centre, available at www.dfait-maeci.gc/iciss-ciis.

Ignatieff, M. (2001) *Human Rights as Politics and Idolatry*, Princeton: Princeton University Press.

Joint Committee on Human Rights (2006a), *The UN Convention Against Torture (UNCAT)*, Nineteenth Report of Session 2005–06, HL Paper 185 I, HC 701-I.

Joint Committee on Human Rights (2006b) *Counter-Terrorism Policy and Human Rights: prosecution and pre-charge detention*, Twenty-Fourth Report of Session 2005–06, HL Paper 240, HC 1576.

Keohane, R. (2003) 'Introduction' in J. L. Holzgrefe and R. Keohane (eds), *Humanitarian Intervention: ethical, legal and political dilemmas*, Cambridge: Cambridge University Press.

Mepham, D. (2006) *Changing States: a progressive agenda for political reform in the Middle East*, London: Institute for Public Policy Research.

Mepham, D. and Cooper, J. (2004) *Human Rights and Global Responsibility:*

an international agenda for the UK, London: Institute for Public Policy Research.

Mepham, D. and Ramsbotham, A. (2006) *Darfur: the responsibility to protect*, London: Institute for Public Policy Research.

Misol, L. (2006) 'Private companies and the public interest: why corporations should welcome global human rights rules', in Human Rights Watch, *World Report*, New York.

Ottaway, M. (2003) *Democracy Challenged: the rise of semi-authoritarianism*, Washington, DC: Carnegie Endowment for International Peace.

Rogers, P. (2006) 'The war on terror: past, present and future', at www.opendemocracy.net/media/article, 24 August.

Rotberg, R. (ed.) (2003) *State Failure and State Weakness in a Time of Terror*, Washington, DC: Brookings Institution.

Sandel, M. (1998) *Liberalism and the Limits of Justice*, Cambridge: Cambridge University Press.

Sen, A. (1999) *Development as Freedom*, Oxford: Oxford University Press.

Sen, A. (2006) *Identity and Violence: the illusion of destiny*, Harmondsworth: Penguin.

Tharoor, S. (2000) 'Are human rights universal?', *World Policy Journal*, 16(4), winter.

World Bank (2003) *Breaking the Conflict Trap: civil war and development policy*, Washington, DC: World Bank.

Zakaria, F. (2003) *The Future of Freedom: illiberal democracy at home and abroad*, New York: Norton.

4

Development and Equity

Kevin Watkins

Asked in 1950 to evaluate the consequences of the French Revolution, Zhou Enlai, then Foreign Minister of China, famously remarked that it was too early to tell. Much the same might be said of the resounding commitments to poverty reduction made by northern governments during 2005.

The 'year of development', as it has been dubbed, saw the UK play a leading role in elevating poverty to the top of the international agenda at the Gleneagles summit of the Group of Eight (G8) – a move that culminated in the adoption of an ambitious plan of action for sub-Saharan Africa. Hard on the heels of the Gleneagles meeting, 191 countries gathered at the United Nations (UN) Millennium Summit to reaffirm a commitment to the Millennium Development Goals (MDGs) – a set of targets for reducing global poverty, cutting child deaths, expanding educational opportunity and meeting other development objectives by 2015. At a time when international cooperation and progressive values are in retreat on many fronts, the cause of global development has been an apparent exception. For this, the UK can claim much credit. Since 1997, there has been a renewed commitment to global poverty reduction backed by an expanding aid programme and international leadership. Ultimately, though, the returns on this investment remain uncertain – and the UK could do far more to advance a global social justice agenda.

This chapter argues that a commitment to international social and economic justice should be central to a progressive conception of UK foreign policy. A progressive politics worth its name cannot focus on improving the human condition at home while turning a blind eye to mass poverty overseas, or to the obscene inequalities that divide rich and poor nations. Moreover, action to combat poverty and to promote equitable development can also reinforce other progressive foreign policy goals, including the achievement of greater common security and shared prosperity. While the international development agenda is very broad, encompassing issues of governance, conflict prevention and resolution, corruption and the management of natural resources, the focus in this chapter is on two issues: aid and trade. These are areas in which action by northern governments has the potential to make a real difference, creating opportunities for poor countries and poor people to escape from poverty. During 2005, commitments on aid and trade figured prominently in the pledges made by northern governments. Unfortunately, there is a large gap between pledge and delivery.

On aid, the progress report is mixed. Overall financing levels are rising, albeit from a low base and far too slowly. These resource flows need to be sustained and expanded. Some commentators argue that increasing aid is a futile exercise in throwing good money after bad. But this armchair aid cynicism is ill-informed and unhelpful. There is plenty of evidence that aid can act as a powerful force for social justice and human progress. At the same time, the serious problems in aid governance have to be acknowledged. Many of these problems are traceable to donor practices. Improving aid quality is a precondition for enhancing effectiveness in poverty reduction, and for sustaining public support.

The record of delivery on trade is more straightforward. It is also less impressive. Launched in 2001, the Doha Round of World Trade Organization (WTO) negotiations has delivered nothing of substance. An occasional spasm of negotiating activity has prompted some to suggest that Doha Round obituaries are premature and that there may yet be life in the WTO negotiations. But measured against its original purpose, the 'development round' is long deceased. Six years ago, the ambition was to achieve an outcome that would share the benefits of rising global prosperity more equitably between rich and poor countries. Today, the ambition is to achieve a face-saving formula that will leave intact a set of trade rules that skew the benefits of trade in favour of rich countries.

Looking beyond the immediate losses for global poverty reduction, the demise of the Doha Round has wider implications for multilateralism. When rich countries choose to sacrifice the integrity of a rules-based international system in order to defend agricultural subsidies and the claims of narrow commercial interest groups, what hope is there for successful multilateralism in tackling challenges such as climate change, international security or terrorism? Developing a poverty-focused, rules-based multilateral system should be seen as an integral part of the wider progressive foreign policy agenda. The importance of the project cautions against leaving multilateral trade negotiations to the mercy of the mercantilist interest groups whose views carry far too much weight in the considerations of ministers dealing with trade and agriculture.

This chapter outlines strategies for aligning aid and trade policies with a commitment to progressive values and global economic justice. It also makes specific policy recommendations for the UK. However, it starts with a brief overview of the problem that aid and trade policies must address: the vast scale of human deprivation in an increasingly prosperous and interdependent world.

The development challenge

'The true test of any civilization', wrote Samuel Johnson in 1776, 'is how it treats the poor.' Measured against this criterion, civilization in the era of globalization is failing the test. We live in a world of unprecedented prosperity. Global average incomes have doubled since 1980 and future projections point to more of the same. According to the World Bank, global output will double again by 2030, reaching $72 trillion (World Bank 2007). Many developing countries are being lifted up on the tide of this rising wealth. In fact, average incomes in the developing world are rising twice as fast as those in the rich world. Many social indicators are also moving in an upward direction. Globally, average life expectancy is increasing, child mortality is falling, and there is real progress on literacy and school attendance. However, without downplaying these important achievements, a global average is not necessarily the best indicator for assessing progress in human development, particularly if we are concerned with the plight of the very poorest.

What does the dynamism of the world economy mean for global poverty and for the distribution of opportunity worldwide? The World Bank is unequivocal. Commenting on its own growth projections, it observes: 'This is good news for the world's poor. The implications of sustained growth for reducing poverty around the world are nothing short of astounding' (World Bank 2007: xiii). But is this really the case? What is more astounding is the slow pace of human development in the midst of the vast expansion of wealth generated by globalization. Pervasive poverty and deepening inequalities between and within countries are just as much hallmarks of the current era of economic integration as the emergence of global markets and production systems.

Income is one important dimension of human development. Absolute poverty, as measured by the international threshold of $1 a day, has fallen by about half since the 1980s, largely as a result of rapid economic progress in East Asia. Even so, around 1 billion people, or 20 per cent of the world's population, survive on less than $1 a day. Twice that number live perilously close to the absolute poverty threshold on less than $2 a day (United Nations Development Programme 2005).

Extreme inequality is one of the defining features of the global economy. Much ink has been spent in addressing the question: is globalization making the world more or less equal? There is no clear-cut answer to this. Measured in terms of average income, the gap between the citizens of the world's richest and poorest countries has probably been widening. For example, since 1990, average income in the UK as a multiple of that in Tanzania has increased from 41 to 46 times. However, if countries are weighted for the size of their population, inequality is shrinking, thanks largely to the high growth achieved in China and India. Stripping away national borders and treating all people as though they were living in a single country produces a 'no-change' income distribution trend (Milanovic 2005). That is, faster growth in large emerging economies has partially offset rising inequality within countries.

Notwithstanding the heat generated by debates over globalization and income distribution, it is easy to lose sight of the scale of global inequality. The 2006 *Human Development Report* used a global income distribution model based on national data to examine the level of inequality in the world. The pattern that emerged was that of a champagne glass, with a heavy concentration of income at the top. Average annual income worldwide is around $5,533. Median income, or the mid-point in the distribution, is $1,700 (United Nations Development Programme 2006). The very large gap between the two figures is an indicator for extreme inequality. The average income of the top 20 per cent is some fifty times higher than for the poorest 20 per cent. Meanwhile, the poorest 40 per cent of the global income distribution account for about 5 per cent of global income. Opinion surveys in the UK consistently reveal a high level of concern over levels of national income inequality (Hills 2004). Yet global income distribution patterns are far more skewed against the poor. The poorest 20 per cent in the world account for 1.5 per cent of global income. In Britain, the poorest 20 per cent account for 6 per cent of national income.

Income poverty is just one aspect of human deprivation. Much has been made of the convergence in life expectancy between the developed and the developing world – and the gap is continuing to close. It has closed by about two years in the past thirty years, though there are huge regional variations. Average life expectancy in developing countries is now 65 years, compared with 77 in developed countries. Here too, though, averages conceal as much as they reveal. Numbers may be coming down, but over 10 million children die each year before they reach their fifth birthday, and average life expectancy in sub-Saharan Africa is only 46 years. It has been estimated that one-quarter of children born in Mali in 2007 will not reach the age of five, compared with well under 1 per cent in the UK (United Nations Children's Fund 2007).

Poor people around the world also die of diseases that are easily preventable or treatable in rich countries. Malaria is one the world's most preventable and treatable afflictions, yet it claims 1 million lives a year, mostly children and almost exclusively in the developing world. The HIV/AIDS pandemic has been an unprecedented setback for human development. Headline figures, such as the 3 million deaths and 5 million reported new cases in 2006, tell only part of the story. Europe and North America accounted for 20,000 of these deaths, sub-Saharan Africa for over 2 million. The HIV/AIDS crisis is also revealing deep-rooted gender inequalities. Women now account for 60 per cent of HIV/AIDS infection in sub-Saharan Africa (Joint UN Programme on HIV/AIDS 2006).

Inequality in access to medicine and public health provision is merely one determinant of unequal survival prospects. During the nineteenth century, the UK took a great leap forward in the creation of wealth but only a tiny step towards reducing the high child death rates that plagued cities like London, Leeds and Manchester. The reason: inadequate provision of clean water and sanitation. Today, around 1.6 billion people in the world lack access to clean water and 2.6 billion lack access to basic sanitation. What these figures mean is that millions of young girls and adults spend hours collecting water – and that people have no choice but to defecate in fields, streams or streets. The figures also help to explain the deaths from diarrhoea of almost 2 million children annually. Putting a tap that delivers clean water into a home in Ghana or Ethiopia cuts diarrhoea by more than one-half (United Nations Development Programme 2006). We are therefore part of a global community that allows its children to die, in a perversely literal sense, for want of a glass of clean water and adequate sanitation facilities.

Levels of deprivation in education are no less striking. In most industrial countries, governments have identified education as one of the keys for overcoming social exclusion and the transmission of deprivation across generations. Recognition that globalization has accelerated the shift towards knowledge-based economies has forced education to the top of the social and economic agenda. The flip side of the premium that globalization has placed on education is the penalty attached to educational deprivation. Over 100 million children of primary school age are out of school. Several hundred millions more are in school but subjected to an education without even the most rudimentary teaching materials. Global inequalities widen as children progress up the ladder towards secondary and tertiary levels, especially for girls. The very large educational disparities that we see today will translate into the global income inequalities of tomorrow.

The severity of the development challenge in sub-Saharan Africa sometimes obscures challenges facing other regions of the world. Consider the case of India. Globalization enthusiasts often point to the country as an advertisement for the power of global markets to act as a catalyst for human progress. Unfortunately, the human development indicators are less impressive than the economic growth credentials. Economic take-off has not been accompanied by a take-off in the rate of poverty reduction. More worryingly still, the rate at which child deaths are falling has slowed. Neighbouring Bangladesh may be poorer and growing more slowly than India, but it has a far better record in reducing child mortality and has now overtaken India on this front. Indeed, had India matched Bangladesh's performance over the past decade there would be 732,000 fewer deaths this year (United Nations Development Programme 2005).

The mismatch between India's economic advance and the country's social progress is of wider relevance to the debate on globalization. Commentators like Thomas Friedman have argued that global market integration and the rise of information technology is creating a 'flat world' of equalized opportunity (Friedman 2005). But the evidence points in a different direction. Efficiency in delivering high-technology software services to California is no substitute for a concerted effort to tackle the deep gender-based, regional and other income inequalities that blight India's social development. More broadly, making globalization work for the poor requires a commitment to public policies that aim at greater distributional equity.

Inequalities within countries can act as a major brake on development – and rising inequality has been a feature of global economic integration. During the 1990s, economic growth worldwide was accompanied by rising income inequalities in countries accounting for over 80 per cent of the world's population (Cornia 2004). One consequence is that growth has become less inclusive and less pro-poor.

According to one detailed survey of national data, developing countries on average have to grow at three times the rate of the pre-1990 period to achieve the same level of poverty reduction (Lopez 2006). The explanation for this is that poor households are capturing a shrinking share of a growing cake.

What these figures highlight is that equity matters a great deal for human development. The MDGs currently focus on national averages and have little to say on distribution. This is a design flaw which needs to be rectified. One option would be to include within the 2015 time frame concrete distributional objectives, such as halving the gap in child mortality or school attendance between the richest and poorest 20 per cent. Overcoming inequalities in these and other key dimensions of human development could play a critical role in getting the world back on track for the 2015 targets.

Some economists remain wedded to the argument that there is an inherent trade-off between economic growth on the one side and greater equity on the other. That argument is flawed. There is in fact robust cross-country evidence suggesting that high levels of inequality hamper growth and investment (United Nations Development Programme 2005). Greater equity can actually serve to strengthen the link between wealth creation and human development. Building on its development policy to date, it is important that the UK government place more emphasis on the critical issue of inequality and encourage other development donors and the international financial institutions to do the same. Far from being a distraction from the MDGs or related development goals, a greater focus on issues of economic equity and distribution can help to accelerate progress towards them.

The progressive case for aid

'Double aid to halve poverty' proclaimed some of the banners brandished during the Live 8 concerts that preceded the Gleneagles G8 summit. Others pointed to aid as a force that could prevent millions of child deaths. At the summit, G8 leaders pledged to increase aid to Africa by $25 billion a year, more than doubling assistance to the region. Large-scale debt cancellation was another part of the Gleneagles package. The agreement reached at Gleneagles was framed in large measure around the recommendations of the report of the Africa Commission created by Tony Blair (Commission for Africa 2005). So, will the resounding aid commitments made during 2005 help make poverty history or, more modestly, get the world back on track for the MDGs?

This question has become a source of great controversy. The conviction that aid has a role to play in advancing the human condition was powerfully reflected in the messages of the Make Poverty History campaign and the Global Call to Action against Poverty. It also underpinned a January 2005 speech by Gordon Brown calling for a 'Marshall Plan' for the world's poor (Brown 2005). The analogy with the Marshall Plan, which delivered large volumes of aid to the war-ravaged economies of Britain, France and Germany, has been taken up by others, including the American economist Jeffrey Sachs. The idea that a 'big push' on aid can provide the investment in infrastructure, health, education and other sectors needed to unleash rapid human progress is now fundamental to the entire MDG project, and a focal point for social justice activists.

This benign view of aid has not gone uncontested. Perhaps the most articulate critic is William Easterly, whose recent book *The White Man's Burden* directly challenges Gordon Brown and other advocates of increased aid (Easterly 2006). At a superficial level, his argument is compelling. Surveying the record for 1980–2002, Easterly finds that the ten developing countries with the lowest growth rates (most of them in Africa) had the highest aid-to-GDP ratios. Meanwhile, high-growth economies like China, India, Malaysia and Singapore had very low aid-to-GDP ratios. Why, Easterly asks, have the billions spent on aid left so many people in poverty, hungry, diseased and uneducated?

In his view, the culprits for this include poor governance, corruption and institutional deficiencies. The simple version of the aid problem, concludes one group of pessimists, is that 'the countries most in need of aid are often those least able to use it' (Birdsall et al. 2005). Forget the Marshall Plan, so the argument runs, what Africa needs is a drip feed with a flow that increases very slowly as governments demonstrate a capacity to tackle their home-grown problems.

While not without elements of truth, the arguments of the aid pessimists are poorly grounded in evidence. There is a good story to tell about aid, and progressives ought to be telling it with far greater conviction. International aid has contributed to some of the greatest advances in human development. The eradication of smallpox, curtailment of polio and reductions in trachoma and guinea worm, and the spread of vaccination against killer diseases are examples of aid-financed interventions that have saved millions of lives (Levine 2004). Development aid has also financed an increase from $2 billion to $8 billion in spending on AIDS. These resources are providing 1.3 million people with anti-retroviral drugs. The fact that this is far short of the 3 million target set by the Joint UN Programme on HIV/AIDS (UNAIDS) is a case for more aid that is better delivered, not for cutting this essential lifeline. Since the creation in 2001 of the Global Fund for HIV/AIDS, Tuberculosis and Malaria that lifeline has become more effective. The Global Fund has quickly become one of the world's most important instruments for fighting diseases that claim 16,000 lives each day. As well as constituting a focal point for an international partnership on HIV/AIDS and around one-fifth of global funding, it has provided over 11 million insecticide-treated malarial bed nets.

At a national level, development aid is also supporting social progress in some of the world's poorest countries. Much of Bangladesh's success in cutting the number of child deaths can be attributed to aid-financed social programmes for addressing malnutrition, expanding basic health care delivery, and reducing gender inequalities in education. Moreover, in countries such as Tanzania, Uganda, Zambia and Kenya, government revenues saved from debt relief have helped to finance the removal of user fees and have increased financing for education and health. With the abolition of school fees in 2003, enrolments in Kenya have increased by over 1 million children. Beyond social sector investment, aid can also directly support the livelihoods of the poor. In countries such as Malawi and Ethiopia, for example, the UK and other donors support social safety nets and seed provision programmes that protect households affected by drought. The outcomes may not be readily appreciated behind a computer screen in Washington DC, but try asking a mother whose child has a chance to survive malaria, or to get an education, whether aid works.

Like aid, debt relief has been criticized by many commentators as a form of misplaced good intent. The Heavily Indebted Poor Countries (HIPC) Initiative, which to date has delivered debt relief to twenty-nine countries mainly in sub-Saharan Africa, has been a particular target. Providing additional debt reduction by writing off 100 per cent of debt owed by some of the poorest countries to multilateral institutions and extending debt relief to Nigeria was an important part of the Gleneagles commitment. It created an opportunity for governments to use their revenues for investment in people, rather than for transfer to creditors. Of course, government priorities will determine the outcome – and some governments will fail the equity test. Yet, expenditure on poverty reduction in the twenty-nine countries that have received debt relief to date has more than doubled since 1999, increasing by around $6 billion (IMF/World Bank 2006). While this is a tiny burden for creditors to carry, it has helped finance the entry into school or to health systems of some of the world's most vulnerable people.

Critics of aid might claim that progress in social areas misses the point. What ultimately matters is whether or not aid generates the higher levels of economic growth needed to lift people out of poverty. There are two responses to this. First, progress in education and health is not just an important indicator of human progress in its own right; it is also a requirement for the increased productivity required for sustained economic growth. Secondly, there is evidence of a positive relationship between aid and economic growth, albeit with large variations (Clemens et al. 2004; Radelet 2006). The fact that some of the countries in sub-Saharan Africa now enjoying a strong economic recovery – Uganda, Mozambique, Tanzania, Ghana and Senegal among them – are all highly aid-dependent surely says something important. But perhaps the greatest weakness in the aid cynic's argument is that they are telling us yesterday's news. Tracing the relationship between aid and growth over the last quarter-century covers a period distorted by Cold War politics, when selling arms and replenishing the Swiss bank accounts of corrupt leaders was standard practice. Surely the real challenge is to address the problems of today rather than simply reciting the well-known failures of the past.

One of the problems with the current debate on aid is that it suffers from highly polarized exchanges. For this, aid pessimists certainly carry a large share of responsibility. But advocates of the 'big push' approach can also overstate their case and downplay the importance of aid quality. A progressive UK government should be arguing that commitments to increase aid need to be carried through. Recent evidence from the OECD pointing to a decline in core development assistance for Africa despite the G8 commitment suggests that this should be a priority. But success on this front must also be matched by real improvements in the way in which aid is delivered. Building the case for aid is vital if the international community is to address the profound threats now facing some of the poorest people in the developing world.

Development assistance works best when it is harnessed to national plans for poverty reduction, backed by a commitment to transparency, accountability and the rooting out of corruption. No amount of aid can compensate for government failure on these fronts, as the people of Zimbabwe and many other countries will attest. In principle, there is now a broad institutional framework through which donors can coordinate support for national strategies. These are set out in Poverty Reduction Strategy Papers (PRSPs). But aid effectiveness is often hampered by bad practice.

Donors themselves cause many of the problems. Recipient countries are often overwhelmed by a multiplicity of donors pursuing different and often contradictory objectives, disbursing aid through dozens of separate projects, each with their own separate reporting requirements and conditionalities. Countries like Tanzania, with its limited human capacity, host over 1,000 meetings with donors a year and prepare 2,400 reports each quarter (Roodman 2006). The failure of donors to cooperate is at the heart of the problem. It is perfectly reasonable for aid providers to insist on conditions that enable them to account for how they spend their taxpayers' money. But why are only 15 per cent of donor missions undertaken jointly with other donors? And do donors to countries such as Mozambique and Ethiopia really need to operate through over 1,400 separate project implementation units in national ministries (Organization for Economic Cooperation and Development 2005)? So severe are the strains on human capacity that in 2003 Tanzania adopted the novel policy of enforcing a four-month moratorium period during which donor missions could not take place. To make a bad situation worse, most donors refuse to use country systems for monitoring and auditing the use of aid. This has the effect of weakening national budgetary systems, which are such an important part of effective economic management.

Aid delivery mechanisms have a direct bearing on aid effectiveness. The uncertainties and volatility associated with foreign aid can make poverty reduction planning a hazardous affair. Countries such as Ghana and Senegal have in the recent past experienced shortfalls in aid delivery against pledges equivalent to more than 2 per cent of gross domestic product (GDP), disrupting government spending plans. The still widespread practice of tying aid to the purchase of goods and services provided by the donor country creates further waste. On one estimate it reduces the real value of bilateral aid by $5–7 billion annually. Resources that could be used to meet essential needs in poor countries are instead being diverted into the creation of markets for contractors and consultants in rich countries. Donors have been discussing coordination and harmonization for several years. At least two major Organization for Economic Cooperation and Development (OECD) summits have been held on the subject. The last of these, held in Paris in 2005, adopted a series of targets on aid effectiveness. What is striking, though, is the desperately slow pace of progress achieved to date. For example, only 9 per cent of donors report undertaking mutual assessments of partnerships, against a target of 100 per cent (Organization for Economic Cooperation and Development 2006). Even in Tanzania, a relatively good case of donor harmonization, only 5 per cent of the 230 missions conducted by the country's fourteen largest donors in 2003 were jointly undertaken.

The UK has a good overall record on many of these problems and is therefore well placed to push the cause of more effective aid internationally. UK-tied aid has been eliminated and the share of budget support in overall UK aid has increased, to around 15 per cent of the total. More aid is also being provided as part of multi-year commitments, helping to support financial stability in partner countries. In addition, the UK has worked with other donors to pilot joint assistance programmes aimed at reducing transaction costs, for example in Nigeria and Cambodia. However, far more could be done to support national ownership in a practical sense. Building the capacity of aid recipients to manage donors and review donor practices is one area that demands particular attention. At the same time, the UK should be pressing for deeper harmonization and coordination. Donor presence in a poor country is an example of where more means less effective aid and higher transaction costs. Doubling aid in the absence of a more robust and streamlined architecture for aid governance is likely to produce limited results for human development, with attendant dangers for public support (Burall and Maxwell 2006).

A critical issue relating to aid quality is that of conditionality. In practice, almost all aid comes with conditions: the average World Bank loan to a low-income country has around fifteen, supplemented by a comparable number of IMF conditions. Bilateral donors vary in their use of conditionality, though most insist upon compliance with World Bank/IMF conditions. In countries characterized by mixed or weak records on human rights, corruption and economic stability, it is reasonable that a commitment to national ownership of development strategies should be tempered by a concern for responsible aid allocation. But it is also important that donor conditions should not be overly burdensome. Again, the UK has taken some positive steps on this in recent years, and it now implements and advocates less intrusive models of conditionality. However, this is an area in which wider harmonization is urgently needed.

The UK Department for International Development (DFID) also deserves credit for seeking to bring the debate on corruption to the centre of the poverty reduction agenda. This is an area in which many non-government organizations have feared to tread, partly out of a concern to advance the case for more aid, and partly out of an undue sensitivity towards offending governments. This approach is mistaken. In a country like Kenya, where the average citizen pays sixteen bribes a month and where fraud and bribery turnover amounts to 7 per cent of GDP annually, some of it involving senior political figures, it is right to put corruption at the heart of the aid dialogue. The proper response is to support the development of national auditing institutions and organizations in civil society that are equipped to hold governments to account – and DFID is pioneering important work in this area.

But it is also important that the UK should practise what it preaches. Some of the most egregious high-level corruption in sub-Saharan Africa and elsewhere involves international contractors. Subversion of national procurement processes can provide contracts for exporters of everything from arms to hospital equipment, and large pay-offs for politicians. To address this problem the UK adopted legislation that brought the country into compliance with the OECD Convention on Bribery of Foreign Public Officials. However, a Serious Fraud Office (SFO) investigation into the activities of a UK arms company was suspended in December 2006 in the face of intensive lobbying and high-level political intervention. As a statement signed by fifty UK-based non-governmental organizations (NGOs) puts it: 'Future efforts by the UK to prescribe government standards for developing countries in receipt of aid and debt relief are likely to be viewed as nothing less than double standards' (Adams 2007).

As a relatively large donor with a rising stock of political capital in aid debates, the UK has scope to provide leadership and innovation in neglected areas. The Africa Commission Report is one example of leadership in mobilizing a wider political constituency and leveraging additional aid. Another is the development in the Treasury of the International Finance Facility (IFF). Briefly summarized, this would mobilize resources by issuing bonds backed by government, effectively creating an aid-financing capacity today against repayment obligations in the future. In areas that demand up-front investment, the IFF holds out great promise. During 2006 the UK took the lead in mobilizing a group of donors to launch an IFF for immunization, generating $2 million for vaccination – an investment that could save up to 5 million lives by 2015.

Water and sanitation is another sector that merits urgent attention and innovation. Chronic under-financing and poor governance in this area blight the social and economic development of whole countries. More than that, they erode the benefits of aid in education, health and livelihoods. To state the obvious, young girls who spend four hours each morning collecting water, or who get sick as a result of water-related infectious disease, are not likely to flourish in education. It follows that the $15 billion that Gordon Brown has earmarked for spending on aid for education over the next decade would generate a higher return if it were matched by much more substantial progress on water and sanitation. Yet despite its importance, the sector merited nothing more than a passing reference in the Gleneagles communiqué. This is despite the fact that three years ago, an earlier G8 summit pledged to put in place a comprehensive global plan of action on water and sanitation.

The UK should be giving increased priority to investment in clean water and safe sanitation. It should be challenging the lethargy of other donors (and, it might be added, most international NGOs). Achieving the MDG target of halving the twin deficit in water and sanitation would cost around $10 billion annually – or around three days' worth of global military spending. The problem is that much of the investment needs to happen up-front: you cannot deliver clean water or sanitation services without prior investment in infrastructure. This makes water and sanitation a strong candidate for IFF-style financing, within the framework of a wider global plan of action to mobilize resources and build capacity.

There are some commentators who argue that sector-specific aid programmes – or 'vertical funds' as they are known – are unhelpful. The fear is that they will distort national priorities and increase transaction costs. In some countries, the Global Fund on HIV/AIDS appears to have had this effect, though the overall record is positive. Another programme in education, the Fast-Track Initiative (FTI), has provided resources for countries seeking to accelerate progress towards the goal of education for all. Around forty-five countries are receiving technical or financial support under the FTI to achieve more ambitious targets. The results have been impressive. Mauritania, Burkina Faso and Ghana have collectively added 1 million children a year to their enrolments since joining the FTI, and Niger and Guinea have accelerated the rate of increase in enrolment by a factor of three (IMF/World Bank 2006). Far from adding to transaction costs, the FTI has facilitated more effective coordination between donors and strengthened partnerships between national governments and aid donors.

Ultimately, what matters is whether or not governments have a political commitment and a national strategy for delivering water and sanitation at an affordable price to all of its citizens. To the extent that an international plan of action mobilizes the residual resources not covered by national donors, builds capacity and puts the issue at the centre of the donor agenda, it can help to support national efforts. The UK should continue to support these initiatives and advocate the development of a global plan of action for water and sanitation.

International trade

International trade is at the heart of global interdependence. It is one of the most powerful motors driving the integration of national economies and economic growth. Trade is also a potential vehicle for accelerated economic growth, poverty reduction and human development. Integration through trade offers poor countries and their citizens an opportunity to get access to the markets, the technologies, the investment and the ideas that are creating a rising tide of global wealth. Of course, integration also creates risks and vulnerabilities: there are losers as well as winners between and within countries. And some countries and producers are better equipped than others to take advantage of opportunities. The aim of a multilateral trading system consistent with a commitment to the MDGs should be to provide a rules-based framework within which poor countries can secure their interests.

The Doha Round of WTO talks, launched in 2001, began with a communiqué promising that multilateral trade reform would contribute to a more inclusive and equitable pattern of globalization. In 2005, the Gleneagles agreement restated the commitment to reform multilateral trade rules in the interests of the world's poorest countries, notably through an agreement on agriculture. But delivery has fallen a long way short of the commitment.

This is bad news for global poverty reduction efforts. Potentially, trade is a far more powerful, dynamic and sustainable force for poverty reduction than aid. If sub-Saharan Africa enjoyed the same share of world trade today as it did in 1980, its exports would be some $119 billion higher (in constant 2000 dollars). The gain would represent some eight times the amount that the region receives in aid. Like well-designed aid programmes, successful participation in trade can equip people with opportunities to produce their way out of poverty. Conversely, failure in trade is contributing to rising levels of marginalization and global inequality. Ten years ago, exports represented less than one-fifth of global GDP. By 2015 that share will have risen to around one-third. In other words, trade is playing an increasingly important role in enlarging the global economic cake and determining how it is divided up (World Bank 2007).

Developing countries are increasing their share of world trade. However, while the rise of India and China is shifting the global balance, whole regions – notably sub-Saharan Africa, much of Latin America and low-income countries in southern Asia – are being left behind. With 12 per cent of the world's population, sub-Saharan Africa accounts for less than 1 per cent of world exports.

The multilateral trade agenda produces two distinctive sets of challenges. First, there is the immediate challenge of what to do about the Doha Round. The unhappily protracted life of these negotiations has been punctuated by a series of crises. After a breakdown in Cancun in

2003, negotiations resumed but culminated in another deadlock at the end of 2005 at the Hong Kong ministerial meeting. While the final outcome is uncertain and an agreement remains technically possible, the pulse of the Doha Round stopped beating a long time ago. Ambitious goals to open up northern markets, cut agricultural subsidies and establish a system that acknowledges the special needs of poor countries have effectively been abandoned. Developed countries bear much of the responsibility for this failure. Behind the bewildering complexity of the negotiating process, the story is essentially one of the rich world asking for too much and being prepared to give too little.

The second challenge concerns the legacy of the past. During the last round of world trade talks – the Uruguay Round – the developed world imposed an agenda that produced profoundly unbalanced agreements. These agreements, on issues ranging from intellectual property rights to investment, served to skew the benefits of trade integration away from poor countries. Altering the WTO system to address this issue is one of the requirements for the development of a multilateral trading order fit for purpose in the twenty-first century.

The Doha Round provided an opportunity to address some of the worst examples of unfairness in world trade rules. While trade liberalization has gathered pace since the early 1990s, tariffs on exports from developing countries entering northern markets are still far higher than those applied in intra-OECD trade – a reflection of the high protectionist barriers that still face labour-intensive products. An agreement in the Doha Round could have eliminated the tariff peaks facing poor countries.

It could also have tackled the perennial issues of agricultural support in rich countries. Agriculture accounts for a tiny share of income and employment in the industrialized world – under 2 per cent in both the EU and the US – but support to agricultural producers is running at around $280 billion a year. This support, which represents around one-third of the value of output, goes overwhelmingly to wealthy farmers such as those in the Paris Basin. Efficient producers in developing countries lose out at various levels. Their access to northern markets is restricted by high tariffs. Exports from industrial countries (which collectively account for around 70 per cent of world exports in agriculture) push down world prices and deprive developing countries of market share. The $4–5 billion a year that the US spends subsidizing cotton production lowers world prices by around 12 per cent and expands the volume of exports by 44 per cent (Sumner 2003). The losers include millions of desperately poor cotton producers in countries such as Burkina Faso, Mali and Pakistan. Developing world producers have to compete against subsidized imports from the rich world. Rice farmers in Ghana and maize farmers in Central America have both been forced to adjust to competition from subsidized American exports. Meanwhile, the EU retains some of the world's highest tariffs and is a major exporter of sugar – a product in which it has no comparative advantage.

Entering the world of the agricultural negotiators at the WTO is to wander through a hall of mirrors in which form becomes separated from content. Both the US and the EU used the Doha Round to table what appeared to be bold offers on the phasing out of direct export subsidies and the reduction of 'trade-distorting' production subsidies. In fact, direct export subsidies have already been phased out and the caveat 'trade-distorting' is important. The two agricultural subsidy superpowers have over the past five years radically restructured agricultural support to shift subsidies into areas not deemed to be trade distorting for WTO purposes. Under the reformed Common Agricultural Policy (CAP), which still accounts for $4 in every $10 spent by the EU, around 70 per cent of support falls into this category, rising to 80 per cent for the US (Stiglitz 2006).

Why does all of this matter for human development? Because it means that multilateral trade rules will continue to provide limited protection to vulnerable agricultural producers in the developing world. At the time of writing (early 2007), there is hope that the EU, the US and the Group of Twenty (G20) developing countries might conclude an agreement on agriculture. However, the terms of that agreement would effectively allow the EU and the US to *increase* overall agricultural spending (Oxfam 2006c). Most of the subsidies directed to cotton in the US would escape WTO disciplines, as would the bulk of the 'single payments' that deliver billions of euros to farmers in the EU. When it comes to market access in agriculture, the EU is by some way the worst offender in a competitive field. It has the highest tariffs and has proposed only limited cuts (of 39 per cent on average), with sweeping exemptions for sensitive products.

What kind of changes should a progressive UK government be pressing for? Agriculture should be a top priority. In the first instance, that means calling for more radical reform of the CAP, with deep tariff cuts across the board and direct payments decoupled from production and directed into social and environmental policy goals. At the WTO, the UK should be working to align itself with the G20 and reformers in the EU, displaying the same resolve on behalf of the world's poor as the French government has displayed on behalf of the rich farmers of the Paris Basin. An immediate priority should be a demand, supported by the G20, for the billions of dollars of subsidies now exempt from

WTO discipline to be subject to a full review. Within the EU itself, the deeper political challenge is to break the stranglehold over agricultural policy exercised by Gaullist populism in France. Sacrificing a key element of the multilateral rules regime to accommodate vested interests among large farmers and agribusiness is not a good foundation for trade policy.

Reviving the Doha Round agenda will also require radical surgery on approaches to market liberalization in developing countries – and this is an area where the UK should set down some clear markers. Liberalization has to be seen not as an end in itself, but as a means to poverty reduction. In this context, the golden rule is that developing countries must be left with sufficient policy space to design trade policies consistent with a commitment to human development. That rule is not widely respected. The US in particular has linked negotiating offers on liberalization to demands for rapid and deep cuts in import barriers in developing countries, including those applied to agriculture. The EU has been more cautious on agriculture, doubtless aware of the implications for liberalization of the CAP, but has adopted a similarly robust liberalizing line for manufacturing. Led by the G20, developing countries have argued for longer timelines for liberalization and shallower cuts. In practice, of course, countries like India and China are already undergoing rapid economic liberalization. And in many areas liberalization is vital for accelerated growth and poverty reduction. However, the case for retaining a residual right to protect agriculture on the grounds of food security and the distorted state of world markets is overwhelming. While the UK should make the argument for properly sequenced import liberalization as part of an overall development strategy, it should resist attempts at using the WTO as a lever for prising open markets.

Import liberalization is re-emerging as a wider issue in trade negotiations. Currently, the EU is negotiating with its former African, Caribbean and Pacific (ACP) partners over the development of six regional Economic Partnership Agreements (EPAs). The terms of the negotiating mandate include reciprocal liberalization for 'substantially all' EU exports to the countries in question. How the EU will interpret this mandate remains uncertain. What is certain is that across-the-board, rapid liberalization would have detrimental implications not just for competition on local markets (with African farmers competing against subsidized CAP exports), but also for revenue. Tariff revenue is a major source of government revenue in most of the countries in question – and the EU is their major trade partner. One estimate suggests that three-quarters of the countries involved could lose 60 per cent or more of their tariff revenue from

EU sources (Stevens 2006; Oxfam 2006a). That is an outcome that would have grave implications for government financing in areas such as health and education. While critics of EPAs sometimes overstate the threats, the UK should take the lead in pressing for a comprehensive review of the potential human development outcomes associated with import liberalization.

None of this is to imply that the EU should evade its own responsibilities to liberalize. EPAs create an opportunity to open up areas still protected by the CAP to agricultural producers in Africa and other regions, partly compensating them for the loss of preferences that some are sustaining as a result of liberalization at the WTO. The EU needs also to revamp its increasingly anachronistic 'rules of origin' regime. These rules specify the value added or processes that must be undertaken before a country is deemed eligible for preferential entry to EU markets. In comparison with the rules applied in Canada and the US, the EU sets the bar too high. Firms and producers in Africa claim to face problems because they are often unable to source locally the packaging or products they need to meet EU standards.

Trying to make the rules-based multilateral trading system more consistent with progressive values will require the UK to think again about the international rules on intellectual property, specifically the Agreement on Trade-Related Aspects of Intellectual Property Rights (TRIPS). Reduced to its essentials, TRIPS imposes US-style patent protection on developing countries. That is good news for patent holders (over 90 per cent of which are northern companies) and bad news for technology-importing countries (because patents inflate prices). While efforts have been made to soften the impact of TRIPS on drugs prices, these provide only partial protection (Oxfam 2006b). The more stringent application and enforcement of patents by pharmaceutical companies will increase the price of vital medicines. More widely, it will stifle technological innovation and limit technology transfer – an outcome that will certainly hamper efforts to foster the adoption of the clean technologies needed to cut carbon emissions in India and China. To make matters worse, the US in particular has used bilateral and regional trade agreements to secure 'WTO plus' intellectual property accords. For example, the Central America Free Trade Agreement enshrines far more stringent intellectual property rules than the WTO, further increasing the patent holder's monopoly.

TRIPS is not an isolated example. The application of WTO rules on investment also restricts the scope for many developing country governments to develop active industrial policies, creating an environment in which firms can successfully innovate and climb the technology ladder. Admittedly, much of what has passed for state intervention in industrial policy in the developing world has been flawed. Yet the development of an engineering industry in Korea in the 1960s, the Chinese electronics sector in the 1980s, and the Indian auto-components sector in the 1990s, all depended upon forms of intervention – including restrictions on foreign ownership and technology transfer obligations on foreign investors – that the WTO would now rule inadmissible and illegal. Indeed, most of the developing country success stories that can be identified in world trade today have followed a path very different from that charted by existing multilateral rules.

In a visit to India in early 2007, Gordon Brown argued that multilateral institutions need to be recast to tackle the problems of the twenty-first century. Nowhere is this more apparent than in the case of the WTO. The Doha Round has stretched the credibility and, in the eyes of much of the developing world, the legitimacy of the institution to breaking point. There is today a real danger that the rules-based multilateral system represented by the WTO will become increasingly marginalized. This would have seriously negative implications for the poorest countries. The weakening of the multilateral rules-based system would give an added impetus to the fragmentation of world trade through bilateral and regional trade deals. Such an outcome could see a drift towards hostile trading blocs and a 1930s-style implosion of world trade. Ultimately, though, the gravest risks are those faced by multilateralism in a broader sense. Strengthening rules-based multilateralism in trade would be one small step away from the destructive unilateralism that blights international cooperation in so many areas. Weakening multilateralism in trade would have the equal and opposite effect.

The UK government urgently needs a strategy for bringing trade into the heart of development policy. The immediate question is this: given the limited achievements of the Doha Round, is a weak deal better than no deal? On balance, and provided that the deal does not impose rapid liberalization on the developing world, the answer is yes. For all of its shortcomings, an agreement on agriculture will create a framework that prevents the EU and the US from reverting to the worst practices of the past. Looking ahead, a progressive UK government should play a leading role in reshaping the politics of the WTO: for example, by working more closely with the G20 grouping.

Conclusion

Social and economic progress in developing countries will depend primarily not on the aid, trade and wider policies of governments in rich countries, but on the policies of governments and the efforts of people in poor countries themselves. Exaggerated claims about the potency of aid and trade as forces for poverty reduction are therefore unhelpful. That said, and as this chapter has sought to show, in the right circumstances aid and trade can make a significant contribution to development. A progressive UK government, building on the development achievements of the last decade, should be a powerful global advocate of more and better aid and fairer international rules of trade. In the last analysis, progressive governments or social movements in rich countries cannot make poverty history in other parts of the world. But what they can and should do is help to create an enabling global environment in which the poorest people have a chance to consign their poverty to history.

References

Adams, C. (2007) 'Blair pressed on corruption inquiry', *Financial Times*, 15 January; available at: www.ft.com/cms/s/45922d1e-a43d-11db-bec4-0000779e2340.html.

Birdsall, N., Rodrik, D. and Subramanian, A. (2005) 'How to help poor countries', *Foreign Affairs*, 84(4), pp. 136–52.

Brown, G. (2005) 'Words into action', speech given on 25 January at Lancaster House, London; available at www.hm-treasury.gov.uk/newsroom_and_speeches/press/2005/press_09_05.cfm.

Burall, S. and Maxwell, S. (2006) *Reforming the International Aid Architecture: options and ways forward*, London: Overseas Development Institute.

Clemens, M., Radelet, S. and Bhavani, R. (2004) *Counting Chickens When They Hatch: the short-term effect of aid on growth*, Working Paper 44, Washington, DC: Centre for Global Development.

Commission for Africa (2005) *Our Common Interest: report of the Commission for Africa*, London.

Cornia, A. (2004) *Inequality, Growth and Poverty in the Era of Globalization*, Oxford: Oxford University Press.

Easterly, W. (2006) *The White Man's Burden: why the West's efforts to aid the rest have done so much ill and so little good*, New York: Penguin.

Friedman, T. (2005) *The World is Flat: a brief history of the twenty-first century*, New York: Farrar, Straus and Giroux.

Hills, J. (2004) *Inequality and the State*, Oxford: Oxford University Press.

IMF/World Bank (2006) *Progress Report for the Education for All Fast-Track Initiative*, Development Committee, Washington, DC.

Joint UN Programme on HIV/AIDS (2006) *AIDS Epidemic Update*, Geneva: UNAIDS/World Health Organization; available at: www.unaids.org/en/HIV_data/epi2006/default.asp.

Levine, R. (2004) *Millions Saved: proven successes in global health*, Washington, DC: Centre for Global Development.

Lopez, H. (2006) *Did Growth Become Less Pro-poor in the 1990s?*, Working Paper 3931, Washington, DC: World Bank.

Milanovic, B. (2005) *Worlds Apart: measuring global and international inequality*, Princeton, NJ: Princeton University Press.

Organisation for Economic Cooperation and Development (2005) *Harmonisation, Alignment, Results: report on progress, challenges and opportunities*, Paris: OECD.

Organisation for Economic Cooperation and Development (2006) *Survey on Harmonisation and Alignment of Donor Practices*, Paris: OECD.

Oxfam (2006a) *Unequal Partners: how EU–ACP Economic Partnership Agreements (EPAs) could harm the development prospects of many of the world's poorest countries*, Oxford: Oxfam.

Oxfam (2006b) *Patents versus Patients: five years after the Doha Declaration*, Briefing Paper 95, Oxford: Oxfam.

Oxfam (2006c) *A Recipe for Disaster*, Briefing Paper 87, Oxford: Oxfam.

Radelet, S. (2006) *A Primer on Foreign Aid*, Working Paper 92, Washington, DC: Centre for Global Development.

Roodman, D. (2006) *Aid Project Proliferation and Absorbtion Capacity*, Working Paper 75, Washington, DC: Centre for Global Development.

Stevens, C. (2006) 'The EU, Africa and Economic Partnership Agreements: unintended consequences of policy leverage', *Journal of Modern African Studies*, 44(3), pp. 441–58.

Stiglitz, J. (2006) *Green Box Subsidies: a theoretical and empirical assessment*, mimeo, Geneva: United Nations Conference on Trade and Development.

Sumner, D. (2003) 'A quantitative simulation analysis of the impact of US cotton subsidies on cotton prices and quantities', paper presented to WTO Cotton Panel, October; available at: www.fao.org/es/esc/en/20953/222215/highlight_47647en_sumner.pdf.

United Nations Children's Fund (2007) *The State of the World's Children*, New York: UNICEF.

United Nations Development Programme (2005) *International Cooperation at a Crossroads: aid, trade and security in an unequal world*, Human Development Report 2005, Oxford: Oxford University Press.

United Nations Development Programme (2006) *Beyond Scarcity: power, poverty and the global water crisis*, Human Development Report 2006, London: Palgrave Macmillan.

World Bank (2007) *Global Economic Prospects 2007: managing the next wave of globalization*, Washington, DC: World Bank.

5

Sustainability and Foreign Policy

Nick Mabey

Environmental and resource issues should be at the very heart of a progressive approach to UK foreign policy. Foreign policy should rightly be concerned with issues of security and prosperity, but in an interdependent world that is pressing up against or exceeding many environmental and resource limits, a radically different approach will be required to achieve these traditional goals.

History is a guide to understanding the challenges facing us. A key lesson of European industrialization in the nineteenth and early twentieth centuries was that unless expanding economic opportunities are matched by a greater sense of responsibility to manage economic change equitably and sustainably, then social instability and conflict will result. The development of the British welfare state was an attempt to manage and civilize this economic process and the social and environmental dislocation to which it gave rise. We are now repeating the experiment of industrialization on a global scale, and in turn will need to manage the global difficulties this creates. Implicitly, we think of the future as being similar to our current world, albeit on a larger scale with a faster pace. However, the challenges we face today are quantitatively and qualitatively different from those of the past, and they will need to be accompanied by profound shifts in how we organize society and the economy, and in relationships between countries.

This chapter starts by highlighting the scale of the global environmental challenge, with a particular focus on climate change. It looks, too, at the critically important linkages between environmental pressures and violent conflict. The chapter then sets out some concrete steps that a progressive UK government could take to respond to these issues. Three clear priorities are identified. First, action needs to be taken to improve the UK's own performance on environmental issues: for example, to reduce our greenhouse gas emissions, as well as to enhance the coordination and coherence of UK policy making on the environment. In this section, I also suggest that the UK should be doing more through its international development efforts to help the world's poorest countries and communities manage environmental problems and resource conflicts more effectively. Secondly, the UK should be promoting a bigger role for Europe in tackling environmental problems. Thirdly, there are measures that need to be taken at the global level, to strengthen global environmental governance and to enhance international cooperation on environmental issues. This cooperation is not just intergovernmental; there are important global initiatives involving the private sector and civil society that the UK should support strongly.

Global environmental challenges

The world faces massive environmental challenges, with most of the major international environmental trends moving in the wrong direction. One critical factor, likely to worsen these trends still further, is the enormous growth in the global population. In the 1940s this totalled 2.5 billion; currently the figure stands at 6 billion; but in the next twenty to thirty years it could rise to between 8 and 10 billion. The next half-century will also see huge numbers of people undertaking the transition from agrarian to industrial societies. Another difference is the growth and size of the global economy and the pressure that this is putting on the earth's natural limits. The world economy has nearly doubled since the end of the Cold War, and it is on track to quadruple by the middle of this century. This implies that by 2050, global GDP will increase by eight times the cumulative growth seen between 1989 and 2006.

But as Kevin Watkins notes in chapter 4 of this volume this enormous growth in global wealth is very poorly distributed, with billions of people still living in acute poverty and with large and growing levels of inequality. Without a fundamental change in the way we generate and distribute wealth, it will be impossible to reduce these levels of poverty in the developing world or to maintain living standards in developed countries. In short, the continuation of our existing resource-intensive and polluting economic behaviour is a recipe for global ecological catastrophe. The traditional foreign policy-making establishment, in the UK and elsewhere, has been slow to wake up to this fact and the far-reaching implications that flow from it.

A few facts serve to illustrate the scale of the problem. If present consumption patterns continue, two-thirds of the global population will live in water-stressed conditions by the year 2025. More than two-thirds of the world's fish stocks are currently being fished at or beyond sustainable levels. Losses from natural disasters are now around eight times higher than in the 1960s, and an estimated 25 million 'environmental refugees' have emerged as a result of weather-related disasters. Meanwhile, poor environmental quality contributes to 25 per cent of all preventable ill-health in the world (United Nations Environment Programme 2000).

However, the single biggest environmental challenge facing the world is climate change. The impacts of global climate change are already being felt. Current levels of greenhouse gases in the atmosphere are higher than at any time in the past 650,000 years, and average global temperatures have already risen by 0.7°C since 1900 (Stern 2006). The latest report from the Intergovernmental Panel on Climate Change (IPCC) suggests that global temperatures will continue to rise over this century. The IPCC predicts that by 2100, global temperatures could increase by between 1.1°C and 6.4°C (IPCC 2007). It also suggests that sea levels are likely to rise by 28–43 cm (driving millions of people from their homes in low-lying areas), parts of the world will see an increase in the number of heatwaves and there is likely to be an increased intensity of tropical storms.

These predicted rises are extremely disturbing. There is a growing consensus that beyond a certain level the adverse impacts of climate change increase markedly (Retallack 2005). If average global temperature exceeds 2°C above the pre-industrial levels for a sustained period, then the evidence suggests that billions of people worldwide will face water shortages, crop losses will hit major food-exporting countries and irreversible damage may be done to whole ecosystems, such as coral reefs and the Amazon rainforest. Climate change will also undermine public health, with higher temperatures making it easier for diseases to spread. The worldwide risk of catching malaria could double by 2080 (Martens et al. 1999). And more frequent floods, particularly in areas of poor sanitation, increase the risk of water-borne diseases such as cholera (Pascual et al. 2000).

There are also large economic implications. Sir Nicholas Stern's review of the economics of climate change estimated that unless immediate action is taken to reduce global emissions, the overall costs and risks of climate change could amount to a permanent reduction in annual global gross domestic product (GDP) of up to 20 per cent by

2100 (Stern et al. 2006). Even this figure is likely to be an underestimate, however, as the Stern review was unable to determine the costs of climate change in reducing the supply of broad ecosystem services: for example, the role of vulnerable wetlands in removing water pollution or how climate damage to coral reefs may reduce the productivity of ocean fisheries.

For progressives, it should be a particular concern that the costs arising from worsening environmental trends will affect disproportionately the world's poorest people. Roughly three in four natural disasters – such as droughts, floods and cyclones – are weather related. And 97 per cent of deaths from natural disasters occur in developing countries (Department for International Development 2006). This is because these communities are more dependent on natural resources and more vulnerable to extreme natural events, and because they possess fewer resources with which to adapt to changing conditions. In 2000, devastating floods in Mozambique left 700 people dead and half a million homeless; as a result, economic growth fell from 8 per cent in 1999 to 2 per cent in 2000. Droughts in Kenya in the late 1990s cut GDP by over 20 per cent as hydropower capacity was reduced and crops failed.

The Millennium Ecosystem Assessment (MEA) has developed scenarios of different levels of ecosystem degradation, showing how the internationally agreed Millennium Development Goals (MDGs) for reducing poverty by 2015 could be undermined by deteriorating environmental trends. The MDG goal to halve hunger is missed in all four MEA scenarios, and progress is slowest in areas that suffer the greatest ecosystem degradation: south Asia and sub-Saharan Africa (Millennium Ecosystem Assessment 2005).

Worsening environmental trends can also increase the risks of instability and violent conflict. Though every violent conflict has its own unique dynamic based on local politics, economics and history, there are some common patterns. For example, natural resource wealth is often associated with poverty and conflict rather than economic success and stability. Over the last forty years, developing countries without major natural resources have grown two to three times faster than those with high resource endowment (World Bank 2005). Politicized revenue allocation from natural resources based around ethnic, religious or regional lines has been a major driver of these internal conflicts. A clear example of this phenomenon is Sierra Leone in the late 1990s, where trade in 'conflict diamonds' funded rebel groups in their war against government forces.

In many other countries, politicized allocation of water and land is driving low-level conflict. This can erupt into major violence when linked to ethnic, national and other divisions. By 2025, 63 per cent of the global population will be living in countries of significant water stress. Freshwater shortages are predicted to become more acute in already unstable regions of north Africa and sub-Saharan Africa, the Middle East and central Asia. Migration away from environmentally degraded regions causes confrontation across borders and inside countries, from Africa to Latin America.

However, despite a few high-profile exceptions such as the action to control trade in 'conflict diamonds', there has been a lack of concerted international effort to address the resource and environmental roots of instability. Cases that have been addressed have required extensive campaigning from non-governmental groups to secure action. Environment and resource management issues are not yet main-streamed into conflict prevention and development policy. In a world of rising scarcity this reactive approach will not be sufficient. The links between the environment and conflict provide an additional security rationale, alongside the economic and moral imperatives, for more concerted international action on the environment.

It should be stressed that although some of these worsening environmental trends are now well advanced, none of the worst-case scenarios is inevitable (Stern 2006). A combination of stronger national environmental management and international coordination could mitigate most of these problems. The technology and knowledge are there. A wealth of experience exists on managing environmental disputes and designing governance systems, anti-corruption measures and mechanisms for sharing resources. The fundamental challenge is to generate the political will and the national and international action necessary to address these issues. This involves highlighting the costs of inaction, which will rise the longer the action is delayed; but also focusing on the real benefits that could accrue from better environmental management. And it means learning lessons from recent successes and failures.

There is clear evidence, for example, that global environmental problems can be tackled successfully when there is a convergence of means and motives. Stratospheric ozone depletion was one such global environmental threat addressed by the international community. The destruction of the ozone layer threatened human health, agricultural productivity and biodiversity on a massive scale. However, effective implementation of the Montreal Protocol could result in the recovery of the ozone layer to pre-1980 levels by the year 2050 (United Nations Environment Programme 2006).

Awareness of environmental problems is also increasing internationally. At the regional level, Europe has taken a lead in tackling its environmental problems. The quality of rivers, lakes and urban air have all improved as a result of new environmental policies and standards. Emissions of pollutants contributing to acidification and eutrophication are declining. And deforestation has been arrested and reversed in many parts of the continent. Elsewhere, governments are devoting significant resources to the problems produced by climate change. For example, China has taken some recent decisive steps to try to address the problem. It has agreed far-reaching plans to increase energy efficiency by 20 per cent in five years and to source 15 per cent of its electricity from renewable sources by 2020. India is also making increasing investments in renewables. These examples may be far from typical, but they do demonstrate what is possible.

The UK's role: from words to action

The UK has come a long way from when it was considered the 'dirty man of Europe'. UK international leadership on the environment was instrumental in delivering the Kyoto Protocol in 1997. More recently, the UK put climate change at the very top of its agenda for the Gleneagles Group of Eight (G8) Summit, was a powerful advocate for the World Bank's Low Carbon Investment Framework in 2005 and commissioned the influential Stern review that reported in 2006.

The UK was one of the first countries to set ambitious domestic targets to reduce greenhouse gas emissions that went further than its obligations under Kyoto: committing itself to reduce UK carbon dioxide (CO_2) to 20 per cent below 1990 levels by 2010 and 60 per cent by 2050. To help secure these targets, the government made the UK the first country to adopt a domestic emissions trading scheme and it led efforts to introduce an EU trading scheme.

Since 1997, the UK government has taken steps to improve government-wide coordination and effectiveness on the environment. Environmental issues were highlighted in the International Development White Papers of 1997, 2000 and 2006. The UK has led efforts to strengthen environmental diplomacy though the creation of a dedicated department in the Foreign and Commonwealth Office (FCO), and by initiating the European Green Diplomacy Network. In 2006, the FCO adopted a new climate security goal and appointed a Special Representative on Climate Change.

The government has also sought to encourage greater involvement in sustainability issues by UK companies and investors, and with some success. UK firms and institutions have been at the cutting edge of incorporating environment and sustainable development into their core business practices. The UK has the highest level of third-party auditing of company environmental reports in the G8, and a strong environmental investment sector. The UK has pioneered approaches to sustainable finance, including the Carbon Disclosure Project. Through this scheme, major investors press companies that they invest in to measure their CO_2 emissions. UK non-governmental organizations (NGOs) and institutes are also leaders in developing new approaches to creating markets for environmentally sound goods and services – from timber to pensions. For its efforts in all of these areas, the government deserves credit.

However, there are other respects in which the government's record has fallen short of its ambitious environmental rhetoric. There are five areas in particular worth highlighting here, and where an enhanced effort by the UK is required.

First, a progressive UK government should be working for deeper reductions in UK greenhouse gas emissions. Although UK CO_2 emissions did fall until 2002, since then they have started to rise again. Instead of achieving a 20 per cent reduction in CO_2 emissions below 1990 levels by 2010, as it had aimed for, the government's own projections suggest it will only achieve a 16.2 per cent reduction in emissions. This is at a time when the international consensus suggests the need for much more radical CO_2 reductions all round. Across the board, the UK should be looking for ways to curb its emissions and to reduce damage to the environment. This obviously includes road, rail and air traffic policy, energy policy, as well as incentives for changed behaviour on the part of companies and individuals. The more that the UK is able to do at home, the more credibility it will have internationally.

Secondly, the UK should increase its funding for global environmental initiatives. The UK currently spends around £130 million annually on international environmental action, including its contribution to the Global Environment Facility, which was established in 1992 as the major international fund for environmental action in developing countries. But the UK figure is below that of many other European countries. The recent initiatives on low-carbon technology cooperation launched at the Johannesburg Sustainable Development Summit in 2002 and the Gleneagles G8 Summit in 2005 have also been hamstrung by a lack of serious financing.

Thirdly, by building on its international development achievements of the last decade, the UK should be doing much more to help developing countries cope with environment challenges. As noted already, it is the world's poor that suffer disproportionately from bad environmental conditions and negative environmental trends. But many of the actions required to address these issues also need to be taken at the national or the local level.

There is a critical need, for example, to use development cooperation policies to help poorer countries better manage their environmental capital and services. The UK could help develop a network of governments engaged in natural wealth accounting, and develop processes for incorporating these new measures into national decision making, with a specific focus on how natural assets underpin poor people's livelihoods. The UK should also work with developing country governments to agree bilateral instruments to prevent trade in illegally harvested resources, building on the success of existing European initiatives in this area.

And the UK can and should work with other international development agencies to set standards for improving poor people's access to natural resources. This includes action to support land reform and reforms to tenure systems, and new approaches to water allocation systems and forestry-use rights. The UK could build on its existing support for government/NGO initiatives, such as the Partnership for Principle 10 (www.pp10.org). This monitors and helps to implement the rights to environmental justice, consultation and redress agreed at the Rio and Johannesburg Conferences.

The UK should further expand and deepen its Sustainable Development Dialogues with emerging economies like India, China, Mexico, Brazil and South Africa. These dialogues should become a primary vehicle for building a global politics of environmental responsibility. The existing UK partnerships with business and civil society in areas such as forestry, water, finance, energy and tourism should be examined critically and reformed or reinvigorated where necessary.

Fourthly, the UK can and should improve its internal coordination and the quality of its decision making on environmental issues. The UK should make risk management of environment and resource issues a core competence at the centre of government by building a specialized Sustainable Development Unit inside the Cabinet Office with responsibility for monitoring these risks. This could usefully work in partnership with the existing external watchdog body, the Sustainable Development Commission. Key departments should also agree a joint international strategy, ensuring that environmental and resource issues are truly mainstreamed into the main international departments.

Taking forward this ambitious agenda will require government to have new skills and expertise. Though the UK government has taken steps to open up its structures to external expertise, this has been limited. Many of these areas require high levels of professional skill and experience, and the UK has a wealth of talent to use outside government to advance its interests. The Department for Environment, Food and Rural Affairs (DEFRA), DFID and the FCO should agree on a range of civil service posts in these areas, including at least 60 per cent of senior grades, which will become permanently open to external competition.

Fifthly, there is a need for greater democratic accountability and oversight of the UK's international policy on environmental issues, starting with the creation of a clear UK international environmental strategy that includes climate change, but is wider than this. As part of broader reforms, a more powerful Parliamentary Environmental Committee could be created, combining the existing bodies, with dedicated analytical support (similar to that given to the Sustainable Development Commission.) The Climate Change Bill planned for 2007 will have a powerful and independent climate committee to oversee UK domestic action, but there is no comparable oversight of the international agenda. The Climate Committee should be given powers to examine the government's international cooperation in this area.

Europe as a global leader on the environment

A progressive UK foreign policy should also promote an enhanced role for Europe on global environmental issues. At present, European energy and environmental policies are too often formulated in a narrow framework of perceived national interests. And they can be based on an outdated view of sovereignty which ignores the growing reality of interdependence. But this is a huge missed opportunity. Europe is the only major power with the scale, resources and political clout to lead the global energy and climate agenda at the pace required. Europe also has most to lose from a world where cooperation on energy and climate security is lacking. The UK should press for a broader European perspective that looks beyond narrow institutional silos and recognizes the benefits to Europe of a more joined-up approach to energy and climate security.

The changing geopolitics of energy, illustrated by the accelerating global scramble for resources, represents a major threat to the international rules-based order. The anti-democratic changes in Russia are an example of the direction the world might move in as geopolitical competition for fossil fuels emboldens authoritarian regimes. The strengthening Chinese engagement with repressive leaders in resource-rich African countries embodies an even more serious risk. China argues that it is driven to engage with these countries because it is excluded from investment in other areas by the West.

Europe has a vital interest in preventing and managing these pressures in non-military ways. A recent Pentagon study argued that, in the event of rapid climate change, the US should abandon Europe and retreat behind its natural borders of the Atlantic and Pacific (Schwartz and Randall 2003). While the ability of the US to isolate itself from climate change impacts may be exaggerated for political reasons, it does have lower vulnerability than Europe to mass migration. Europe has no realistic 'defensive' option to remove itself from the destabilizing impacts of climate change in Africa, the Middle East and Asia, and the resulting migratory and other pressures. Furthermore, the UK should argue that the successful management of global energy and climate security is not simply an issue of economics or morality, but an essential component of European strategic interest. Such leadership is required in order for Europe to preserve its future prosperity and stability while living in accordance with its fundamental values. There are two particular steps that the UK should be pressing the European Union (EU) to adopt.

First, the EU needs to reduce significantly its own carbon emissions and to reduce its dependence on imported energy. By setting an aggressive unilateral target to cut carbon emissions by 30 per cent by 2020, and putting in place the policies to deliver this, Europe could demonstrate that ambitious change is possible. Strong European action would also increase confidence in its fledgling carbon market, which would give a clear signal to investors to develop the technologies needed for a low-carbon economy.

Secondly, Europe can help to leverage global improvements. The most optimistic scenario sees a new international climate change agreement to succeed the Kyoto protocol being negotiated in 2009–10. The EU should argue for a web of global deals on energy and climate security between major energy-consuming nations as a pragmatic step to producing a stable global regime. This could include deals with India and China on trade and investment in energy-efficient technologies, renewables and zero-emission coal power plants; deals with the US and Japan on cooperation rapidly to develop and deploy efficient aircraft and vehicle technologies; and vitally, a deal with the US on the level at which it sets a domestic cap on carbon emissions in return for access to the economic benefits of the European emissions trading market.

These relationships would provide the political, investment and trade underpinning of a new international climate change agreement. Europe can use its enormous economic weight to drive such changes, especially in its relationships with India and China. The industrial boom in China – mainly fuelled by European investment and consumption – means that it is currently building coal-fuelled power stations at the unprecedented pace of a major plant every four days. The lifetime emissions of the coal power plants built by 2030 will equal two-thirds of total global emissions over the last two decades. Europe cannot stop India and China building coal power stations to meet their energy needs, but it could help to prevent them dramatically increasing their future carbon emissions by assisting them to deploy carbon capture and storage (CCS) technologies. These remove carbon emissions and store them underground. The EU has already agreed to build a commercial-scale CCS demonstration plant with China. While this is a good first step, unless the planned completion date of 2020 is moved forward it will have little impact on climate stability. A plant could be built by 2010, if the right level of political and financial investment within Europe could be mobilized.

China has also set an extremely ambitious target of improving its overall energy efficiency by 20 per cent by 2010. It is in Europe's interest to act decisively to help China achieve this, in parallel with developing a more aggressive domestic energy efficiency policy: for example, by harmonizing efficient product standards in the EU and China and lowering relevant tariffs. The energy and climate security benefits of cheap and highly efficient Chinese appliances in Europe outweigh any possible 'competitiveness' issues around tariff reduction. In the same way, Europe (and the rest of the world) has a greater interest in ensuring energy and climate security than in overprotecting intellectual property rights (IPR) around clean technologies. Fears around IPR protection are holding up EU–China and EU–India cooperation in renewable energy technologies, coal, efficiency and other areas. However, many European companies already manage access to IPR as part of their commercial and governmental relationships in China and India, showing that a strategic balance of risk and reward can be found if ultimate objectives are clear. Action in both these areas could help significantly in tackling climate change and other global environmental problems.

Strengthening environmental cooperation and global governance

A progressive UK approach to environmental sustainability should also promote more effective forms of international environmental cooperation and global environmental governance.

But improving the level of international cooperation on environmental issues will involve a willingness to face up to the difficult politics surrounding this, particularly when it comes to resources. Historically, western industrialized countries have been the biggest polluters, accounting for roughly 80 per cent of CO_2 build-up in the atmosphere to date (World Resources Institute 2003). And this is still true today. Although emerging economies are catching up fast, more than 60 per cent of new CO_2 emissions globally still originate in industrialized countries, where only 20 per cent of the world's population resides. Without a concern for equity and burden sharing, there will be no prospect of securing a global deal on climate change or many other environmental issues, between developed and developing countries. This is at its heart a problem of diplomacy and foreign policy, not of technical environmental management, and solutions will be found in Foreign Ministries rather than Environment Ministries.

The majority of investments to tackle global environmental issues – particularly climate change – will need to be carried out in rich and middle-income countries, which are the biggest part of the problem. As the Stern review has argued, the costs of doing this are significant but entirely manageable in the context of developed country budgets – around 1 per cent of global GDP by 2050 (Stern 2006).

China and India may have sufficient resources to reduce their carbon emissions, but they see responsibility for the problem lying in past emissions from developed countries, and so expect financial compensation for their actions in the short term. Poor developing countries face serious resource constraints on funding environmental action, given many other pressing calls on national resources. Funding from richer countries is therefore an essential part of the political and ethical partnership underlying successful international environmental cooperation. This should not be seen as a replacement for national political action in developing countries, but it is unrealistic and wrong to think that the action will happen without higher resource flows from developed countries.

Current estimates are that US$60–90 billion per annum will be required to address environmental goals over the next ten to fifteen years, excluding climate change (Poverty Environment Partnership 2005). Current adaptation costs to manage climate change in developing countries are estimated at $10–40 billion per annum, depending on how quickly we reduce the pace of global warming (World Bank 2006). The costs of mitigating climate change to keep below a 2°C rise are higher with estimates of $40–150 billion per annum in developing countries.

Set against this estimated cost, the international response has been pitiful. The major international financing instrument in this area – the

Global Environment Facility – has delivered an average of only $330 million per annum to developing countries over the last fifteen years, well below the 1 per cent needed. The Clean Development Mechanism, which allows private sector funding of greenhouse gas reductions in developing countries to count against emission targets in the developed world, is worth around $3 billion per annum in additional low-carbon investment. This is less than 5 per cent of what the International Energy Agency (IEA) estimates is needed in new clean investment (IEA 2006). Developed countries, including the UK, will need to commit to higher resource transfers to the developing world in order to address this challenge and to get international agreement to a post-Kyoto deal on capping emissions.

More effective global institutions are also crucial. There is currently no lack of institutions for global environmental governance, but these have largely failed to prevent the worsening of environmental trends over the past thirty years. There are over 200 international environmental agreements supported by cross-cutting agencies (UN Environmental Programme (UNEP), Global Environment Facility), overarching coordinating structures (Environment Management Group, Commission for Sustainable Development, UN Economic and Social Council) and the international legal framework (Environmental Chamber of the International Court of Justice). Environmental issues are included to some extent in the work of key global economic institutions (World Bank, World Trade Organization and International Monetary Fund), and official institutions are complemented by a huge number of private sector initiatives (e.g. codes of conduct, eco-labels, NGO activities). The question is: why have these bodies been ineffective in achieving their stated objectives?

One reason is that high-level leadership on environmental issues is often weak. Good environmental governance produces joint benefits, but is often frustrated by special interests both nationally and internationally: for example, the role of member nations of the Organization of Petroleum Exporting Countries (OPEC) in blocking action on climate change and the actions of national forestry interests in Asia in preventing binding global forestry standards. Overcoming these blocks requires strong leadership to identify common problems and potential benefits, and to help pull together political coalitions to solve them. International environmental agreements are poorly coordinated and weakly enforced. Each is negotiated separately – tailored to specific problems with different objectives, membership, funding and compliance mechanisms, as well as institutional and reporting arrangements.

Progress in negotiating and ratifying agreements has not translated into effective implementation at the national level. Blame has often been levied on weak enforcement mechanisms, with calls for tough World Trade Organization-style compliance and dispute mechanisms to punish free-riders. But countries seem reluctant to bring environmental disputes, even though existing institutions are available to provide legal remedies. Part of the problem lies with the developmental nature of many non-compliance issues. Lack of resources, capacity, technology and skills is often the root cause of poor implementation of environmental agreements in developing countries. Poorer developing countries will need carefully designed assistance to come into compliance rather than coercive measures which could make them poorer and would fail to benefit the environment.

A progressive UK government should also press for a series of achievable steps towards a World Environment Organization (WEO). It is unrealistic to think that a full shift to a WEO can be achieved at once given existing political resistance in many quarters, not least the US. An evolutionary approach would see UNEP increase its status by becoming a specialized UN agency with increased levels of compulsory UN funding. Leadership could be strengthened by working to ensure that a high-level political leader is appointed, and increasing UNEP's role in the core tasks of leadership, scientific analysis, information gathering and assessment of priorities. International environmental agreements should also be clustered into functional groups, and umbrella conventions should be negotiated under UNEP to improve policy coordination.

To be effective, financing would need to be increased by broadening the mandate of the Global Environment Facility (GEF) so that it funds all international environmental agreements and reflects developing country priorities more strongly. The GEF should eventually be brought under UNEP control. The resulting organization could then be consolidated and renamed as the World Environment Organization. The guiding ethos of this WEO would be one of informed, principled and powerful leadership, and its role would be the global environmental watchdog that identifies future environmental challenges and threats to the integrity of the global commons. Much of the practical work of the WEO should be embedded in webs of agreements between a wide range of different partners from governments, business and civil society.

But securing international support for a WEO will require persuasive arguments. The Stern review has set out, more clearly than ever before, the economic consequences of failing to tackle environmental problems and the real financial benefits of doing so in the medium to long term. Stern argued that it costs between five and twenty times less to invest in reducing greenhouse gas emissions than to face the consequences of doing nothing. This analysis is profoundly important and it has the potential to shift public attitudes and the policies of governments in a way that traditional environmental arguments have so far failed to do. The UK should continue to promote this report and its analysis very assertively. The social and health consequences of climate change and other environmental problems are also becoming increasingly apparent. And as I have highlighted earlier, there is growing awareness of the security implications of a further deterioration in the global environment. Progressives should deploy all of these arguments in building support for greater international cooperation and better global governance arrangements for the environment. In essence, the case needs to be made for a new politics of interdependence, cooperation and mutual benefit. This approach will be a challenge to the existing mindset in foreign policy, which largely continues to view issues as a process of win–lose negotiation.

There are two other areas where the UK should be pressing for stronger international environmental cooperation and institutional development. First, compliance with environmental agreements could be improved by creating an International Centre for the Settlement of Environmental Disputes (ICSED), inside UNEP, analogous to the World Bank's investment dispute body. This would act as a mediation, arbitration, compliance and problem-solving institution. It could be specified as a referral body in any environmental treaty. This would be backed by streamlined procedures for using the environmental chamber of the International Court of Justice (ICJ), including stricter time limits, assistance for developing countries and encouraging countries to declare compulsory ICJ jurisdiction for bilateral environmental issues.

Secondly, there are a series of important global initiatives on the environment and resource management involving the private sector and civil society. As the home of many major mining and resource companies, the UK has a particular responsibility for helping tackle the negative impacts of badly managed natural resource extraction. This should build on existing UK experience and leadership in developing novel mechanisms to improve the management of natural resource extraction, like the Forest Stewardship Council and the Extractive Industry Transparency Initiative (EITI).

Conclusion

During the last ten years, the UK has positioned itself as a global leader on the environment. Over the next decade it will need to take these issues and this political commitment to a higher level. Much of what the UK is currently doing in this area is broadly along the right lines; however, it is on too small a scale and it is not backed up by sufficiently effective machinery for environmental diplomacy, finance and implementation.

By improving the UK's own environmental performance, strengthening Europe's role and contributing to greater international environmental cooperation and stronger global environmental governance, a progressive UK government could have a serious and constructive impact on these problems. In addition, the UK can and should do more to make use of its pre-eminent networks of non-governmental institutions in the environmental field. This includes organizations like the Royal Society for the Protection of Birds and the World Wide Fund for Nature, scientists at Kew and the Hadley Centre, and universities and professional institutes like the Tyndall Centre. The UK is also host to the British Broadcasting Corporation and the Television Trust for the Environment, which have world-class reputations in environmental programming. The UK should exploit these assets to the full. Governmental action is crucial if we are to tackle more effectively the world's pressing environmental challenges. But the problems cannot be solved by governments alone. A diverse civil society and the private sector must also be part of a progressive response to these critical issues.

References

Intergovernmental Panel on Climate Change (2007) *Climate Change 2007: synthesis report – summary for policymakers*, Geneva: IPCC.

International Energy Agency (2006) *World Energy Outlook*, Paris: IEA.

Martens, P. et al. (1999) 'Climate change and future populations at risk from malaria', *Global Environmental Change*, Vol. 9, Supplement 1, pp. S89–S107.

Millennium Ecosystem Assessment (2005) *Ecosystems and Human Well-Being: synthesis*. Washington, DC: Island Press.

Pascual, M. et al. (2000) 'Cholera epidemics and El Niño southern oscillaton', *Science*, 289 (5485), pp. 1766–9.

Poverty Environment Partnership (2005) *Environment and the MDGs: investing in environmental wealth for poverty reduction*, New York: UNDP.

Retallack, S. (2005) *Setting a Long Term Climate Objective*, London: Institute for Public Policy Research.

Schwartz, P. and Randall, D. (2003) *An Abrupt Climate Change Scenario and Its Implications for United States National Security*, Washington, DC: US Department of Defense.

Stern, N. et al. (2006) *Stern Review: the economics of climate change*, London: HMSO.

United Nations Environment Programme (2000) *World Environmental Outlook*, Geneva: UNEP.

United Nations Environment Programme (2006) http://ozone.unep.org/ Treaties_and_Ratification/2B_montreal_protocol.asp, Geneva: Ozone Secretariat.

World Bank (2005) *Where is the Wealth of Nations? Measuring capital for the 21st century*, Washington, DC: World Bank.

World Bank (2006) 'An investment framework for clean energy and development: a progress report', paper for World Bank Development Committee, Washington, DC: World Bank.

World Resources Institute (2003) 'Developing countries and the Climate Treaty: what's fair, what's possible?', available at http://climate.wri.org/ project_content_text.cfm?ContentID=1284.

6

Recasting the Special Relationship

Andrew Gamble and Ian Kearns

The notion of a special relationship between the United Kingdom and the United States was first articulated by Winston Churchill sixty years ago in a speech in Fulton, Missouri (Churchill 1948). In this speech, Churchill sought to define the UK's role in an international system that had been utterly transformed by the Second World War. The huge sacrifices demanded by the war had visibly shrunk UK power, greatly reducing its strength relative to other great powers. Recognizing this, Churchill suggested that the UK still had a future as a great power, but at the intersection of three circles – Empire, Europe and Anglo-America. For him, the special relationship was one in which the US, because of its greater material and human resources, would now play the leading role in shaping world affairs, with the UK acting both in parallel and as a junior partner in this endeavour.

In the decades that have followed the Fulton speech, the special relationship has been the subject of much mockery and criticism, as UK power and capacity has waned and the US has become more dominant, particularly since the collapse of the Soviet Union in 1991. The UK has been described as the fifty-first state of the US, as America's unsinkable aircraft carrier, and UK leaders (including both Thatcher and Blair) as America's poodle. Moreover, some critics have argued that the special relationship is largely an illusion, that it is valued more highly by the British than it ever has been by the Americans, and that in any case the US has special relationships with many other states – Germany, Japan, Australia, Mexico, Turkey and Israel among them (Dumbrell 2001).

Nevertheless, successive governments have attached huge importance to their relationship with the US and made it a central focus of
UK foreign policy. If anything, this commitment to the US has been
even stronger in the last twenty-five years, under Margaret Thatcher,
John Major and Tony Blair, than it was before.

In this chapter we reflect on the UK/US relationship and suggest a
new approach that would be more consistent with the goals and values
of a progressive foreign policy. The chapter is divided into four sections. The first sets out the interests which shape the UK attitude
towards the US. The second gives a brief account of the evolution of
the special relationship over time. The third section analyses the
strains in the Anglo-American relationship precipitated by the adoption of the Bush doctrine in the US. The fourth section recommends
policy options for the UK for dealing differently with the US.

UK attitudes towards the US

The main reason why the special relationship has had such a hold on
the UK political class is that it has both reflected core and continuing
UK interests, and provided a strategy for the management of UK
decline. This can be seen especially in narratives such as 'America in
Britain's place' on issues of political economy, and in the 'Hug them
close' strategy on security.

'America in Britain's place' was the long-standing project of an influential section of the UK political class to persuade the US that it should
take up the burdens of global leadership once shouldered by the UK,
and guarantee the conditions and institutions for a secure and prosperous liberal world order (Watt 1984). In the 1920s and 1930s it
became clear that the UK could no longer perform that role, but the US
was still unwilling to do so. The UK retreated into protectionism and
the security of the sterling area and its imperial markets. A key issue
for the UK government during the Second World War was whether to
revert to this protectionist policy after the war, or to persuade the US
to take the lead in reconstructing a liberal world order under its leadership. The latter policy was adopted, and building a strong relationship with the US became the cornerstone for protecting UK global
commercial and financial interests, and with them some of the essential features of the UK state and society that had developed over the
previous century and a half. The choice was a painful and controversial one, because it entailed at US insistence the liquidation of the
British Empire, which had been the guarantor of an independent UK

policy. But the UK government accepted subordination to the US in return for a US commitment to restore an international economic order.

This political economy narrative of the special relationship might not have succeeded had it not been complemented and underpinned by a parallel 'Hug them close' narrative on national security. 'Hug them close' was the advice that Bill Clinton gave to Tony Blair on how to handle the incoming Bush team, but it reflects the stance of UK political leaders ever since Churchill (Riddell 2003). This stance is rooted in a hard-headed assessment of the UK national interest. The close wartime alliance between the UK and the US, coupled with the onset of the Cold War Soviet threat, convinced successive governments that the UK's security against military challenges required a close alliance with the US. Maintaining this commitment on the part of the US was seen to depend on the UK staying close to US policy positions, and doing nothing to undermine support in the US for its external security guarantees. Because of this, the US came to be regarded not just as the guarantor of a liberal global economic order, but also as the protector of the UK itself. The combination proved powerful, and helps explain the persistence of the attachment of the UK political class across the political spectrum to the special relationship.

The postwar subordination of the UK to the US, which has continued up to the present, was therefore founded on a particular understanding of the UK's national interest, in terms of both political economy and security. It was also sustained over the years by an emphasis on the shared history and values that unite the two countries. This is one of the hardest aspects of the special relationship to pin down but also one of the most persistent. Its origins are seen to lie in common history and ancestry, which has meant common language and the sharing of many institutions and traditions. Anglo-America in this sense has always been a shared transnational space, and while phrases like 'our Atlantic cousins' and 'brothers across the ocean' are somewhat overblown, there has always been easy communication between UK and US citizens, and often a sense of common identity. UK citizens have tended to identify with the US much more than with Europe. The common language has also facilitated a great deal of cultural exchange between the UK and the US, including in intellectual ideas and fashions, media, films and books. Political debates too have frequently been pursued on both sides of the Atlantic, so that many of the ideological arguments of the twentieth century, from the New Deal of the 1930s to the neoliberalism of the 1980s, have been arguments within Anglo-America and with strong partisans on both sides, rather than arguments between the two states.

This powerful combination of factors underpins much of what UK political leaders do, and is reflected in the everyday assumptions of Whitehall. Support for the US has been the default setting of UK foreign policy. This does not mean, however, that the relationship has been constant and unchanging in the post-1945 period. There have been at least three distinct phases of the special relationship in the last sixty years, the first period lasting up to the Suez crisis of 1956 and the second up to the onset of the new Cold War in the 1970s. The third, the era of Thatcher and Blair, we are still living.

In the first period, the UK saw the special relationship as a partnership, and played a considerable role with the US in establishing and designing the institutions of the new world order. UK involvement in the establishment of the North Atlantic Treaty Organization (NATO), its readiness to re-arm and commit troops alongside the US in the Korean War of 1950–3 and its acceptance with very few conditions of the establishment of permanent US military bases in UK ensured a period of close cooperation. This was reflected in the continuing close contact between the military, intelligence and diplomatic services of both countries.

However, the Suez crisis demonstrated that the special relationship was not really a partnership between equals, because the UK could no longer act independently, at least in a military sense, if the US was strongly opposed to its policy. After Suez there was a major reassessment of UK foreign policy and direction. Links with the US were restored, but withdrawal from Empire was speeded up, and the first approach to joining the European Economic Community (EEC) was made. This was welcomed by the US officials, who now wanted to bury the idea of the special relationship as a partnership. Dean Acheson, former US Secretary of State, declared in 1962 that the UK had lost an empire but not yet found a role, and he warned: 'The attempt to play a separate power role, that is a role apart from Europe, a role based on a "special relationship" with the United States, a role based on being Head of a "Commonwealth" which has no political structure, or unity or strength . . . this role is about to be played out' (Dimbleby and Reynolds 1988: 238).

Despite the initial rebuff of the UK's attempt to join the EEC by General de Gaulle, the drift towards Europe gathered pace in the 1960s. In this second phase of the special relationship, UK leaders displayed more political independence. Harold Wilson refused to send even a token force of UK troops to fight in Vietnam, despite US pressure for him to do so, while Edward Heath, the only postwar UK prime minister who consistently gave greater priority to Europe than to Anglo-America and the special relationship, shocked the Americans by insisting on consulting his European partners before agreeing to the use of US bases in the UK during the Yom Kippur War of 1973.

This second, cooler phase of the relationship came to an end in 1976 amid the most serious political and economic crisis of postwar UK history. During this crisis, the danger of a collapse of sterling was averted only by a deal with the International Monetary Fund (IMF), largely on US terms. A new phase of the special relationship now developed in response to the renewed Cold War between the US and the Soviet Union. This shift became most apparent after Margaret Thatcher became Prime Minister in 1979. Despite the UK's full membership of the EEC, the priority of both the Callaghan and Thatcher governments was not Europe, but once again the special relationship with the US. Both Callaghan and Thatcher were firm Atlanticists, and Thatcher herself was from the start a strong critic of détente and an advocate of a tough position towards the Soviet Union. The close rapport she established with Ronald Reagan created the template for this new phase of the special relationship. However, there was no attempt to disguise the asymmetry between the UK and the US, or to suggest that the UK could pursue a truly independent foreign policy. The new role that was envisaged for the UK was as the US's closest ally, its cheerleader and supporter. There were still conflicts and divergences. Thatcher objected strongly to the US occupation of Grenada, a member of the Commonwealth in 1983. But these were exceptions to the rule, and UK reservations, if there were any, were voiced in private.

In this third phase of the special relationship, which has reached a climax as well as a breaking point under Tony Blair, the identification of the UK with the US in foreign policy has never been so close. Blair consistently opposed any attempt to separate the UK from the US and, despite the increasing Europeanization of the UK state and economy, continued to believe that it was possible to be a strong ally of the US and a strong partner of the European Union (EU), as the EEC became in 1992. He did not accept that a choice had to be made between the two, or even that the UK government had to decide which should be given priority in thinking about UK interests and the place of the UK in the world. Blair has argued that the UK can be a bridge between Europe and the US, and that both have equal priority. After the Labour Party's election in 1997, Blair pursued a strong pro-European policy at first, re-establishing UK influence in the EU and forging links with other European leaders. At the same time he formed a close personal and political bond with Bill Clinton, and cooperated with the US on security questions, including the sanctions regime against Iraq and interventions in Kosovo.

Blair performed this balancing act between the US and the EU with some skill, but his bridge collapsed in the changed global environment following the election of George Bush and the events of 9/11. In the run-up to the war in Iraq, Blair made it absolutely clear that the UK should side with the US and not the EU when major security issues were at stake. After six decades, 'Hug them close' remained the central idea of UK foreign and security policy because in Blair's view, whatever the short-term disagreements and costs, in the long run the world, including the UK, would be a much less secure place if the US ever chose to disengage. However, it is these assumptions that have come under such scrutiny in recent years. It is no longer clear that UK national interests are best served by such a close relationship with the US. Since the collapse of the Soviet Union, the emergence of a unilateralist trend in US thinking and policy about its role in the world has opened a gulf between the US and the UK, which no amount of rhetoric can disguise. It was the perception of common security threats that brought the UK and the US together in the 1940s, but it is the lack of agreement on the new security threat, the so-called 'war on terror', that now requires the UK in its own national interest to rethink the terms of the special relationship.

International security and the Bush Doctrine

A defining feature of the national security landscape since 2001 has been the Bush administration's response to the attacks of 9/11. Elements of this response, such as the removal of the Taliban in Afghanistan, were widely seen as justified, and received broad international support at the time. Others, however, particularly the invasion of Iraq, have caused deep divisions. As an approach to foreign policy, the neoconservative world view believes in the benevolent use of US power for moral purposes, drawing on the national myth of US exceptionalism, while expressing heavy scepticism about the effectiveness of international security institutions, and asserting the right of the US unilaterally to launch 'preventive war' when necessary (Fukuyama 2006; White House 2002).

This approach has been highly controversial, not least because it appears to place the US outside widely accepted norms of international behaviour. So the implicit bargain at the heart of the special relationship, that the US would establish a rules-based multilateral regime in both the economic and the security fields, has been broken. This offence has been compounded by the way in which the US has pursued its new policies. For example, the threat assessment in relation to the Iraqi weapons of mass destruction (WMD) programme was hopelessly inaccurate. This has both damaged the reputation of the US and fed speculation that preventive war was merely a cover story for a more aggressive policy of regime change. This perception has been strengthened by the negative attitude towards international collaboration adopted by many administration officials in public statements. Scepticism toward the United Nations (UN), the International Criminal Court and even the views of allies has often turned into open contempt. Indeed, from President Bush down, US officials in recent years have seemed to go out of their way to assert the right of the US to act unilaterally, regardless of the views of others. The net effect has been to diminish US moral authority, to generate massive anxiety about US intentions around the world, and to undermine domestic UK political support for US foreign policy positions (Dumbrell 2004).

A second problem in sustaining the Anglo-American special relationship is that many of the core ideas of the neoconservative approach go against the grain of wider international developments. In particular, a changed profile of security threats and a shifting geopolitical landscape raise fundamental questions about what has now become known as the Bush Doctrine. The security threats that the US perceives are no longer common to many of its allies, including the UK.

One example of the shift in threat profile is provided by the possibility of terrorist use of WMD. For most security analysts, this has now emerged as the number one national security threat. On both sides of the Atlantic, leading politicians have commented extensively on it. Both John Kerry and George Bush, for example, named it as *the* threat in the first debate of the 2004 presidential campaign. In the UK, Tony Blair and Gordon Brown have given the issue prominence in their public statements: Blair in a series of speeches delivered between the end of 2001 and 2007, and Brown most notably in a speech to the Royal United Services Institute in February 2006. In this latter speech, Brown set out some of the features of the terrorist networks which, he noted, 'raise money in one country, use it for training in a second, for procurement in a third and finally, to commit a terrorist act in a fourth' (Brown 2006; see also Blair 2006). He might have gone on to say that despite the seriousness of developments such as the North Korean nuclear weapons tests in the autumn of 2006, the nuclear threat today is not, for the most part, one concerned with state-led missile-borne attacks. The threat now is that Al-Qaeda, or one of a number of other terrorist groups, will get their hands on either a ready-made nuclear weapon or the fissile material required to make one, that they will smuggle such a weapon or its component parts across international borders into the US or the UK, and that they will then detonate the device without warning in a major city, willingly taking their own lives as well as those of hundreds of thousands of others in the process (Allison 2006).

What is striking about this threat is that it is transnational in conception and execution. Responding to it requires intelligence-led activity coordinated across many states so that the individuals and groups planning and supplying terrorist networks can be disrupted at every stage of their activities. While the full resources of the US state can obviously be used to gain leverage over some of the relevant players here, it is highly unlikely that any amount of unilateral action or ad hoc coalitions of the willing will successfully address the problem. The primary national security threat of the age, in short, requires a coordinated multilateral response of precisely the kind made more difficult by both the content and tone of US foreign and security policy since 9/11. The question that the UK government must ask is whether the UK national interest in sustaining a multilateral security regime is still compatible with a foreign policy that gives priority to remaining the chief ally of the US.

Similar questions arise about the implications of the Bush Doctrine for other issues of the twenty-first century national security agenda, and for the multilateral regimes that the US and its allies so painstakingly constructed after 1945. Climate change, for example, though a less immediate threat, is increasingly being seen as a security problem both in terms of human security and in terms of its impact on resource scarcity, internal state viability and inter-state conflict. Former President Clinton and former Vice President Gore have both argued that climate change is a more significant threat to human existence than terrorism (Gore 2006; Clinton 2006). Here again, however, the problem is no respecter of borders. Solutions to it must be global in reach, and are only possible through intense multilateral diplomacy. Similar observations can be made in relation to the problem of transnational organized crime, the drugs trade that is fuelling the comeback of the Taliban in Afghanistan and several other pressing security problems.

Neoconservative policy prescriptions are ill-suited to such threats and are unlikely on their own to be effective in meeting them. Large majorities inside and outside the US and the UK know this, which is precisely why Bush and Blair were so damaged by being associated with their pursuit. Unless the US changes course, this means that the UK national interest will be poorly served by continuing to stay so close to the United States.

Even had the neoconservative ideas succeeded in providing effective short-term policy solutions, they would still not amount to sensible long-term strategy. Changes in the geopolitical landscape raise questions about how long the period of US unipolar dominance of the international system might last. For some, it is already over, with the foreign policy miscalculations of the Bush administration accelerating the speed of relative US decline (Wallerstein 2006). For most others, the belief that the US remains the most powerful actor in international affairs is tempered by the view that its role will increasingly be challenged over the next fifteen to twenty-five years by China, India and other regional powers. According to the US National Intelligence Council, 'a combination of sustained high economic growth, expanding military capabilities, and large populations will be at the root of the expected rapid rise in economic and political power for both countries [China and India] this century' (National Intelligence Council 2004: 9).

The US then, can no longer hope to achieve the kind of primacy in the international economic sphere that it enjoys in the military sphere. Forecasts indicate that the Chinese and Indian economies will rival those of most western powers except the US by 2020. Although the US will remain by far the largest economy in the world in the first half of this century, the trend shows a slow decline in US economic power relative to the emerging powers of Asia as the century proceeds. Even militarily, the US will suffer some erosion of its position. In its Annual Report to Congress in 2004, the US Department of Defense made clear that it expected Chinese defence expenditure to quadruple in the period to 2025, such that its annual dollar value would amount to over half that of current US defence spending. Even allowing for further increases in US defence expenditure between now and 2025, this will mean a serious challenge to US military dominance, at least in East Asia.

Considering the geopolitical landscape more widely still, it is likely that the scene will be altered further by the continued emergence of Brazil as a major economy and by similar developments in Indonesia. What this all points to is the emergence of a world in which the US is still the most powerful actor in the international system but in which unipolarity gives way to a new multipolarity. The implications of this for the Anglo-American special relationship are considerable, since the UK's interest is not in US primacy but in the US forging and submitting itself to a multilateral regime of rules and institutions that can promote welfare and prosperity throughout the international system. Whether assessed against the current threat profile or the emerging geopolitical landscape, the Bush Doctrine therefore makes no sense from a British perspective. It is putting at risk the very things that the UK has long regarded as necessary for its own security, and is preventing the emergence of new and more viable forms of international collaboration.

Policy options

A progressive UK government will always want good relations with the United States, but these should not be pursued at any price. Consideration of the Anglo-American relationship must be freed from the shackles and the delusions of the special relationship if it is to be placed on a basis that will benefit both sides, and provide effective national security, economic prosperity and legitimacy. This is not such a difficult balance to strike when the actions of the US administration are clearly in our own national security interests and are rooted in progressive values. But the key challenge for a progressive UK government in dealing with the Bush administration, and its successors, is to develop a strategy for dealing with the relationship when these conditions do not apply. The world has changed, and more divergence between the interests of the US and the UK should be expected. Blair did nothing that most of his predecessors did not do, but he got the balance wrong, hugging the Americans close even when US policy was ineffective or counterproductive as a response to national security threats. The mistakes of Blair's policy cast a sharp light on the special relationship, and allow the relationship and the future direction of UK policy to be rethought.

There are no easy answers to this dilemma. All progressive governments walk a tightrope when attempting to manage the relationship with the US. On the one hand, they risk appearing soft on security to their domestic electorate if any divergence of opinion with a US administration becomes visible. Some countries, such as France and Norway, have successfully avoided this problem, but in the context of UK political culture and its media a new UK stance towards the US can very easily be misrepresented and caricatured, and would require great political skill to introduce. On the other hand, if UK governments get too close to US positions, they risk appearing as if they have no independent foreign or security policy of their own. Both extremes can have damaging political consequences. On balance, the greater need today is for the UK to become more independent of the US, and to chart its own course. British political leaders need to become bolder in criticizing the US openly and publicly where they disagree with it, without lapsing into anti-Americanism. To achieve this policy shift, the UK government now needs to do four things.

First, it needs to develop and publish a new, comprehensive national security strategy.[1] This would deal with a wide range of issues and not just the UK's relationship with the US, although this would obviously be a core part of it. It needs to include inputs from non-government as well as government experts and should involve a thorough strategic threat assessment to ensure our policy frameworks, alliances and institutional architectures are demonstrably designed to meet the security challenges of the early twenty-first century rather than those of the last century. The threat assessment itself must consider issues such as the security of WMD-related materials and know-how in locations such as the former Soviet Union, Pakistan and parts of the developing world. It must consider the security implications of growing international pressure on natural resources such as oil and water and the possible re-emergence of multipolar competition among the US, China and a resurgent Russia. Finally, it must consider the long-term security implications of climate change, and the diminishing ability of formal state authorities to keep control of transnational terrorist and organized crime networks. The national security strategy should also spell out our interests and vulnerabilities against the backdrop of this threat profile, and should therefore also provide the explicit rationale for any policies designed and developed to keep us secure in this environment. This national security strategy should replace the 'Hug them close' strategy as the bedrock of UK foreign policy.

Secondly, the government should work to build support for a progressive security strategy. Such a strategy has to establish the security credentials of a progressive government, and act as a criterion against which principled actions could be justified. This task has been made somewhat easier for progressives by David Cameron's shift in the positioning of the Conservative Party in recent months. In a speech to the British–American Project in September 2006, Cameron talked of the need to rebalance our relationship with the US and, in doing so, he pointed to an important policy space between unconditional public support for the Bush administration on the one hand and unconditional public opposition on the other (Cameron 2006). Finding and holding that space is not easy, but it is essential for progressives. The Blair government has found it in some areas: for example, in its support for the Kyoto agreement and more radical action on climate change, and its criticism of US positions in these areas. There is a viable policy space for progressives to occupy and Cameron's speech has made it politically much easier for them to do so without being seen as soft on security, and to champion UK interests, even when these conflict with those of the US.

Third, a comprehensive national security strategy should be used to provide a new basis for policy discussions between London and Washington. While it is likely, as the preceding discussion has implied, that any comprehensive assessment of current threats will generate policy disagreements with the United States, a UK national security strategy would help to clarify and delimit those disagreements while also making explicit the many areas we do and ought to agree on. It is crucial to point out here that rebalancing does not mean wholesale rejection of US policy, even when the latter reflects neoconservative policy prescriptions. Progressives in the UK should acknowledge that the US has in the past been committed to multilateral solutions, and has, however imperfectly, provided certain kinds of public goods and acquired a moral authority by some of the purposes it has pursued. There has always been a benign side to US power, from the use of US resources to create the Bretton Woods institutions in the immediate aftermath of the Second World War, to the Marshall Plan to rebuild western Europe, right through to military intervention in the Balkans. What progressive governments need to do is to remind themselves of some of the positive features of the US role since 1945, and not to be mesmerized by the Iraq quagmire. At a time of serious security challenges and geopolitical flux, the world still needs the US: not the unilateralist US of the recent past, but a multilateralist US that is prepared to engage with the international community and lead it rather than dominate it. The UK position in terms of overall strategic outlook should be one that supports the US when it is performing that role, but not when it reverts to seeking US primacy.

Suggesting that the UK should be more assertive in our relationship with the United States still sets alarm bells ringing for some. But there is now an urgent need to bring some realism into the domestic UK debate on the relationship with the US. It simply lacks credibility, for example, to claim that any public disagreement with a US administration on a national or international security issue would destroy the relationship. There are many examples of other countries, such as most recently Germany, which have strongly disagreed in public with the US, but this has not damaged their relationship. Despite its strident criticism of US foreign policies, even France manages to cooperate with the US when it is in both their interests to do so: for example, in addressing the war in Lebanon in 2006. If it were true that public criticism of the US would damage the Anglo-American relationship beyond repair, it would mean that the UK's entire national security strategy is based on a relationship that is not only brittle, but also fickle and unreliable. All relationships require sensitivity, but some open disagreements will and should exist if the relationship is to be a healthy one, and serve both parties. The special relationship in its present form ceased to do that long ago.

It is also important to bear in mind that the neoconservative view currently prevalent in Washington is not the sum total of US opinion. Many important foreign and security policy analysts in Washington disagree profoundly with the policies of the Bush administration. If we allow all disagreement to be branded as disloyalty, either within the United States or between allies across the Atlantic, we concede important ground to those who seek political advantage in constructing the debate in such a way as to ensure their own favoured outcomes. Moreover, if we treat the views of the current US administration as a permanent feature of the landscape, we fail to acknowledge the obvious point that US politics is dynamic and cyclical. Neoconservative foreign policies often struggle to show results abroad, and can suffer serious loss of popular political support at home as a result. The gains of the Democratic Party in the mid-term elections of late 2006 are evidence of this. US administrations also use the support of allies abroad as important sources of political capital in the ongoing noise of domestic disagreement and debate. We will never know how a UK government refusal to take part in the invasion of Iraq would have played on the US political scene, but we should not underestimate how valuable UK support can be to any US president about to undertake serious and risky military action overseas. The UK contribution in terms of military hardware and personnel may be small, but its moral and symbolic value is well understood, in parts of Washington at least.

Fourth and last, in terms of new policy development, a progressive UK government needs to offer forward-looking and credible policy alternatives to the Bush Doctrine. Other authors in this volume have described what some of these policy alternatives might be. A key motivation for the call for a new and comprehensive national security strategy in this chapter is also the perceived need to give the debate on policy options a central focus while also making it more systematic and identifiably progressive.

If the number one security challenge of the age is the threat of terrorist use of WMD, a UK government rebalancing the relationship with the US should put more energy into multilateral efforts to track down the many loose nuclear weapons and associated fissile materials that may yet fall into the hands of terrorists, and into attempts to shore up the crucial but weakening Nuclear Non-Proliferation Treaty. The Bush and Blair administrations have been insufficiently focused on this problem and more needs to be done to address it. Serious analysts in the US, such as former Assistant Secretary of Defense Graham Allison, have outlined practical policy strategies in relation to the threat of nuclear terrorism. The UK government should put them front and centre in policy debates with the US and in a new national security strategy (Allison 2006: 176, 203).

In addition, the UK government should make a renewed multilateral effort to negotiate a comprehensive Middle East settlement as a condition for further UK support of US policy in the Middle East. Tony Blair has attempted to do this, even though President Bush has largely ignored his suggestions. Although multilateral diplomacy on this issue is fraught with difficulties, the Bush administration's policy of non-engagement has been disastrous. Renewed multilateral efforts to negotiate a settlement of many of the region's interlocking problems are not merely 'nice to have' but are central to the national security interests of the United Kingdom, since one of the greatest threats to the UK comes from the global consequences of a Middle East that is racked by instability.

Conclusion

The US outgrew its special relationship with the UK many decades ago. For the UK it has taken much longer. Although in the 1960s the UK appeared for a time to be acquiring more independence, the special relationship reasserted itself in a new and virulent form in the 1980s and 1990s, culminating in the decision to back the US invasion of Iraq in 2003. The consequences of this decision are still being felt, and they have already caused some major shifts in public opinion in Anglo-America.

The failure of successive UK governments to rethink the terms of the special relationship have been costly, particularly in relation to the UK's relationship with the European Union (Gamble 2003). Giving priority to the US has delayed the development of European identity and European common action, by helping the UK to avoid a full European commitment. This has not prevented the UK from steadily converging with the rest of Europe and becoming recognizably European in its social and economic institutions, and in its public policies. But much of the political class has remained stubbornly attached to the idea that the UK is capable on its own of sharing a special relationship with the United States and helping to sustain US global leadership.

The pro-European position has lost ground in UK politics in recent years, but it remains a crucial component of a progressive foreign policy. Only if Europe is stronger and more independent, and vigorous in championing multilateralist solutions, is there a chance of persuading the US that its best policy is to engage once again in a multilateralist politics with the rest of the world. To make this a reality would involve some painful choices for the UK, such as giving up its seat on the UN Security Council to allow a seat to be given to the EU, and working to establish common EU positions on security, as currently already exist on trade.

Many people in the UK would prefer the country to be tied neither to the US nor to Europe, but to go it alone. This idea for a UK Gaullism, popular in some quarters on the right, or a UK Swedish model, popular on the left, is superficially appealing, but makes no real sense in the light of the security agenda of the twenty-first century. Not even the largest country can choose isolationism, and hope to insulate itself from the problems of the rest of the planet. The need for novel and ambitious multilateral solutions to solve the pressing challenges we face has increased enormously over the last century, and looks set to go on increasing in the present one. Isolationism is a poor response, and could not work for long. But the policy of 'America right or wrong' has also hit the buffers. We need a foreign policy that encourages alliances across nations as well as between states, and mobilizes progressive opinion everywhere in support of the multilateralist solutions the world needs.

Note

1   An ippr Commission on National Security in the 21st Century, chaired by George Robertson and Paddy Ashdown, began work on producing such a comprehensive national security strategy in April 2007. It is expected to produce its final report in early 2009.

References

Allison, G. (2006) *Nuclear Terrorism: the risks and consequences of the ultimate disaster*, London: Constable and Robinson.

Blair, T. (2006) 'A clash about civilisation', speech, London, March.

Brown, G. (2006) 'Securing our future', speech to the Royal United Services Institute, February.

Cameron, D. (2006) 'A new approach to foreign affairs – liberal conservatism', speech to the British–American Project, London, September.

Churchill, R. (ed.) (1948) *The Sinews of Peace: post war speeches/Sir Winston Churchill*, London: Cassell.

Clinton, B. (2006) Speech in Guildhall, London, 28 March, attended by one of the authors.

Dimbleby, D. and Reynolds, D. (1988) *An Ocean Apart: the relationship between Britain and America in the twentieth century*, London: BBC.

Dumbrell, J. (2001) *A Special Relationship: Anglo-American relations in the Cold War and after*, London: Palgrave.

Dumbrell, J. (2004) 'The US–UK "Special Relationship" in a world twice transformed', *Cambridge Review of International Affairs*, 17(3), October, pp. 437–50.

Fukuyama, F. (2006) *America at the Crossroads: democracy, power and the neoconservative legacy*, New Haven, Conn.: Yale University Press.

Gamble, A. (2003) *Between Europe and America: the future of British politics*, London: Palgrave.

Gore, A. (2006) Speech to NYU Law, September; available at http://thinkprogress.org/gore-nyu.

National Intelligence Council (2004) *Mapping the Global Future*, Washington, DC: NIC.

Riddell, P. (2003) *Hug Them Close: Blair, Clinton, Bush and the special relationship*, London: Politico's.

Wallerstein, I. (2006) 'The curve of American power', *New Left Review*, 40, July–August, pp. 77–94, London.

Watt, D. C. (1984) *Succeeding John Bull: America in Britain's place*, Cambridge: Cambridge University Press.

White House (2002) *The National Security Strategy of the United States of America*, September: Washington, DC: The White House.

7

Europe's Global Role

Charles Grant

Whoever follows Tony Blair as prime minister will inherit a much stronger position within the European Union (EU) than Blair himself did in 1997. Conservative governments had marginalized the UK in Europe through futile policies such as the 'empty chair' – when John Major boycotted the Council of Ministers because of the ban on British beef – and through relentless anti-European rhetoric. In contrast, the Blair government has adopted a generally constructive attitude to the EU. Furthermore, it has earned credit with other governments for its positive contributions in areas such as the 'Lisbon agenda' of economic reform, where the UK has been one of the leaders, and the European Security and Defence Policy, which was a Franco-British creation. The consistently strong performance of the UK's economy over the past ten years has underpinned its influence. So has the high calibre of UK officialdom: other governments may disagree with UK policies, but they have great respect for the Foreign and Commonwealth Office (FCO), the Treasury, other ministries and the UK Representation in Brussels.

Yet Tony Blair did not fulfil his potential as a European leader, and to a large degree he failed in his ambition to reconcile the British people to the EU. By 2002 he had emerged as the pre-eminent European leader, and seemed likely to take on the kind of status that Chancellor Helmut Kohl had enjoyed a decade earlier. But then in 2003 came both the Iraq war and the decision not to hold a referendum on joining the euro. Blair's standing in the EU never recovered from these blows.

The UK's 'soft power' – which may be defined as its attractiveness to people in other countries – has long suffered from the perception that its first loyalty is to the US. The Blair government's decision to join the US in invading Iraq greatly strengthened that view. Of course, plenty of other governments supported the Iraq war. But none has been so uncritical of US foreign policy, particularly on the question of Israel and Palestine. Public opinion throughout the EU is strongly hostile to George W. Bush and his foreign policy. Some of that sentiment has rubbed off on to Blair and the British.

The decision not to join the euro has not harmed the UK economy. But it did cause many EU leaders to question the strength of the UK's commitment to the Union. Those doubts were reinforced by the UK's shunning of the 'Schengen area' – which would require it to scrap passport controls – and its consistent opposition to treaty changes that would erode national sovereignty. Indeed, the Blair government's enthusiasm for enlargement but horror of treaty change led some to suppose that its underlying vision of Europe remained that of Margaret Thatcher. She wanted to keep on enlarging the EU in order to weaken its institutions and sense of solidarity, in the hope that it would become little more than a glorified free trade area. That would be an unfair caricature of the Labour government's attitude. But many influential continental commentators, officials and politicians genuinely believe that UK strategy remains fundamentally Thatcherite.

Such prejudices have been reinforced by the UK press, sections of which report on the EU with a venom and lack of respect for facts that is unmatched in any other member state. Decision-makers and opinion-formers in other countries read the cuttings from British tabloids, and sometimes take them more seriously than do many Britons. The UK media's style of covering European issues also limited the ability of Blair and his ministers to win the argument for the EU at home. The government considered the hostility of much of the press to the EU to be a given, which constrained the tactics, if not the substance, of its approach to negotiations with EU partners.

This chapter asks what the central tenets of a post-Blairite European policy should be. It sketches out some of the ways in which the UK could help to steer the EU towards becoming a more effective and progressive global actor. It focuses in particular on foreign and defence policy, on enlargement and neighbourhood policy, and on climate change. But first it considers some of the changes under way in the EU, and some of the challenges facing both the Union and a post-Blair UK government.

The recent enlargements

The entry of twelve new members (ten joined in May 2004, followed by Bulgaria and Romania in January 2007) is transforming the character of the European Union. Those who predicted that the new members would all line up with the UK in support of free markets, US foreign policy and the retention of national vetoes were mistaken. For example, Poland sometimes echoes France in its protectionist instincts and support for farm subsidies, while Slovenia would willingly give up many national vetoes.

Nevertheless, enlargement is in most respects good news for the UK. In a union of twenty-seven countries, the Franco-German alliance, however resilient it may be, cannot dominate. It is now almost impossible for the UK to become isolated: on tax questions, treaty change, labour market regulation or policy towards some obscure corner of the globe, the UK will almost always find an ally. The old federalist ideology – that in a 'political union' the Commission should become an executive government, responsible to both the European Parliament and the Council of Ministers (transformed into an 'upper house') – still has adherents in Belgium, Germany, Italy and a few other places. But none of the new members subscribes to this ideology.

One consequence of the Union embracing such a diverse collection of countries, at contrasting stages of economic development, and with different priorities, is that it is no longer feasible for every member state to take part in every EU activity. 'Variable geometry' is on the rise. Only half of the member states are in the euro. Some opt out of the Schengen area or European defence arrangements. New sub-groups have emerged: the 'EU3' of the UK, France and Germany, with the support of foreign policy 'High Representative' Javier Solana, handles the problem of Iran's nuclear programme; the 'G6', the interior ministers of the six largest member states, focuses on counter-terrorism; and the signatories of the Treaty of Prüm – the Benelux three, France, Germany, Austria and Spain – have agreed to share sensitive information on policing and security.

The UK has traditionally opposed the creation of new *avant-garde* groups, fearing that its absence from some of them would diminish its influence in the broader union. But in fact variable geometry may create opportunities for the UK. At times it may wish to opt out of integrationist initiatives, as it did with the euro. But on other occasions it may welcome the chance to team up with like-minded countries in particular areas, such as defence, foreign policy or counter-terrorism, without having to worry about the views of all the other governments.

The coming institutional challenges

One dark cloud hanging over the EU is the uncertainty surrounding its treaties and institutions. The 'no' votes in the French and Dutch referendums on the constitutional treaty have effectively killed it. There is no chance of all twenty-seven member states being willing or able to ratify the document. However, most EU governments believe that the current treaties are inadequate and need amendment. At the time of writing (early 2007) it seems likely that an attempt will be made to hold an intergovernmental conference (IGC) in the second half of 2007, to amend the treaties.

Yet there is currently no consensus on the scope of a new IGC. Countries such as Germany, Italy and Spain will want to use an IGC to salvage large parts of the constitutional treaty. Others, such as France and the Netherlands, will probably only want a 'mini-treaty', so that they can avoid having to ratify the result by referendum. The innovations desired by the larger countries, such as the creation of the post of 'foreign minister' and the reduction of the role of the rotating presidency, are unpopular with many smaller countries, which have their own priorities. The effort to forge an agreement on a new treaty and then get it ratified in twenty-seven member states will be fraught.

The arguments over treaty revision present a number of challenges for the UK. It has a particular interest in reviving those elements of the constitutional treaty that would facilitate a more coherent EU foreign policy (see below). And it has a general interest in seeing a new institutional settlement, because of the strong connection between institutional reform and enlargement.

Since the 1970s, there has been a close link between 'deepening' (the movement towards a more integrated Union) and 'widening' (the enlargement of the Union). Political elites in countries such as France, as well as some federalists, have always been reluctant to widen the EU, believing that a larger Union could never become the political union they desire.

But despite these reservations, the EU has continued to expand – in 1981, 1986, 1995 and 2004. Those sceptical of enlargement swallowed their doubts because they extracted a price: a series of treaties that created a more integrated Europe, culminating in the constitutional treaty that was signed in 2004. The UK, Scandinavians and some other enthusiasts for enlargement were never particularly keen on treaty-based integration, but accepted it as the quid pro quo for enlargement. The Germans wanted deepening and widening – the former, because of their federalism, and the latter to promote stability and prosperity in their immediate neighbourhood.

This implicit bargain between deepeners and wideners has driven the EU forward for the past twenty years, so the demise of the constitutional treaty has not only brought an end to treaty-based integration for the foreseeable future, but also created major obstacles to further enlargement. If the UK has an interest in keeping the process of enlargement alive – and I will argue below that it does – it should be enthusiastic about trying to improve the institutions.

A new IGC will in itself do little to improve the legitimacy of the EU in the eyes of many Europeans. But a successful IGC should lead to reforms that make the institutions more efficient and transparent, and in the process build wider public support for the Union. In the meantime the Union can do a lot to show that EU action improves the quality of Europeans' lives. For example, the recent introduction of the European arrest warrant makes it easier for EU governments to bring terrorist suspects to justice; the reform of the EU's carbon emissions trading scheme that is due in 2007 should enable the Union to take the lead in tackling global warming; the establishment of the new European Research Council should focus research and development funds on centres of academic excellence, thus improving the performance of Europe's universities; and measures in the pipeline should lead to more stringent energy efficiency standards.

External challenges

For most of its history, the EU has evolved in response to economic and political developments within Europe. Member states worked to build a single market and a single currency. They embarked on an endless series of attempts to reform the institutions. And then in reaction to the democratic revolutions in southern and eastern Europe, they decided to extend the Union's frontiers across much of the continent.

However, in the coming decades, the key drivers of change are likely to come from beyond Europe. How can the EU respond to the economic challenge posed by China and India? How can it persuade those countries and the US to help tackle global warming? How can the EU best deal with a resurgent and increasingly authoritarian Russia? And what can the EU do to help resolve the Israel–Palestine problem?

Since enlargement will – at best – move only very slowly, the EU will need to find new ways of transforming its neighbourhood. An arc of instability stretches from Belarus to North Africa, passing through

Ukraine, Moldova, the western Balkans, the Caucasus and the Middle East. Unless the EU redoubles its efforts to promote stability, security, prosperity and good governance in these countries, it risks paying a heavy price – whether through increasing numbers of illegal immigrants, criminal gangs and refugees entering the EU, or the obligation to send battalions to keep the peace in conflict zones.

The EU, its policies and institutions must evolve to deal with these and other challenges. A progressive UK government will be well placed to help strengthen the EU's global role.

Climate change

Take the case of climate change. Ever since global warming first became a concern, the EU has led international efforts to tackle it. The Union deserves praise for its role in helping to create the Kyoto protocol, and for being its principal champion. The EU's emissions trading scheme (ETS), which began operating in 2005, is the first international effort to use carbon pricing to curb the emission of greenhouse gases. It works by setting a 'cap' on each member state's total carbon emissions: energy-intensive companies are free to buy or sell the 'right' to emit carbon dioxide. Companies that manage to emit less than their entitlement can sell certificates on the open market. Firms that emit too much can buy those certificates or invest in carbon abatement projects in developing countries, through the United Nations' Clean Development Mechanism. The point is to create economic incentives to reduce carbon emissions.

But the ETS is flawed. The EU governments set their own caps, with the Commission only having the power to say whether the caps are consistent with the member states' Kyoto commitments. In the first phase of the scheme, most governments ended up with emissions allowances set at higher levels than projected emissions. That left the price for carbon permits too low to motivate businesses to change their behaviour. Moreover, governments distributed the vast majority of permits to industrial users free of charge, rather than auctioning them to the highest bidder. They did this so as not to damage the international competitiveness of energy-intensive industries. But the result has undermined incentives to invest in more efficient technologies.

So the scheme needs reform. The EU should agree on a Europe-wide cap, based on scientific advice, and then apportion carbon quotas to each member state on a fair basis. A new, independent authority should be created – perhaps modelled on the European Central Bank – to take the politics out of these crucial decisions. The reformed carbon-trading scheme should be extended to the aviation and road transport sectors, which are responsible for increasing amounts of greenhouse gas emissions. The EU needs to be clear about the duration of the scheme, so that businesses have the incentives to plan ahead and invest in new technology. Furthermore, the EU should also encourage the many American states that are developing their own caps on carbon emissions to establish links with the ETS.

In the international negotiations on a framework to replace the Kyoto Protocol in 2012, the EU should argue for a 30 per cent binding target of cuts in greenhouse gas emissions by 2020 (from 1990 levels). This would create major incentives for the development of new technologies that can help to solve the problem. Since it negotiates as one block, the EU is in a good position to play a decisive role in securing the commitment of the US, China and India to take part in future schemes to curb carbon emissions.

The UK is home to the nascent global market in carbon trading. And it has produced the report by Nicholas Stern on the economics of climate change – a document that several European leaders have taken to quoting in their speeches (Merkel 2006). The UK has also a reasonably good record in reducing its own carbon emissions. It is therefore strongly placed to lead European efforts to tackle climate change.

A stronger common foreign and security policy

The UK should champion a more effective EU foreign policy through the Common Foreign and Security Policy (CFSP). That does not mean creating a single EU foreign policy. There will be foreign policy issues on which the UK and other EU states will differ. But on many of the key global challenges, the UK and the other member states share similar interests. On such issues the UK can often achieve more by acting through the Union than on its own. On the Balkans, for example, the UK has had no specific policy for the past dozen years. The EU's economic aid and political engagement – supported by the North Atlantic Treaty Organization (NATO) and then EU peacekeepers – have brought stability to the western Balkans. There have also been particular diplomatic successes: Javier Solana helped to broker the Ohrid accord, which prevented Macedonia from sliding into civil war in 2001, and then intervened the following year to prevent a rupture and possible war between Serbia and Montenegro.

As long as the EU has a common position to represent, the High Representative can play a useful role. The Europeans are usually more or less united on the Israel–Palestine problem, which allows Solana to be constructive – as when in 2005 he negotiated for EU monitors to police the border between Gaza and Egypt at Rafah. In the EU's dealings with Iran, the 'big three' (the UK, France and Germany) and Solana have represented the Union. Iran's subtle diplomatic games failed to divide them, and they persuaded an initially hostile US to support their stick-and-carrot strategy of engaging Iran. The united EU line also persuaded Russia and China to harden their position on Iran. However, the diplomacy fizzled out in the autumn of 2006 when Iran refused to abandon its enrichment of uranium. A more successful example of EU diplomacy was the intervention in Ukraine during the 'orange revolution' in 2004. The presidents of Poland and Lithuania, and Javier Solana, persuaded President Leonid Kuchma to re-run the flawed presidential election that Viktor Yushchenko had 'lost'.

The UK shares common interests with its European partners in many other domains, even where – for now – there are no common policies. A stronger CFSP would make it easier for the UK to achieve several of its foreign policy objectives. The two biggest challenges for the CFSP are currently the Middle East and Russia.

EU policy towards the Middle East

One structural weakness that often undermines EU foreign policy is that the UK and France have very different approaches to transatlantic relations. The UK tends to line up with the US on the most important strategic issues, and works to prevent the CFSP from coming into conflict with US policy. The Blair government has also tended to avoid public criticism of the US, on the grounds that it would undermine the UK's private influence. In contrast, France is often critical, supporting the idea of an EU that stands up to the US and helps to promote a 'multipolar' world (as opposed to a 'unipolar' or US-dominated world).

This British–French divergence has undermined the EU's effectiveness on the Israel–Palestine question. The Europeans generally share a similar analysis of what kind of solution would offer the best hope of long-term peace: they believe that the Palestinian state should be based on Gaza and the West Bank, with frontiers similar to those of 1967, though with land swaps that would allow Israel to keep some of its settlements in occupied land. However, whenever European policy shows signs of diverging from that of the US in response to particular events in the region, Blair has sought to bend it towards the American line. For example, in 2004 President Bush shifted US policy by saying that 'facts on the ground' meant that the Palestinians could not hope for their state to include all of the West Bank. Blair, at that moment on a visit to the US, refused to take a different line, which made a coherent European response impossible. Again, in July 2006, when Israel reacted to the kidnapping of two soldiers by attacking Lebanon, the UK – along with Germany, the Netherlands and Poland – prevented the EU from condemning the Israeli response as disproportionate (see chapter 8 in this volume).

Declaratory diplomacy may not achieve very much, but other things being equal, the Europeans are more likely to be listened to if they speak with one voice. In the post-Blair era, the UK should work to strengthen the EU's diplomacy in the region. There is a solid foundation on which to build. The EU is the biggest provider of aid to the Palestinian Authority, and is Israel's largest trading partner. And many Arabs have a grudging respect for the EU. In the last few years the EU has become more engaged in the Middle East, for example through the border mission at Rafah, a scheme that is training the Palestinian security services, and the dispatch of European troops to southern Lebanon in the summer of 2006. However, a settlement between Israelis and Palestinians evidently requires active American engagement, since only the US has the ability to lean on Israel.

The EU needs to make a priority of persuading the US to engage in this conflict more energetically and even-handedly. While the UK tends to pride itself on having the ear of Washington, a united EU would carry more weight in Washington than the UK alone. In particular, if the UK and France collaborate, they should be able to help forge an EU position that has some influence on the US and a positive impact on the region.

Dealing with Russia

A second big challenge for the CFSP is Russia. The member states have very similar interests in Russia. They want it to become a strong and successful economy that welcomes foreign investment and is a reliable source of energy. They want the slide towards authoritarianism reversed. They want Russia to be an ally in the fight against terrorism and in opposing the proliferation of dangerous weapons.

And they want it to respect the sovereignty and independence of the countries in the common neighbourhood that it shares with the EU.

However, the Europeans do not work together on Russia. The UK, France, Germany and Italy have run separate policies, each at various times seeking a special relationship with President Vladimir Putin. These bilateral relationships have been competitive, allowing Putin to play the member states off against each other. In recent years, two of Putin's closest allies, Gerhard Schröder and Silvio Berlusconi, have left office. Yet the EU still divides into three distinct groups: the 'pro-Russian' camp led by France, Germany and Italy; the 'anti-Russian' camp led by Poland and the Baltic states; and others in the middle, such as the UK. Whenever the EU tries to develop a line on Russia, or react to a specific event – such as the Russian blockade of Georgia in October 2006 – it proves unable to agree on much beyond the most anodyne of statements. Some of the most influential member states simply do not want the EU to do anything that might upset Russia.

The EU does have a working relationship with Russia on many technical matters. The Commission takes the lead in dealing with Russia on some crucial issues like trade and visas. And the EU and Russia will open negotiations on a new 'partnership and cooperation agreement' in 2007 (assuming that Poland lifts its veto). However, the Kremlin always prefers – if it can – to work through bilateral relationships with the key member states. The EU as a whole has proved unable to develop a coherent political strategy for dealing with Russia. This is unfortunate, given Russia's importance to the EU as an energy supplier, market and neighbour with a global foreign policy.

Russia is proving an increasingly difficult partner for the EU (Barysch 2006). Apparently seeing no need for help in developing its oil and gas industries, it seems intent on reducing the role that foreign firms play in them. Russia's political system is increasingly authoritarian. Stung by the 'colour' revolutions in Georgia and Ukraine, the Kremlin is focused on ensuring that similar events do not unfold in other former Soviet republics. It also appears to be trying to undermine the relatively democratic regimes in Georgia and Ukraine.

A priority for a progressive UK government should be to push the EU to forge a common approach to Russia – based on five principles. First, the EU should maintain a constant dialogue with Russia. The EU and Russia have so many shared interests that they should always be in close contact, whatever happens inside the country. Secondly, the EU should recognize that it has a limited capacity to influence Russia's domestic politics. If the Russian government violates human rights, the EU should complain, but it should not expect dramatic changes in its behaviour. Probably the best hope for changing the internal politics of Russia would be the example of a successful and prosperous democracy in Ukraine. Thirdly, the EU should make clear to Russia that the closeness of the institutional links that the EU is willing to offer Russia will depend on European perceptions of whether it shares European values. Fourthly, the EU should ask for Russia's assistance in tackling some of the key problems of international politics, such as the Iranian nuclear programme. Russia likes to see itself as a great power and should be treated as such, when it can be helpful.

The fifth and most important priority for the EU should be to focus on the neighbourhood area that it shares with Russia. The EU should resist any Russian attempt to reintegrate neighbours such as Georgia, Moldova and Ukraine into its political system, especially if in doing so it seeks to undermine the relatively pluralistic societies that have emerged in some of these states. The EU and its member states must be unrelenting in pointing out to Russia that it has an interest in seeing strong, prosperous and democratic countries on its borders. The EU should also tell Russia – in private – that that there are red lines that must not be crossed: if it imposed an undemocratic regime on one of these neighbours, it would no longer be welcome in the Council of Europe or the Group of Eight.

The EU cannot feasibly offer membership to its eastern neighbours, at least for the foreseeable future. Nor should it be in a hurry to extend NATO membership to Ukraine and Georgia. That would provoke Russia to an unnecessary degree, and – because of the US's involvement in NATO – would complicate the EU's relations with Russia in the common neighbourhood. But the EU should take these countries much more seriously than it has done. Too few ministers or prime ministers from EU governments visit them. The EU should increase aid to the regimes under pressure, and to democracy-building non-governmental organizations (NGOs) throughout the region. It should seek to bind the more democratic countries closer, through an enhanced neighbourhood policy.

The long-term destiny of the borderlands between the EU and Russia is unclear. They could move closer to the EU, or become dominated by Russian authoritarianism. To its credit, the US has taken this region rather more seriously than have many EU governments. But the EU should not allow the US alone to deal with Europe's far east or the southern Caucasus. All Europeans share an interest in ensuring that political and economic reform takes root in their neighbourhood.

Institutional reform

The imperfect nature of the EU's foreign policy institutions is not the main cause of its sometimes poor performance. If EU governments cannot muster the political will to forge a common position during a crisis like that over Iraq, even the strongest institutions will not guarantee unity. That being said, the EU's currently ramshackle foreign policy machinery often prevents it from acting effectively. Countries beyond the EU are fed up with having to deal with the rotating presidency, which puts a new member state – each with its own priorities – in the driving seat every six months. They also complain about the lack of coordination between the various pieces of the EU machine, and slow decision making. Those parts of the Council of Ministers responsible for CFSP (led by Solana) and those parts of the Commission dealing with external relations (led by Commissioner Benita Ferrero-Waldner) sometimes work at cross purposes, even seeing each other as rivals rather than partners.

The EU's constitutional treaty would have introduced important reforms, such as merging the High Representative and the Commissioner for External Relations into a 'foreign minister', who would have taken over some of the tasks of the rotating presidency. The treaty would also have created an 'external action service', bringing together officials from the Council, Commission and member states, under the leadership of the foreign minister. Such reforms would have made it easier for the EU to join up the various trade, aid, judicial, diplomatic and military policies that it runs in various parts of the world, and thus to be more effective at promoting stability and security.

The loss of the constitutional treaty therefore creates real problems for EU foreign policy. In the treaty negotiations that are likely to lie ahead, the UK's priority should be to insert some of the key foreign policy provisions of the constitutional treaty into the new document. However, if efforts to revise the treaties fail, EU governments could still implement some useful reforms on the basis of the current treaties (Grant and Leonard 2006). For example, the High Representative could replace the presidency in chairing foreign ministers' meetings and in representing the EU externally. And key officials from the Council, Commission and member states could be brought into one building to work as a single team.

Building up European defence

The EU is uniquely well placed to bring security, better governance and economic aid to troubled regions. NATO has no tools for development, and the World Bank no soldiers. In contrast, the Union possesses a broad range of assets, such as trade policies, technical assistance, aid for reconstruction, police officers, legal officers, administrators and soldiers, which, if coordinated well, are a powerful force for stability. The EU's track record in the Balkans shows that it does not always succeed in joining up its various policies. But, overall, the EU has been quite effective in places such as Bosnia and Macedonia. And in Afghanistan the EU has helped NATO by providing some of the civilian instruments that it lacks, and by sending judges, aid workers and administrators to the provincial reconstruction teams.

In fact, the EU's growing ability to stabilize conflict zones has been one of its unsung successes. From its conception at the Franco-British summit at St Malo in 1998, the 'European Security and Defence Policy' (ESDP) has achieved real results. Sixteen separate missions have been launched, including customs officers to the border between Ukraine and the breakaway Moldovan region of Transdnestria, border monitors to Rafah, police officers to Bosnia and Kosovo, and civilians to monitor the peace accord in Aceh in Indonesia. Some missions have been military, such as the two separate forces sent to the Democratic Republic of Congo to stabilize particular areas at the behest of the United Nations (UN), and the 6,000 peacekeepers currently in Bosnia. Some missions have been very complex, such as the one backing the African Union (AU) in Darfur: in addition to sending transport planes to support the AU peacekeeping mission, the EU has provided military observers and police officers, as well as training and equipment. The recent 'Unifil 2' deployment to southern Lebanon is technically a UN force but is in practice European-led, with European forces playing the predominant role.

In 2007, thirteen 'battle groups' are due to become operational – battalion-sized rapid reaction forces that can stabilize a conflict zone at the request of the UN. The UK and France devised the concept of battle groups. Ever since St Malo, the UK has taken a lead on European defence because of its evident advantages in this area. It has the most proficient armed forces in Europe. Its overall spending on defence is the highest in Europe (£29 billion a year). And it spends more on procurement than any other nation – a quarter of the total defence budget. If the UK and France – the second nation in European defence – can reach an agreement, others in the EU are likely to follow.

Another reason why this is a good area for the UK to lead is that defence is 'intergovernmental'. Decisions on ESDP will always require unanimity, since no country will allow others to vote by majority on the deployment of its troops. For a sovereignty-conscious country such as the UK, defence is a 'safe' area for European cooperation.

However, the main reason why the UK should strive to keep up the momentum for European defence is that a strong defence capability is an essential component of an effective CFSP. The EU governments learned this the hard way in the Balkans during the early 1990s. They issued any number of joint declarations, urging Slobodan Milosevic to change his behaviour. He felt free to ignore them, since the EU had no battalions. After the Bosnian war broke out, the Europeans provided the bulk of the UN peacekeeping force, but the rules governing that mission rendered it ineffective, and prevented it from stopping the Srebrenica massacre in 1995. Finally the Americans and NATO became involved, which led to the Dayton peace accords, and then in 1999 the Kosovo air campaign. But the US quite rightly regards Europe and most of its peripheral areas as the long-term responsibility of the EU, which is why it has – most of the time – encouraged the ESDP. If one accepts that the EU gains through forging common foreign policies on some issues, one also has to support a defence capability for the Union.

The most disappointing aspect of the ESDP, so far, is that it has failed to generate significant improvements in military capability among the member states. In many of them, the armed forces lack sufficient transport planes, troops that can serve abroad at short notice, and secure communications systems. Defence budgets are flat or declining in most EU countries, while the cost of developing new equipment and technology is rising much faster than inflation. So how can the EU countries improve their military capabilities, at a time when the demand for European forces to deploy in various parts of the world is likely to increase?

The answer is to spend more wisely. The twenty-seven governments' defence budgets currently add up to about €180 billion – almost half the American defence budget – though the combined military capabilities of the twenty-seven are only a small fraction of those of the US (Langton 2007). The problem is that the Europeans spend most of their money on large conscript armies that cannot serve overseas, on huge and inefficient national defence bureaucracies and on defence industries protected by pork-barrel politics. The UK should therefore encourage its European partners to embrace a series of changes.

Firstly, many EU governments need to reform their armed forces. Those countries that still rely on conscription should scrap it and shift towards smaller, better-equipped, better-trained and more deployable forces. Secondly, the EU should move towards a more open defence market. There is no chance of governments opening up the procurement of sensitive military items. But they may be attracted by the savings that could flow from freer procurement of non-sensitive items. Thirdly, the EU should encourage role specialization. Not every member state has the resources to maintain every sort of military capability. But if a country gives up capabilities in some areas, it needs to be able to trust its partners to provide them when needed. The UK and France can afford to maintain many sorts of military skill – but even they are finding that budgetary pressures are forcing them to specialize. For example, the UK now relies on France's capability to build some sorts of satellite and missile, while the French are buying a UK aircraft carrier design rather than developing their own.

Fourthly, EU governments could save a lot of money by pooling military capabilities. For example, the countries buying the A400M military transport plane could choose to put their planes into a common pool, involving just a small number of bases and a single support organization. Already, the French are talking of stationing their tanker aircraft at the base used by British tankers, to save money. A similar logic could apply to ship and vehicle repairs, medical units or catering organizations. Of course, defence bureaucracies tend to oppose such ideas. Ultimately, however, the constraints on defence budgets will probably persuade bureaucracies to accept pooling – as well as role specialization, open procurement and military reform (Buckley 2006).

Promoting enlargement

Between April 2004 and January 2007, the EU enlarged from fifteen members to twenty-seven – the biggest expansion in its history. So it is hardly surprising that many governments and voters in the EU are hostile to further 'widening' of the Union (Grant 2006). For example, in Austria, France and Germany, six out of ten people want no more countries admitted to the EU. France even changed its constitution in 2005 so that no country seeking to join after Croatia can do so without a positive French referendum.

Croatia can hope to join in about 2010, but the accession talks with Turkey – which began in 2005 – will be long and difficult, and it is far from certain that they will result in an accession treaty. Although the EU has accepted in principle that the states of the western Balkans should join the Union when they are ready, there is little chance of them moving towards accession in the near future. Countries further afield that aspire to membership, such as Georgia and Ukraine, are a long way from even being considered as candidates.

One reason for this hostile climate is the uncertainty hanging over the EU's institutions. Political elites in many EU states believe that if the EU takes in more members without making radical reforms to its institutions, the speed, quality and effectiveness of EU actions and decisions will decline drastically (and they claim that the May 2004 enlargement has already had an adverse effect). Commission President José Manuel Barroso speaks for these elites when he says that the EU cannot admit more countries without a new institutional settlement.

Ordinary voters tend to oppose enlargement for other reasons. They fear that immigrants from new member states will take their jobs or depress their wages. There is a close correlation between the member states with the highest levels of unemployment and the strongest opposition to enlargement – though even in the UK, which enjoys relatively low unemployment, there has been concern over the impact of Bulgarian and Romanian immigrants on labour markets. Amongst some voters, cultural factors are also important. The fact that most Turkish citizens are Muslim is one reason why the French and the Austrians are particularly against Turkey's accession.

Despite the hostility in some quarters to further widening, the UK should continue to lead the EU's pro-enlargement camp. It should remember that one of the Union's greatest successes has been to entrench democracy, prosperity, security and stability across much of the continent. Of course, there has to be a geographical limit at some point: the EU treaties restrict membership to 'European' countries. North African countries are not in Europe and so cannot join. But a permanent delimitation of the EU's borders at this time would have a disastrous impact on would-be members beyond those borders.

If the EU ended talks with Turkey, hard-line Islamists and nationalists in the country would gain strength against liberals and modernizers. But the impact of the EU shutting the door on the western Balkans would be much worse. Would fragile constructions such as Bosnia and Macedonia hold together? Would Serbia ever be able to swallow the bitter pill of independence for Kosovo without the prospect of EU membership for itself? If the western Balkans area were excluded from the European mainstream, economic reform and foreign investment would suffer. Endemic problems such as organized crime, corruption and ethnic tension would worsen, and could spill over into the EU. And if the EU said 'never' to countries such as Ukraine, Moldova, Belarus and Georgia, its ability to influence their development would be hugely weakened.

Neither the UK nor the EU should view enlargement as a form of phil-anthropy. Enlargement benefits not only the accession countries but also the older members. The recent expansion of the EU into a diverse group of European economies, creating a single market of nearly 500 million people, is allowing more economic specialization within the Union. The east European states are now applying, more or less perfectly, EU rules on trade, investment, business regulation and competition. The accession countries have fast-growing economies, offering west Europeans demand for their products, opportunities for investment, and supplies of skilled labour. Further enlargement would bring similar benefits.

Enlargement also enhances the security of those who live within the Union. Neither criminal gangs nor terrorists respect the EU's external frontier and stay outside. But the member states' various law enforcement agencies are better able to combat them when they are on EU territory than when they are nearby. If the EU decided that the western Balkans should remain permanently beyond its boundaries, as a kind of black hole on the map of Europe, it would not be immune from the criminal networks centred there. During the accession process, the EU helps candidates to tackle organized crime and other security threats: for example, by strengthening police forces and border guards through the provision of better training and new equipment.

Finally, enlargement brings strategic gains. A wider Europe, with a larger population, a stronger economy and a broader geographical extent – so long as it learns to speak with a single voice – would be more influential. For example, an EU that included Turkey, Bosnia and Albania would be listened to in the Muslim world with more respect. It would stand a better chance of helping to shape the Middle East peace process. But an EU that rejected Turkey would be seen by many in the Islamic world as anti-Muslim.

For all these reasons, a progressive UK government should keep banging the drum for enlargement. This means, specifically:

- Encouraging economic reform to boost the performance of the core Euroland economies, so that the workers in them become less fearful of change.
- Supporting all efforts that will improve the EU's legitimacy. If the Union is unpopular, the idea of enlarging it will also be unpopular.
- Urging the accession candidates to accelerate reform. The best advocates of further enlargement are the candidates themselves, through the way in which they transform their economies, societies and political systems.
- Leading UK public opinion. In recent years, too few ministers have

explained that enlargement is good for British security and prosperity. Unless the government gives a lead, populist politicians may exploit public concerns and rally opposition to enlargement.

- Accepting the need for a fresh institutional settlement. The UK should also welcome greater use of variable geometry. If the more integrationist countries can establish *avant-garde* groups among themselves – thus achieving a measure of 'deepening' – they are less likely to oppose widening.

A stronger neighbourhood policy

Given that the enlargement process will move slowly in the coming years, the European Neighbourhood Policy (ENP) will become increasingly important. This policy is the EU's main tool for promoting political and economic reform in its neighbours – both those that could in theory join the EU one day, such as Ukraine and Moldova, and those that cannot because of geography. Under the ENP, the EU negotiates an 'action plan' with each neighbour. Each plan guarantees trade, aid, participation in EU programmes and political contacts, in return for precise commitments to reform. Since the ENP began in 2004, action plans have been negotiated with Armenia, Azerbaijan, Georgia, Israel, Jordan, Moldova, Morocco, the Palestinian Authority, Tunisia and Ukraine. At the time of writing (early 2007), plans with Algeria, Egypt and Lebanon are in the final stages of negotiation.

Some of these action plans have been modestly successful. Ukraine has adapted some of its laws and standards to comply with those of the EU, and will gain an easier visa regime. Morocco and Moldova have improved their border controls. Jordan, Morocco and Tunisia have set up forums that discuss governance, democracy and human rights. But the ENP is failing to transform neighbours in the way that the accession process transformed much of eastern Europe. The carrots offered by the EU are not juicy enough to motivate political elites to undertake the very painful reforms required.

The EU's conundrum is that it needs to create a more effective neighbourhood policy, without being able to offer membership. The German government, which took over the EU presidency in January 2007, has sought to beef up the policy. It has ideas for integrating neighbours with EU energy markets and transport networks. Meanwhile, the Commission plans to offer Ukraine and other neighbours a 'deep free trade area' with the EU. That would mean scrapping not only tariffs but also some non-tariff barriers (Emerson 2006).

These ideas are useful. However, the UK – given its expertise and leadership role in the Common Foreign and Security Policy – should propose strengthening the ENP in another way. The best-performing neighbours should be offered a stake in the CFSP. If countries such as Georgia and Ukraine make steady progress towards becoming liberal democracies, the EU should ask them to become 'security partners'. They would then have the opportunity to take part in discussions on policies of common interest, such as Black Sea security, non-proliferation, counter-terrorism and illegal immigration. The security partner would send a team of diplomats to be based in the Council of Ministers in Brussels. The partners would help to shape EU policy but, not being members, could not vote on it. Once EU governments had decided a policy, the partner would be free to sign up to it, or not.

Neighbours that joined the CFSP would gain several benefits. The politicians and bureaucrats of the security partners would learn about the EU's ethos of compromise. And the neighbours would find it much easier to adopt the *acquis communautaire* in foreign policy – much of which comprises declarations – than in other areas. Adopting the rules of the single market, for example, can be hard work, technically and politically. Above all, joining the CFSP would make countries such as Ukraine and Georgia feel a little safer. Many Georgians and some Ukrainians would view NATO membership as the best guarantee of their security. But since that goal remains a distant prospect, they may favour closer ties with the EU as an interim step.

This scheme should also be offered to candidates for EU membership, which are currently excluded from discussions on CFSP. There is a risk that too many governments around the table could slow down decision making. So the scheme should begin with just a few chosen topics. If it worked well, the EU and the partners could decide to extend it to more policy areas. In any case, if the EU governments thought the security partners (and candidate countries) in the room were being difficult, they would be free to move ahead and take their own decision.

These proposals for strengthening the ENP will work only if they are seen as 'membership neutral'. Some Georgians and Ukrainians will sniff at any offer that does not mention the goal of membership. But when they realize that full membership is not in the pipeline for the foreseeable future, they may welcome other ways of moving closer to the EU. Similarly, some EU countries hostile to enlargement will be reluctant to give neighbours a status that could be seen as a stepping stone to membership. But in time they may see that the EU has a strategic need to foster reform in its neighbours and that it must therefore give them a closer embrace. Despite being geographically distant from the EU's neighbourhood, the UK has a strong interest in helping the Union to build a more effective neighbourhood policy.

Conclusion

Ten years of Labour government have left the UK with strong foundations for its European policy. Post-Blair governments will be well placed to build on these and strengthen the UK's position in the Union. Enlargement has changed the dynamics of EU politics in the UK's favour. The UK will continue to hold powerful cards, such as its vibrant economy, global connections and pragmatic approach to many European issues. A fresh face in No. 10 will offer the UK an opportunity to dispel some of the dark clouds that the Iraq war has left hanging over its reputation.

A post-Blair European policy should be based, in part, on continuity. It should stick to solid support for EU enlargement and economic reform, leadership in European defence and a non-ideological approach to institutions. In other areas, the UK's European policy should go further than it did during the Blair years: there should be a greater emphasis on the EU's role in tackling climate change, and a stronger effort to forge effective EU foreign policies on the Middle East and Russia.

But on some other issues, UK policy needs to take some genuinely new directions. It should welcome greater use of 'variable geometry' in the EU's institutional arrangements. It should work to find new ways of binding neighbours more closely to the Union. And a post-Blair UK should make a special effort to work with post-Chirac France, in particular to develop a common approach to dealing with the US. These two countries should collaborate with their partners to build an EU that is friendly towards the US, and that offers it practical help in dealing with global problems. But they should also favour a Union that can act autonomously and which, on matters of vital importance, is capable of pursuing policies different from those of the US. Such a Union would have more global influence than the EU does today.

References

Barysch, K. (2006) *The EU and Russia: from principle to pragmatism*, CER Policy Brief, London: Centre for European Reform, November.

Buckley, E. (2006) 'Britain and France must pool parts of their defence', CER Bulletin 49, London: Centre for European Reform, August.

Emerson, M. (ed.) (2006) *The Prospect of Deep Free Trade between the EU and Ukraine*, Brussels: Centre for European Policy Studies.

Grant, C. (2006) *Europe's Blurred Boundaries*, London: Centre for European Reform, October.

Grant, C. and Leonard, M. (2006) *How to Strengthen EU Foreign Policy*, CER Policy Brief, London: Centre for European Reform, May.

Langton, C. (ed.) (2007) *The Military Balance 2005–06*, London: International Institute for Strategic Studies.

Merkel, A. (2006) Speech outlining Germany's plans for its EU presidency, delivered at the Deutsche Gesellschaft für Auswärtige politik e. V. (German Council on Foreign Relations), Berlin, 8 November.

8

The Middle East: A New Agenda for UK Policy

David Mepham

While the Middle East is enormously diverse, and while some of its people are enjoying growing prosperity and opportunity, as a region it performs poorly on many international indicators of democracy, governance and human rights. It also faces a series of profound challenges and 'harbours unparalleled potential for crisis, including steady demographic expansion, worsening environmental conditions, stagnating economies and endemic political, ethnic and religious tensions' (Gnesotto and Grevi 2006: 9). In recent years, regional instability has increased significantly as a result of the war in Iraq, the international stand-off with Iran over the nuclear issue, and the worsening situations in the Palestinian Territories and Lebanon. These conflicts are often interrelated and they have serious knock-on consequences across the region and globally. While there is a powerful critique to be made of recent international interventions in the Middle East, it makes no sense to advocate international disengagement from the region. Progressives should be pressing for a very different kind of relationship with the Middle East, one that is realistic and nuanced rather than evangelical, but one rooted in a commitment to some basic universal values (Halliday 2006).

This chapter looks specifically at policy towards Iraq, Iran and the Israel–Palestine conflict. It also addresses some wider thematic issues, including the regional prospects for political and economic reform and the rise of political Islamist movements. The chapter reflects on some of the key aspects of UK government policy towards the region over the last decade, and the lessons to be learned from this; but the main focus is forward looking. While it is always perilous trying to predict future developments in the Middle East, and while the current moment is remarkably uncertain, the chapter suggests some of the major challenges likely to face the region over the next few years, the way in which Middle Eastern governments and societies may try to deal with them, and the potential opportunities for the UK to influence these processes for the better.

The historical context

However, before we can look forward, it is important to reflect briefly on the past. The position of the UK in the Middle East is weaker today than it was ten years ago. As a former colonial power that, with France, largely determined the territorial borders and state structures of the region at the end of the First World War, that did so without regard for the wishes of the region's people, and that misled Arab leaders in 1916 about what political arrangements the UK would support at the end of the war, the UK has always been treated with a strong element of suspicion and hostility across the Arab world (Owen 2005). Nonetheless, the period from 1914 to 1956 was one in which the UK was the dominant colonial power in the region, a period described by the historian Elizabeth Monroe as 'Britain's moment in the Middle East' (Monroe 1963).

It was the Suez crisis that marked the decisive turning point in this regional role, bringing an end to the UK's residual colonial presence in the Gulf and accelerating the decline of UK influence in the Middle East (Woollacott 2006). Surprisingly though, during much of the last century, suspicion and animosity towards the British coexisted with grudging respect for them, at least in some quarters. Particularly amongst western-oriented Arab elites, there was a sense that the UK understood the region in a way that the US and others did not. However, there are very few people in the region who would argue this today, even privately.

The primary reason for this is Iraq; a secondary reason is the closeness of the Blair government to the Bush administration, and the fact that Blair backed Bush on highly controversial regional policies. The UK has paid a particularly heavy price, in terms of regional influence and credibility, for its involvement in the Iraq war. To say this is not to suggest that the decision over intervention in Iraq was unproblematic for progressives. Saddam Hussein's regime was exceptionally brutal and repressive. And there was a humanitarian case for intelligent and coherent international action to try to weaken or remove him, and to help support the emergence of a broad-based alternative government and better arrangements for the protection of human rights in Iraq.

But the case for intervention should clearly have been considered alongside the likely costs and consequences of military action, including the loss of life resulting from armed intervention, the radicalization of Muslim opinion that might result from this, the spur given to global terrorist movements, the very real danger that Iraq might disintegrate into civil war and the financial (and therefore the opportunity) costs of action. There were also huge legal issues: most international legal opinion regarded military intervention without a further explicit United Nations (UN) resolution as unlawful. There were issues, too, about the way in which any intervention led by the Bush administration would be likely to be carried out. As I argue in chapter 3 in this volume, for a military intervention to have a benign outcome in humanitarian terms, it is necessary, though certainly not sufficient, that humanitarian concerns should be uppermost in the minds and plans of the intervening powers. It is very clear that this was not the case with Iraq. Taken together, therefore, these factors should have indicated a need for extreme caution, the serious exploration of other policy options, and the building of an international consensus before any military action was contemplated.

Working to a very different agenda, the US did not allow any of these concerns to get in the way of a war that some people in the administration had been planning to wage for a number of years (Cockburn 2006). It was strongly supported in this by the UK government. Tony Blair was genuinely convinced that Saddam Hussein posed a threat that needed to be dealt with. However, to secure public support for war, Blair and Bush were selective in their use of intelligence information in a way that made the threat from Saddam appear more alarming and more immediate than it was. Blair also believed that it would be dangerous for the world if the US acted unilaterally, but while he sought to gain UN authorization for action, he had no hesitation in backing Bush without it when his attempts failed.

Within weeks of the intervention it became clear that the threat from Iraq was not so great as to justify the premature curtailment of the UN weapons inspections process. Indeed, no evidence of weapons of mass destruction (WMD) or even weapons programmes has been discovered over the last four years. It was only after their claims about WMD were found to be false that the US and UK chose to give greater prominence to human rights and democracy as a retrospective justification for military action in Iraq.

But judged in these terms, the action has also been a monumental failure. Although there has been some political progress, with an elected government now in office in Baghdad, this government lacks the capacity to govern effectively or to contain the escalating levels of violence in the country – indeed, through its alliance with various Shia militia it is also responsible for large-scale violence and human rights violations (Human Rights Watch 2006).

There are many reasons for this failure, including a catalogue of errors on the part of the intervening and occupying powers. Some of these mistakes are set out in George Packer's fascinating book on the conflict: *The Assassin's Gate* (Packer 2006). He highlights the widespread ignorance on the part of the US administration of Iraqi history and society, and the poor management of the occupying forces, which led, amongst other things, to the abuses of Iraqi prisoners at Abu Ghraib. Other mistakes resulted from weak strategic planning, including the decision to disband – almost overnight – the Iraqi armed forces, a decision that contributed to the breakdown of public order in Iraq and provided ample recruits for the insurgents. He notes the disastrous consequences of blanket de-Baathification and crude counter-insurgency operations, like that in Falluja in 2004. He also highlights the appalling lack of preparation for the occupation phase, including the deliberate exclusion by the US Department of Defense of people in the State Department and elsewhere with experience in post-conflict reconstruction issues.

While the Blair government raised doubts about some of these specific policies, it appears to have been largely unsuccessful in altering the course of US policy. And in the eyes of much of the Arab world the UK was joined at the hip with the Bush administration in pursuing a deeply unpopular and destructive war.

While there are many examples of good work by the UK in individual countries in the Middle East – by diplomats, development agencies, the British Council and by UK non-governmental organizations (NGOs) – the perception of the UK amongst large sections of the region's public has been powerfully and negatively shaped by Iraq. This is the backdrop against which a post-Blair UK foreign policy in the Middle East will need to be developed.

Iraq – is there a way out?

However misguided recent UK policies towards Iraq may have been, those on the progressive wing of politics should clearly want to see the emergence of a stable and reasonably democratic government there, and an end to the horrific levels of violence and human rights abuse. But the chances of achieving this look extremely slim.

The report of the US-commissioned Iraq Study Group, chaired by James Baker and Lee Hamilton, which was published in December 2006, provided a very sombre account of the situation in Iraq and its immediate prospects (Iraq Study Group 2006). As they put it:

> Some 3000 Iraqi civilians are killed every month . . . Violence is increasing in scope and lethality. It is fed by a Sunni Arab insurgency, Shiite militias and death squads, Al Qaeda, and widespread criminality . . . If the situation continues to deteriorate, the consequences could be severe. A slide towards chaos could trigger the collapse of Iraq's government and a humanitarian catastrophe. Neighbouring countries could intervene. Sunni–Shia clashes could spread. And Al Qaeda could win a propaganda victory and expand its base of operations. (2006: xiv)

But with the Bush administration having rejected the broad thrust of the Study Group's recommendations in January 2007, the situation in Iraq continues to deteriorate. It may well be too late to pull Iraq back from all-out catastrophe, but a post-Blair UK government has an obligation to propose a different approach. There are three areas in particular where this is required and where the UK should try to use its diplomatic influence to best effect.

First and foremost, the UK should argue for enlisting a broader set of international actors behind a shared endeavour to help stabilize Iraq. Critically, this should involve key countries in the region, including Saudi Arabia, Egypt and Turkey, but also Iran and Syria. Enlisting the support of the last two will be extremely difficult. These countries are already heavily involved in Iraq. Iran, for example, is now the dominant external power in the country (Chatham House 2006). It will require a major diplomatic effort to convince the Iranians and the Syrians to adopt a new approach. That in turn will depend on persuading them that existing US/UK policy towards Iraq and the wider region will change and that Iranian and Syrian interests in Iraq are not diametrically opposed to western interests. While the odds may be stacked against it, and while current US policy is moving in the opposite direction, there is a powerful case for dialogue with the Iranians and the Syrians to see what common ground can be established (Malley and Harling 2006).

Secondly, greatly increased international pressure and support is required to help secure a new political compact and reconciliation process within Iraq. While the international debate about Iraq is currently dominated by security concerns, it is clear that military power alone will not reverse Iraq's sectarian violence and civil war. Only a re-energized political process that is more inclusive and equitable can help to do this.

One of the weaknesses in the Iraq Study Group report, and in existing US and UK policy, is the assumption that the current government in Iraq is a 'government of national unity' and 'broadly representative of the Iraqi people'. It is not. As the International Crisis Group notes,

> The government is not a partner in an effort to stem the violence, nor will its strengthening contribute to Iraq's stability. The Sunni Arab representatives it includes lack meaningful support within their community and have no sway with the armed opposition groups that are feeding civil war dynamics. Conversely, its most influential Shiite members control the most powerful militias, which are involved in brutal sectarian violence. (2006a: 1)

Nor are the prospects of greater stability and political reconciliation in Iraq well served by calls for a formal partition of the country between Sunni, Shia and Kurdish areas (Galbraith 2006). Despite considerable movement of population, in response to violence and the fear of violence, most of Iraq's population still lives in areas that are confessionally mixed. Far from stabilizing the country, therefore, proposals for formal partition are more likely to trigger further violence, instability and population displacement.

Making political progress in Iraq also means facing up to the failures of the recent constitutional process. The 2005 drafting of the country's permanent constitution was hugely divisive. Most Sunnis regarded it as a naked attempt by the Shia and Kurds to exclude them from the country's wealth and power, and the process greatly exacerbated sectarian divisions. Current trends suggest that the constitutional review process is unlikely to make much difference.

As an alternative, the international community should be pressing much harder for compromise and political accommodation within Iraq, including the question of equitable revenue sharing from oil, gas and natural resources. A new political compact for Iraq will need to involve agreement on the nature of Iraq's federal system, the passage of a broad amnesty for those who agree to put down arms, a timetable for international troop withdrawal, a new electoral law and strengthened provisions to protect human rights. Both international and regional actors will need to use a combination of generous carrots and big sticks to help secure this kind of political accommodation on the part of Iraq's various factions.

Thirdly, there needs to be a strengthened international effort to help build up Iraq's institutions. The overthrow of Saddam

Hussein's regime in April 2003 precipitated the collapse of almost all of Iraq's existing institutions. This scenario was not predicted by the US or planned for. As Condoleezza Rice put it in an unguarded moment, 'The concept was that we would defeat the army, but the institutions would hold, everything from ministries to police forces' (Dodge 2006: 126). But this premise proved to be profoundly flawed.

In most cases, Iraqis need assistance to build new institutions literally from scratch. This includes help with developing the basic administrative capacity of the state. While the UK has already been active in this area, there is potentially a bigger role for the European Union (EU) and the UN, drawing on their experience of institutional development and capacity building in other parts of the world.

Further international support is needed to help develop a more effective and professional Iraqi police force and military, which is not only technically proficient but subject to proper civilian accountability. It is essential that this process be approached in the wider context outlined above. The issue of US and UK troop withdrawal from Iraq also needs to be approached in this broader framework. The 21,000 extra US troops deployed in early 2007 are clearly not succeeding in improving the security situation for ordinary Iraqis: a predictable outcome given the failure of the US to change its existing military strategy and given the absence of a more inclusive political process, to help bring Iraq's fractured communities together. In the short term, a new UK government should press for a less aggressive military posture in Iraq on the part of US forces. This should include a significant reduction in heavy-handed counter-insurgency operations, which continue to make things worse, a specific focus on protecting the civilian population and a more central role for new Iraqi-trained armed forces and police.

It is desirable that there should be an early withdrawal of US and UK troops (significant numbers of UK forces have already been withdrawn from the south of the country in 2007), but the precise timing and sequencing of the final withdrawal of international troops is something that should be discussed in the context of a new political compact for Iraq, rather than it being determined by reference to an arbitrary timetable or through a policy of 'cut and run'.

While there is no guarantee that this kind of three-pronged effort will succeed (indeed, with each passing month, the prospect that external players can exert constructive influence over developments in Iraq recedes), an approach along these lines represents Iraq's best and last hope. By contrast, the continuation of the existing US strategy will lead to yet further bloodshed and regional instability.

Iran – averting all-out confrontation

A post-Blair UK foreign policy will also need to give real priority to the situation in Iran. The seizure and subsequent release of fifteen UK naval personnel in March/April 2007 will not make the adoption of a new UK approach towards Iran any easier, but neither does it make it any less urgent or necessary.

In the next few years Iran could very easily become the single biggest foreign policy and security issue facing the UK, not just in the Middle East but globally. What would guarantee this is a declaration by the Iranians that they were withdrawing from the Nuclear Non-Proliferation Treaty (NPT) or Tehran carrying out a nuclear test, or a decision by the US or Israel to launch a pre-emptive military strike against Iranian nuclear facilities in an attempt to prevent the second outcome. There is a serious possibility that one of these scenarios will materialize in the next year or so if a diplomatic solution cannot be found to defuse the tense stand-off between Tehran and the international community over the nuclear issue.

What happens in Iran also matters to the UK in economic and political terms. Iran has the world's second largest reserves of oil and natural gas, as well as an abundance of copper, gold and uranium. Any reduction in Iranian oil output, for example, could have a big impact on the global and therefore the UK economy. This chapter has already noted that Iran has now become the dominant external player in Iraq (more influential than the US), and that engagement with Tehran is therefore necessary to make progress there. But Iranian influence is very significant and growing across the Middle East as a whole and in other surrounding countries (Chatham House 2006). From a UK perspective, Iran is crucial to events in Afghanistan, Pakistan, Syria, Lebanon and Israel–Palestine – countries where the UK is heavily involved.

A progressive UK foreign policy should be concerned about Iranian policy on human rights and its support for violence abroad. Iran's human rights record is poor and deteriorating. The government regularly uses torture and ill-treatment in detention, including prolonged solitary confinement, to punish so-called dissidents. The judiciary, which is accountable to the country's Supreme Leader Ali Khamenei, has been responsible for many serious human rights violations. Paramilitary groups often violently attack peaceful protestors and intelligence services run illegal secret prisons and interrogation centres (Human Rights Watch 2006). Various remarks by the Iranian President, Mahmoud Ahmadinejad, have also produced serious concern about Iran's future intentions. On several occasions Ahmadinejad has called into question the veracity of the Holocaust and in 2005 he suggested that Israel should be 'wiped off the face of the earth'.

In the closing months of his premiership, and in response to these comments and recent Iranian actions, Tony Blair argued that Tehran was the main obstacle to peace and progress in the Middle East and that the UK and the wider world needed to wake up to the challenge it posed and confront it (Blair 2006). While he was right to be highly critical of many aspects of Iranian policy, calls for direct confrontation, let alone military action, are likely to make things much worse not better.

A post-Blair UK foreign policy needs a more nuanced approach towards Iran. This should display a better appreciation of UK/Iranian history. It was the UK that imposed a series of unequal treaties on the Iranians in the nineteenth century and in the early years of the last century. It was also the UK, along with the US, which in 1953 overthrew the democratically elected Iranian President, Mohammed Mossadegh, and then supported the undemocratic and increasingly repressive Shah until the Islamic revolution of 1979 (Woollacott 2006). Iranians have not forgotten this and the coup was a defining moment in the emergence of modern Iranian nationalism (Hiro 2005). A new approach towards Iran also requires a better understanding of Iranian society, its political system and its interests, and the factors that may help to shape Iranian thinking and policy.

There are two distinct but closely related priorities that ought to shape UK policy towards Iran over the next few years. First and most obviously, there is the nuclear issue. It would be extremely undesirable for Iran to acquire a nuclear weapons capability. This is because any increase in the number of states with nuclear weapons weakens the NPT and the existing international norm against the acquisition of nuclear capabilities, and increases the risks of their use. In the case of Iran, there would be additional concerns about the nature of the Iranian regime (anxieties heightened by the election of Mahmoud Ahmadinejad and his inflammatory remarks about Israel). There would be a further concern that an Iranian bomb would trigger a process of nuclear proliferation across the Middle East as a whole, with countries like Egypt, Saudi Arabia and Turkey then making the decision to seek a nuclear weapons capability. There is perhaps no region of the world where the proliferation of nuclear weapons would be more dangerous than the Middle East. Vigorous and intelligent diplomatic efforts should therefore be made to try to avoid this outcome, and the UK should make a constructive contribution to these.

At the time of writing (spring 2007), existing diplomatic efforts to address the nuclear issue – in which the UK, France and Germany have been centrally involved since 2003 – have stalled. Iran has been censured by the UN Security Council and international sanctions have been imposed. If there is to be a resumption of diplomacy, and if this is to have a greater chance of producing results, fresh thinking is therefore required about the kind of carrots and sticks most likely to persuade the Iranians to forgo the development of a nuclear weapons capability. While economic and trade issues may be an important part of a 'grand bargain' between the West and Iran, what is likely to matter more to the Iranians is a concrete international guarantee that the US and others will not launch a military attack on Iran or otherwise seek to destabilize or bring down the regime. In return, western governments would clearly want to see a shift in Iranian policy towards Hamas and Hizbollah and in relation to Iraq. While it will be much harder to pull off such a deal today than would have been the case during the period of the Reform Movement in Iran (1997 to 2005), such a bargain remains the best hope for a negotiated solution and the UK government should seek to reinvigorate diplomatic efforts along these lines.

More hawkish voices, particularly in the US and Israel, argue that diplomacy will not succeed and that it is simply unacceptable that Iran should go nuclear under any circumstances – and hence, by implication, that all means, including the use of military force, should be taken to prevent this outcome. However, the case against military action against Iran is currently overwhelming. While the UK government would be most unlikely to be involved directly in any military action – with this being undertaken by the US or Israel – a progressive UK government should be using all of its diplomatic influence to dissuade these states from adopting such a thoroughly misguided and dangerous policy.

If the Iranians are serious about acquiring nuclear weapons (and this is a reasonable assumption, despite their protestations that they seek only civilian nuclear capacity) then it is impossible to believe that they will not have taken measures to conceal their fledgling programme. The idea, therefore, that there are some obvious targets that can be easily taken out through strategic bombing is naïve. But a bombing strategy would almost inevitably produce civilian casualties. If nuclear material is hit, there is a danger of widespread contamination and large-scale fatalities. In a highly nationalistic country like Iran, this is likely to rally public opinion behind the existing regime rather than driving a wedge between the two. Relations between Tehran and western governments are already extremely strained, but an attack on Iran would make them immeasurably worse.

The Iranians are well placed to hit back at the West, most obviously in Iraq, where any prospect of Iran playing a constructive role in stabilizing the country would be lost. An end to any form of Iranian engagement would also cause serious problems for the UK in Afghanistan, where there has been a degree of cooperation with the Iranians. The Iranians have considerable influence, too, in Syria, Lebanon and Palestine, and they would be emboldened to support aggressive actions through their allies in each of these countries. And although the Iranians are predominantly Shia and Al-Qaeda is a Sunni movement, it is highly likely that a military attack on Iran would provide a further stimulus to global Islamic radicalism and to anti-western Islamic terrorism. Oil prices would be likely to go through the roof, particularly if Iranian commanders retaliated by disrupting tanker traffic through the Strait of Hormuz.

The assumption that Iran is intent on regional aggression or that it would represent an existential threat to Israel if it acquired nuclear weapons is also dubious. The Iranian political system is highly complex. While Mahmoud Ahmadinejad is the Iranian President and while he has made some highly offensive and disturbing remarks about Israel in recent years, he is not the most powerful person in the Iranian political system (the Supreme Leader Ali Khamenei is more influential); moreover, Ahmadinejad does not have direct control over Iranian nuclear policy (Chatham House 2006). There is evidence of increasing disaffection with Ahmadinejad, with poor results for his supporters in local elections and with motions critical of his policies being passed in the Iranian Parliament. Moreover, while Iran has regional interests and agendas, the regime's foreign policy is more pragmatic and less ideological today than it was in the period immediately following the 1979 revolution.

It is worth reflecting on how Iranians perceive their security environment. They have land borders with seven neighbouring states, and two of their neighbours – Iraq and Afghanistan – are currently characterized by large-scale violence and insecurity. The US, which describes Iran as part of an 'axis of evil', has large numbers of troops in both countries, as well as military bases in Turkey, central Asia and the Persian Gulf. In this context, it is not wholly unreasonable for Iranians to feel threatened. The Iranians also note a profound double standard when it comes to western policy on nuclear weapons. Israel has nuclear weapons but has never suffered any western criticism as a result. India and Pakistan have recently become nuclear weapon states, but both enjoy good diplomatic and strategic relationships with the US and UK. None of this means that we should be remotely naïve about Iran's current leadership or lessen our determination to deny it a nuclear bomb. But we should be fully aware of the disastrous consequences of military action and explore more intelligently some of the saner alternatives.

A second priority for a progressive UK government should be pressing for greater respect for human rights and movement towards political reform in Iran. There is clearly a tension between the desire to do a deal with the Iranian regime on the nuclear issue and to gain its cooperation on Iraq and wider regional issues, while at the same time criticizing its human rights and governance record. But the latter goal should not be abandoned to the former: indeed, an Iran which better respects human rights, allows its people a bigger say in government and upholds the rule of law would be one of the best ways to advance the security and stability of the whole region. Western governments failed to provide sufficient support to the former Iranian President, Mohammad Khatami, in the late 1990s, at a time when he was making efforts to liberalize and reform the Iranian political system. It was a very serious missed opportunity (Ansari 2006).

While the prospects for reform look much less favourable today, it would be a grave mistake to ignore the diversity, vibrancy and youthfulness of Iranian society and the underlying yearning for change amongst many Iranians (Keddie 2006). Although this should clearly be done sensitively, the UK has a moral *and* a security interest in seeking political reform and respect for human rights in Iran, and Iran's own reformers would welcome the right kind of international support. As the Iranian Nobel Peace Prize winner, Shirin Ebadi, has argued, 'the West can keep Iran's human rights record in the spotlight and the Islamic regime has shown itself to be sensitive to such criticism' (Ebadi 2006: 215). But it is also worth heeding her thoughts on the consequences for human rights and political reform of a more confrontational or military approach:

> I can think of no scenario more alarming, no internal shift more dangerous than that engendered by the West imagining that it can bring democracy to Iran through either military might or the fomentation of violent rebellion . . . If the clerics in power detect military strikes on the horizon instead of a negotiated solution, then they will find no incentive, no credibility gained, in safeguarding the rights of their citizens. (2006: 215)

Israel–Palestine – breaking the impasse

After Blair, the UK government should continue to remain strongly focused on the Israel–Palestine conflict and on Israel's relations with its immediate Arab neighbours. Progress here matters most obviously to the peoples of the countries and territories concerned, but there is a wider regional and international strategic interest. As the International Crisis Group has noted,

> perpetuation of the Arab/Israeli conflict, with all the anger it generates, fuels extremist, jihadi movements in the Muslim world; intensifies animosity towards the West; radicalises Muslim populations in Western Europe; discredits pro-Western governments; deepens the damaging divide between the Islamic and Western worlds; and, as both Syrian and Israeli officials have warned, sows the seeds of the next Arab–Israeli war. Resolving the conflict clearly would not be a sufficient condition to tackle such deep-seated problems; but it is, on all available evidence, a necessary one. (2006b: i)

However, at the time of writing (spring 2007), the prospects for progress look very bleak. The modicum of trust that once existed between the two sides has gone and it is hard to see how it can be easily regained. Amongst the Palestinians, there are profound divisions between supporters of Fatah and Hamas (Hroub 2006). The Palestinian Territories, particularly Gaza, are now characterized by pervasive insecurity, and Palestine's political and administrative institutions teeter on the verge of outright disintegration.

This political and security crisis has been compounded, and to a large extent caused, by the Palestinians' desperate economic plight. Even before the victory of Hamas in the January 2006 legislative elections, a majority of Palestinians were living in poverty, primarily as a consequence of Israeli occupation and associated restrictions on Palestinian movement and access, although poor economic management and corruption on the part of the Palestinian Authority also played their part. The imposition of western sanctions on the Palestinian Territories and Israel's freeze on the transfer of tax revenues following Hamas's victory has further deepened Palestinian suffering. In this context, the Palestinians are not well placed, or well disposed, to take early initiatives of their own or to offer a coherent negotiating position to the Israelis.

The Israeli side is marked by incoherence, uncertainty and pessimism, particularly following the debacle in Lebanon in 2006. While Ehud Olmert's Kadima government was elected on a pledge to undertake some unilateral disengagement from parts of the West Bank (the so-called 'convergence plan'), Israel's inconclusive military performance during the Lebanon war of July–August 2006 has greatly damaged its sense of self-confidence and military invulnerability, and has left this plan in tatters. Israel has increased its military assaults on Gaza following the end of the Lebanon conflict, agreed to the building of further illegal settlements in the West Bank and showed little interest in the resumption of a meaningful peace process with the Palestinians.

In this situation, international pressure and encouragement is essential if there is to be any kind of progress towards a lasting resolution of the conflict. The UK should attempt to make a constructive contribution to this process. But Blair's successor will need to appreciate how much the UK's standing with the Palestinians and surrounding Arab states has been damaged, not just by the Iraq war but also by Blair's policy on the Israel–Palestine conflict itself and by his stance during the 2006 Israeli military action in Lebanon.

Although the 2003 'Road Map to a permanent two-state solution to the Israel/Palestine conflict' called for the terms of a final settlement to be negotiated between the two parties, in 2005 Ariel Sharon undertook a policy of unilateral disengagement from Gaza, and was supported in this by the US administration and by the Blair government, to the dismay of the Palestinians.

Following Hamas's election victory, the UK also backed Israel and the US, as did other European countries, in halting direct aid transfers to the Palestinian government (unless and until it renounced violence, recognized Israel and accepted previous agreements relating to the conflict). While Hamas does need to shift its policy on these issues, it is not unreasonable to ask why comparable demands are not made of the Israelis, given Israel's continuing large-scale military action in Gaza, its refusal to withdraw from occupied Palestinian territory and its consistent violation of previously signed agreements with the Palestinians, including the Oslo Accords and the Road Map.

UK influence was further weakened by Tony Blair's response to Israel's military assault on Lebanon in July–August 2006. While Hizbollah triggered the crisis, through the capture and killing of Israeli soldiers (and while this action should be strongly condemned), the Israeli response was a gross overreaction. During the course of the conflict, over 1,200 Lebanese civilians were killed (almost a third of them children), 400,000 were wounded and a million people were displaced. The economic damage to Lebanon from the war was estimated at $7 billion, or 30 per cent of gross domestic product (Salem 2006). This action has severely destabilized Lebanon's fragile political system, raising the spectre of another Lebanese civil war. While most of the rest of the world was highly critical of Israel's response and called for an immediate ceasefire, the Blair government sided with the Bush administration and declined either to support an early ceasefire or to describe Israel's action as 'disproportionate'. This stance provoked enormous anger on the part of many ordinary Lebanese and Palestinians, and across the Arab world more broadly.

If the UK is to play a more constructive, influential and progressive role in relation to the conflict in the immediate future, a significant shift in approach will therefore be required. An important starting point would be to recognize that there is a basic asymmetry at the heart of the Israel–Palestine conflict – an asymmetry between an Israeli occupying power and an occupied Palestinian people. This does not mean that a resolution of the conflict will not require compromise and flexibility on all sides. Nor does it mean that the international community should stop pressing Hamas to change its policy in key areas. But there can be no realistic possibility of resolving this conflict, or limiting the dreadful toll of human suffering that results from it, without an end to the Israeli occupation. Yet far from ending it, Israel is actually intensifying its control over the occupied territories.

In 1967, when Israel first began its occupation of the West Bank and Gaza Strip, it claimed that its settlements were a temporary security measure. Forty years on, these settlements have been hugely expanded; there are now 400,000 Israeli settlers living illegally in occupied Palestinian territory, including East Jerusalem. All the evidence suggests that Israel plans to retain the vast majority of these settlements, by formally annexing them to Israel, and to limit severely the amount of land in the West Bank that might potentially constitute a future Palestinian state. Israel's wall, or 'security barrier', is a crucial part of this strategy. Israel is not building the wall on its 1967 pre-occupation border (which it would be entitled to do under international law); rather it plans to build 80 per cent of the wall inside Israeli-occupied Palestinian territory. This has led the independent Israeli human rights organization B'Tselem to argue that the route of the wall was 'completely unrelated to the security of Israeli citizens' and that 'a major aim was to build the barrier east of as many settlements as possible, to make it easier to annex them to Israel' (B'Tselem 2005).

Through the construction of the wall, Israel is de facto annexing Palestinian agricultural lands and water resources, restricting Palestinian freedom of movement, separating Palestinians from schools, health facilities and jobs, and depriving thousands of Palestinians of their livelihoods. The route of the wall, the pattern of Israeli settlements and the building of a highway network (linking Israeli settlements with Israel and for the exclusive use of Israeli citizens) have a combined impact of destroying the contiguity of the territory left for a potential Palestinian state. Such a state would be unviable, and yet without a viable Palestinian state, there can be no viable peace.

A progressive UK government should be urging its European partners and the Americans to play a more active and even-handed role in trying to resolve this dispute. The Saudi-brokered Mecca Agreement between Hamas and Fatah in February 2007, with its commitment to a Palestinian national unity government, offers the chance of a fresh start – one that local parties and international actors should seize with both hands. For their part, the UK should be calling for a lifting of the international ban on economic assistance to the Palestinian Authority and the resumption of direct negotiations between Palestinians and Israelis. At the same time, it should continue to press the Palestinian authorities to pursue a comprehensive and reciprocal ceasefire with the Israelis and to resolve intra-Palestinian disputes through dialogue not violence. The UK should also support pressure being exerted on Israel to end its policy of targeted assassinations, house demolitions and land confiscations in the occupied territories, to halt new settlement activity, to lift Israel's own economic restrictions and penalties on the Palestinians and to enter substantive negotiations with them. While the US would be best placed to bring this pressure to bear (and shows very little interest in doing so), the EU does have some significant economic and diplomatic leverage with the Israelis, which it should be encouraged to use more assertively: for example, through its economic and trading relationship.

The international community should be promoting a comprehensive and inclusive approach that addresses the Israel–Palestine question within the wider framework of Israel's relations with its Arab neighbours. Relations with Syria and Lebanon are particularly critical. The Syrian President, Bashir al-Assad, has indicated a willingness to enter into negotiations unconditionally with the Israelis (International Crisis Group 2006b). The Israelis should be urged to respond to this offer. And there needs to be a sustained international focus on the situation in Lebanon to help prevent a further round of violence there.

At the outset of negotiations, there also needs to be a clearly articulated end goal:

> The goal should be unambiguously stated as security and full recognition for Israel within internationally recognised borders, an end to the occupation for the Palestinian people and an independent, sovereign state based on the 1967 borders with East Jerusalem as its capital, a just resolution of the refugee issue, recovery of lost land by Syria and a fully sovereign and secure Lebanese state. (International Crisis Group 2006b: ii)

In addition, there could be more of an effort to engage the Arab states in the search for a solution. The 2002 Arab League Initiative (which called for full normalization of relations with Israel in exchange for its full withdrawal from the occupied territories) was also a groundbreaking statement by them, which deserves greater debate in the

Arab world and internationally. If the Arab states are serious about this proposal, they should be publicizing it at every opportunity, including through direct public diplomacy aimed at Israelis. International partners should also focus global attention on the initiative as a potentially valuable way in which a meaningful Arab/Israeli peace process could be revived.

On all of these issues, international pressure and encouragement cannot substitute for a lack of willingness or commitment to negotiate by the parties themselves. But in the right conditions, it can increase the costs of belligerency and defiance of international law, and it can make more attractive the prospects for dialogue and accommodation.

The wider prospects for reform

The issues of Iraq, Iran and Israel–Palestine are likely to dominate UK policy towards the Middle East over the next few years, although Lebanon, Saudi Arabia and Egypt could also move very rapidly up the international policy agenda, depending on developments there. But a progressive UK strategy should also have something to say about the region as a whole. While the Iraq war has been a disaster, the conclusion that progressives should draw from this is not that we should abandon the cause of human rights or democracy in the Middle East, but rather that we should develop more thoughtful and sophisticated ways of advancing these goals.

As already noted, the Middle East performs poorly on global indicators of democracy, governance and human rights, and it suffers from widespread and deeply entrenched authoritarianism (Posusney and Angrist 2005). While there has been economic advance in some countries, the region also suffers from profound economic and development challenges. The region attracts a mere 1 per cent of foreign direct investment flows to developing countries. The region's manufactured exports to countries in the Organization for Economic Cooperation and Development (OECD) are minuscule and interregional trade is low (North Atlantic Treaty Organization 2005). According to the World Bank, roughly 100 million new jobs will need to be created in the next twenty years to absorb the growing workforce. Weak economic performance also translates into poor development outcomes in many countries: 32 million people in the region are undernourished, the maternal mortality rate is double that of the Caribbean and Latin America and four times that of East Asia, and about 65 million Arabs are illiterate, two-thirds of them women (United Nations Development Programme 2002).

The Arab Human Development Reports have been right to stress that it is the people of the region themselves who must take primary responsibility for addressing these problems. But the wider international community also has an important role to play. While every case is different, and while there is no substitute for good analysis and a close understanding of political, economic, social and cultural context, there are three areas in particular where the broader international community could better assist the cause of human rights, better governance and development in the Middle East. A progressive UK government should highlight these issues.

First, western governments need to recognise that their own policies can reinforce authoritarianism in the region (Bellin 2005; Mepham 2006). This takes a number of forms, including diplomatic cover and financial assistance to some of the region's more repressive but pro-western regimes, such as Egypt and Saudi Arabia. Arms sales are also part of this. Urged on by western arms salesmen, encouraged and financed by western governments, the Middle East represents a huge part of the global market in military equipment. This relationship between western and Middle Eastern security establishments contributes to the heavy militarization of societies in the region and the high proportion of the population engaged in the state's security agencies. A much more restrictive UK approach to weapons transfers to the region is essential, as is a more conditional approach to financial assistance, linked to greater progress by recipients on human rights and good governance. At the moment, the UK is moving in the opposite direction: promoting new arms sales to countries like Saudi Arabia, while in December 2006 halting a Serious Fraud Office investigation into allegations of corruption against a British company relating to a   previous arms deal to the Saudis: the Al-Yamamah project.

Secondly, there is more that can and should be done in respect of economic justice in the Middle East. Illiberal and extremist forces thrive in situations of economic marginalization, poverty, unemployment and falling living standards. Broad-based economic development, job creation and action against poverty are certainly not a guarantee of political moderation, human rights and democratization. But over the medium term at least, they can help create conditions in which these developments become more likely. Much of the existing international aid to the region has a weak developmental impact. Development resources could be better spent strengthening the capacity of Middle Eastern countries to secure pro-poor growth, enhancing the quality and accountability of institutions, supporting an impartial rule of law, a free press and media, and strengthening human rights, particularly the rights of women and minority communities. On trade, many of the biggest obstacles are those that Middle Eastern states erect between themselves, but the EU also imposes significant barriers to Middle Eastern exports in relation to agricultural commodities and petro-chemical products. These should be reduced or eliminated.

Thirdly, there needs to be a more intelligent approach to the phe-nomenon of political Islam in the Middle East. While media and polit-ical attention focuses disproportionately on violent Islamic extremists, political Islam in the Middle East (and elsewhere) is marked by con-siderable diversity: 'Islamists cover a wide spectrum: radical and mod-erate, violent and peaceful, traditional and modern, democratic and anti-democratic . . . and the moderate side of the spectrum vastly out-weighs the more dangerous, violent and radical segment' (Fuller 2005: 38).

In Iran, Shia religious authorities hold decisive power in the state. In Iraq, Shia parties now dominate the government. And in Lebanon, the Shia movement Hizbollah, emboldened by its clash with Israel in summer 2006, has become a much stronger force. Elsewhere in the region, Shia forces appear to be undergoing something of a resurgence (Nakash 2006). This trend is a source of anxiety to the leaders of countries like Jordan and Saudi Arabia who fear its potentially desta-bilizing consequences.

Meanwhile in Morocco, Egypt, Jordan, Kuwait and Yemen, some Sunni Islamist groups have adopted more moderate and pragmatic positions after decades of failed opposition to existing regimes. Their moderation involves a formal rejection of violence to secure their political ends, support for the rule of law and an acceptance of plu-ralistic politics. In some cases, these positions are relatively new. There is also a degree of ambiguity about where some of the mainstream Islamist movements stand on particular issues (Brown et al. 2006). This raises a legitimate concern in some quarters that this new-found interest in democracy is a cynical ploy rather than a genuine conver-sion: that were Islamists to come to power through democratic means, they would then tear up these institutions and rule through violence and repression. Those who advocate engagement with Islamist groups should not dismiss this concern out of hand, but neither should this argument be overstated, or used to block constructive dialogue. In all cases, groups should be judged by what they do as well as what they say. However, there is sufficient evidence that many Islamist groups have changed their approach in recent years to justify engagement (Hamzawy 2005; El-Din Shahin 2005).

A dialogue with political Islam obviously does not imply that the positions taken by Islamist groups – even 'moderate' ones – are not open to criticism. For example, some Islamist groups have reactionary attitudes or policies towards women that run directly counter to universal principles of equality and non-discrimination. There are additional concerns about the stance of some Islamist groups in respect of freedom of expression. In countries like Kuwait and Egypt, for example, Islamist groups have actively sought to limit intellectual freedom, instituting legal proceedings against any writings on Islam they disagree with and persecuting those who write them. These policies should clearly be opposed very strongly.

The argument here is rather about the best means to encourage progressive political change in the Middle East, including judicial independence, representative government and respect for human rights. In many countries in the region, Islamist movements command significant public support and are the main source of opposition to existing regimes. Moreover, the repression of Islamists by existing rulers and the ostracism of them by international actors has been a singularly ineffective and indefensible strategy. A willingness to engage with its moderate elements, at the same time as engaging with other social forces, could help improve the prospects for regional political reform and the avoidance of further political and religious radicalization.

Conclusion

There are no quick fixes when it comes to the myriad problems of the Middle East. The key decisions will be those taken by the people of the Middle East themselves. The Iraq war has shown how much damage can be done by ill-conceived and poorly executed external interventions. But the state of the region, not least the frightening security situation and the region's lamentable record on human rights, should also convince progressives from outside the region that continuing international engagement is necessary, albeit of a form markedly different from recent policy. It is ironic, to say the least, that in the last few years a right-wing US president should have been the most vocal global advocate for democratic change in the Middle East. His policies have been an unmitigated disaster. But the cause of democracy and human rights in the region should be a real priority for progressives (Mepham 2006; Mathieson and Youngs 2006). A new UK government will need to make major changes in its strategy towards the region if it is to regain the trust of local parties and an element of influence over regional developments. Post-Blair, there is no area of UK foreign policy where a radical shift in policy is more urgently required.

References

Ansari, A. (2006) *Confronting Iran: the failure of American policy and the roots of mistrust*, London: Hurst.

Bellin, E. (2005) 'Coercive institutions and coercive leaders', in M. Posusney and M. Angrist (eds), *Authoritarianism in the Middle East: regimes and resistance*, London and Boulder, Colo.: Lynne Rienner.

Blair, T. (2006) Speech in Dubai, 20 December.

Brown, N., Hamzawy, A. and Ottaway, M. (2006) *Islamist Movements and the Democratic Process in the Arab World: exploring the gray zones*, Washington, DC: Carnegie Endowment for International Peace.

B'Tselem (2005) *The Separation Barrier*, at http://btselem.org/english/separation_barrier.

Chatham House (2006) *Iran, Its Neighbours and the Regional Crisis*, London.

Cockburn, P. (2006) *The Occupation: war and resistance in Iraq*, London: Verso.

Dodge, T. (2006) 'Iraq: a European perspective', in I. Daalder, N. Gnesotto and P. Gordon (eds), *Crescent of Crisis: US/European strategy for the Greater Middle East*, Washington, DC, and Paris: Brookings Institution and EU Institute for Security Studies.

Ebadi, S. (2006) *Iran Awakening*, London: Rider.

El-Din Shahin, E. (2005) 'Political Islam: ready for engagement?', FRIDE Working Paper, February, Madrid: Fundación para las Relaciones Internacionales y el Diálogo Exterior.

Fuller, G. (2005) 'Islamists and democracy', in T. Carothers and M. Ottaway (eds), *Uncharted Journey: promoting democracy in the Middle East*, Washington, DC: Carnegie Endowment for International Peace.

Galbraith, P. (2006) 'The case for dividing Iraq', *Time*, 5 November.

Gnesotto, N. and Grevi, G. (2006) *The New Global Puzzle: what world for the EU in 2025?*, Paris: Institute for Security Studies.

Hamzawy, A. (2005) *The Key to Arab Reform: moderate Islamists*, Washington, DC: Carnegie Endowment for International Peace.

Hiro, D. (2005) *Iran Today*, London: Politico's.

Hroub, K. (2006) *Hamas*, London: Pluto Press.

Human Rights Watch (2006) *World Report*, New York.

International Crisis Group (2006a) *After Baker-Hamilton: what to do in Iraq*, Middle East Report No. 60, 19 December.

International Crisis Group (2006b) *The Arab–Israeli Conflict: to reach a lasting peace*, Middle East Report No. 58, 5 October.

Iraq Study Group (2006) *The Iraq Study Group Report*, New York.

Malley, R. and Harling, P. (2006) 'Talks with Iran and Syria will not be an easy ride', *Financial Times*, 14 December.

Mathieson, D. and Youngs, R. (2006) 'Democracy promotion and the European Left: ambivalence confused?', Madrid: Fundación para las Relaciones Internacionales y el Diálogo Exterior (FRIDE).

Mepham, D. (2006) *Changing States: a progressive agenda for political reform in the Middle East*, London: Institute for Public Policy Research.

Monroe, E. (1963) *Britain's Moment in the Middle East 1914 to 1956*, London: Chatto and Windus.

Nakash, Y. (2006) *Reaching for Power: the Shi'a in the modern Arab world*, Princeton, NJ: Princeton University Press.

North Atlantic Treaty Organization (2005) *Economics and Security: economic transition in the Middle East and North Africa*, spring, Brussels: NATO Parliamentary Assembly.

Owen, R. (2004) *State, Power and Politics in the Making of the Modern Middle East*, London: Routledge.

Packer, G. (2006) *The Assassin's Gate: America in Iraq*, London: Faber and Faber.

Posusney, M. and Angrist, M. (eds) (2005) *Authoritarianism in the Middle East: regimes and resistance*, London and Boulder, Colo.: Lynne Rienner.

Salem, P. (2006) 'The future of Lebanon', *Foreign Affairs*, 85(6), November–December, pp. 13–22.

United Nations Development Programme (2002) *Creating Opportunities for Future Generations* (Arab Human Development Report 2002), New York: UNDP.

Woollacott, M. (2006) *After Suez: adrift in the American century*, London and New York: I. B. Tauris.

9

Looking East: The Rise of China

Steve Tsang

With the transfer of the sovereignty of Hong Kong to China in 1997, the United Kingdom's relationship with China changed. Although British Hong Kong had been hailed as a model of success where paternalistic colonial rule delivered good governance, respect for human rights and the rule of law, the UK's presence there was seen by the Chinese as the last vestige of nineteenth-century European imperialism. The handover of Hong Kong in 1997 put Sino-UK relations on a new footing. It presented the UK with the opportunity to review its interests and policies in the region as a whole. Much has happened over the last ten years, but there is still real scope for the UK to develop fresh thinking and to pursue a new approach towards this part of the world.

How then should the UK deal with the rising economic importance and political influence of China? What are the basic interests of the UK in China and are these interests in conflict with those of China? And what would a progressive UK foreign policy look like? This chapter addresses these questions. It first examines the basic factors that determine China's foreign policy and how China has sought to manage its growing economic, political and strategic power. It then outlines briefly the UK's main interests in China. It ends with a proposal for how the UK and the wider international community should deal with the rise of China, consistent with a commitment to progressive values like human rights.

The rise of China

China has undergone extraordinary economic expansion since the late 1970s, following reforms introduced by Deng Xiaoping. Before this, China's economy was largely insulated from the global economic system. This changed as China's economic reforms took hold, turning the country into a major manufacturing nation and the leading source of inexpensive consumer products. China's economy is now so well integrated into the global economy that consumers in the UK or elsewhere in the West would feel a serious impact should the Chinese economy be suddenly cut off from the outside world. Similarly, having transformed itself into the leading importer of various commodities or raw materials for manufacturing, a major economic slowdown in China would have a substantial impact on global commodity prices, and particularly on economies that depend heavily on the export of commodities.

However, rapid and significant as its economic expansion has been, China's economic importance can be overstated. There are also big question marks about the sustainability of China's economic growth. The headline figures do look impressive. China has a US$202 billion trade surplus with the United States (for 2005), an $89 billion trade surplus with the European Union (EU) including $14.8 billion with the UK (for 2004), and a $1 trillion foreign exchange reserve. China is now the third largest economy in the world – after the US and the EU (Lum and Nanto 2006). There is also a widespread sense in the West that China's economic growth will translate into political power: that China is an alternative superpower in the making. Whether this perception is accurate or not, it colours much of western commentary about China.

However, the story of China's economic development is more complex than is often suggested. Much of China's economic might is based on foreign investments, technologies and management know-how. Some of the fastest-growing parts of the Chinese economy are essentially foreign-run businesses manufacturing for export markets, and these companies could be relocated to other low-cost countries if foreign investors chose to do so. The importance of foreign direct investment (FDI) is reflected in its dramatic growth: it rose from US$109 million in 1979 to US$72 billion in 2005 (UN Conference on Trade and Development 2005: 1). China is now the largest recipient of FDI in the developing world. Indeed, foreign-invested enterprises account for 40 per cent of China's economic growth, even though they employ only 24 million of the 752 million Chinese working population (Whallay and Xin 2006: 1 and 20). This suggests that China's phenomenal economic expansion is very heavily dependent on, and vulnerable to, external developments.

It is also important to view China's recent economic progress in a historical context. On the basis of purchasing power parity calculations, China was estimated to have produced 13 per cent of global GDP in 2004 (*The Economist* 2004). In comparison, China was responsible for producing 26.2 per cent of world gross domestic product (GDP) 2,000 years ago, 22.7 per cent in the year 1000, 25 per cent in 1500, and 32.9 per cent in 1820, before a century of decline commenced (Maddison 2001: 263). It means that China's contribution to world output today is still substantially below its historical average.

Over the last twenty-five years, China has averaged annual growth rates of 9.7 per cent. But it should be remembered that China started from a very low base, accounting for less than 5 per cent of global GDP in the 1970s even though it was home to 20 per cent of the world's population (Elwell et al. 2006). Even the size of its foreign exchange reserves reveals a more complex picture than is often recognized. These reserves may be the largest in the world but their continuous rise beyond the requirement of financial prudence reveals an inability to use this huge resource efficiently (Browne 2006).[1]

Focusing on growth figures also ignores the huge costs that China's economic development model has imposed on the environment and the health of China's citizens (Economy 2004). The horrendous scale of pollution and the depletion of vital resources such as water in northern China in turn impose significant limits on China's capacity to sustain its economic growth over the longer term. The most important river in north China, the Yellow river, is the main source of water for 155 million people and for 15 per cent of China's farmland. However, only 40 per cent of the water in this 5,646-kilometre river is now fit for human consumption after treatment (Shi 2006). The breakneck rush to development has also produced a level of environmental degradation that seriously harms people's health. For example, in the Huai river basin in central north China, pollutants that have seeped into the groundwater have caused many residents to develop intestinal and liver ailments. Indeed, with an estimated 70 per cent of some parts of the Huai river being 'wastewater', scientists believe this 'has contributed to a regional death rate that is 30 per cent higher than the national average' (Beach 2001: 735).

Putting China's economic expansion in context is significant for two reasons. First, it is a useful counter to the 'China fever'. Secondly, because the Chinese themselves frequently invoke history, it can help outsiders to get a better understanding of how the Chinese view current developments within a longer time frame. This is important if we are to understand what the Chinese mean by their 'rightful' place in the world.

It is also critical for understanding China's policy for managing its own rise or re-emergence. The Communist Party's approved version of history describes China as the most advanced country and the centre of civilization, at least since it was united under the First Emperor in 221 BC.[2] This pre-eminence was then undermined by western imperialism, spearheaded by the British, in the nineteenth century. The Chinese leadership conclude from this historical narrative that China and the world flourished when China was a united country and when it dominated the world within its reach. Amongst the leadership, there is also an unspoken understanding that restoring China to the superior position it enjoyed historically will be a positive and civilizing development for the world (Tsang in de Burgh 2006: 20). The present rise of China is seen in this light.

Of course, the Chinese leadership is aware that it still has a long way to go before it can regain its former level of international power and influence. This restoration remains China's objective. In the meantime, the Chinese government would prefer the rest of the world not to see it as a threat, which might lead the major powers to seek to thwart China's rise. Hence the Chinese President, Hu Jintao, talks of China's 'peaceful development'. This rhetoric is meant to make China's rise appear less threatening to the outside world. It is with this long-term goal in mind that China has chosen to avoid asserting itself politically in the international community, although its apparent economic rise has given it scope to do so.

The guiding principle behind this approach is the concept of the 'United Front'. This is not a policy but a methodology. In essence, the United Front requires the Chinese government to identify a principal enemy, and then to win support from the intermediate zone – members of the international community that are neither friend nor foe of China – to defeat it. This is a dynamic process. After one enemy has been conquered, the Party will move on and identify from the intermediate zone a new principal enemy. This will become the target of focused attack in this new stage until it too is destroyed. The process is to be repeated until all in the intermediate zone have embraced Chinese leadership (Tsang in de Burgh 2006: 22).

In the context of the current international situation, Chinese diplomacy is directed at two objectives, as required by the idea of the United Front. The first is to pre-empt or stop Taiwan from asserting de jure independence. This is despite the fact that, in reality, Taiwan has existed as a state for as long as the People's Republic of China itself.[3]

The second is to reassure the rest of the world that even in the event of China using force against Taiwan, this would still be compatible with the 'peaceful development' of China. Underlying this objective is the argument that the question of Taiwan is a 'domestic' Chinese affair and that its resolution does not imply that China has territorial or hegemonic ambitions elsewhere.

In assessing China's rise, it is also essential to recognize that China is in the midst of great change. This has political and economic implications. It is unclear, for example, whether China's authoritarian system, based on the monopoly of power by the systemically corrupt Communist Party, can last in the longer term. Similarly, how sustainable is China's economic growth when it is being driven by foreign investments? Should the Chinese economy be hit by a major recession or a significant downturn, does the state have the capacity to deal with the many problems that were created or exacerbated in the last quarter-century?

These problems include environmental degradation, frequent incidents of major social unrest (87,000 of which occurred in 2005 alone), widening gaps between rich and poor as well as between the rural and urban areas, unemployment, a disappearance of social safety nets, and social problems created by a huge gender imbalance. In such a scenario, the Communist Party is likely to be challenged. Its capacity to reassert its authority and sustain itself will be sapped further should there be an intense struggle for power at the top. In other words, China's autocratic political system and economic juggernaut are both brittle in nature. Superficially they appear to be strong, but they can disintegrate quickly if their weak points are put under pressure (Tsang in de Burgh 2006: 26).

If China can sustain high levels of economic growth, there will probably be a dramatic expansion of the Chinese middle class in the next few decades. Despite tight government control over the media, communication and the Internet, the growth of a Chinese middle class will have political implications. Like people the world over, once they have a taste of a middle-class lifestyle, most Chinese will increasingly find the Leninist authoritarian system stifling, repressive and intolerable. When sufficient momentum has been gathered for political reform, the Communist Party will either have to face down such a challenge by repression or reform itself drastically (Tsang in de Burgh 2006: 26–7). Under Hu Jintao the Chinese government has chosen to strengthen its capacity to take the first option, though it has also tried to eliminate the need to do so by redressing some of the iniquities of Chinese society. Despite the Communist Party's determination that its basic political system and outlook should be maintained, there is no guarantee that it will be successful in this aim.

Whether the Chinese government can achieve its goal of restoring China to its 'rightful' place in the world will not be known for many decades. In the meantime China is a rising power that demands attention from the international community, including the UK. The Chinese government may be focusing its diplomacy on reassuring the world that its rise will be non-threatening in order to buy time for it to build up its 'comprehensive national strength'. But this also means that its government is at the moment publicly committed to a policy of 'peaceful development' and that it seeks to make the most of multilateralism, particularly within the United Nations (UN) framework (Zhuqing 2005).

Whether the Chinese government is sincere in its commitment to a 'harmonious world' is, in some ways, irrelevant. An international community that treats the rise of China or, for that matter, any rising great power as a destabilizing factor will almost certainly produce a self-fulfilling prophecy. It is in the interest of the international community that the emergence of China should not be destabilizing. The fact that the Chinese government is committed, at least in principle and in the immediate term, to ensure that its rise will be peaceful is an important basis on which the rest of the world should relate to China. For the international community the crucial question is how to ensure that China's publicly articulated good will and intention will be turned into reality. This is the context within which the UK should think about its foreign policy towards China.

UK interests in China

From a realist perspective the UK's primary interests in China today are trade, investment opportunities and stability. On this definition, there would seem to be little conflict between UK and Chinese interests. But a progressive UK foreign policy should also be concerned with human rights and democracy. The current leadership of China is not committed to these things; indeed, it sees liberal democracy as subversive and it rejects outside interference in countries' internal affairs.

But as a post-colonial power in Asia, where the UK no longer has vested interests to protect, the gap between what UK foreign policy in China should be on the basis of realist and progressive calculations is now much smaller than previously. In the post-colonial and post-Cold War era, for UK companies and investors to enjoy the best access to

trade and investment opportunities in China, they do not need the protection that was historically provided by physical bases and a capacity to project power. As the UK does not compete against China for
power and influence or trading and investment opportunities in East
Asia, the rise of China's standing in the region does not pose a threat
to UK interests. What UK companies need is a stable and prosperous
environment where politics and judicial outcomes are basically predictable, individual and corporate freedoms are upheld, and the
danger of war or regional conflicts is reduced.

It is therefore in the UK's interests to endorse and support China in
its public commitment to building a 'harmonious world'. But to say
this does not mean that the UK government should lose sight of the
basic differences it has with the Chinese government on issues like
democracy and human rights.

A progressive foreign policy for the UK in China requires the UK government to support liberalization and democracy in the region. This
should include Taiwan, where a vibrant democracy has existed since the
1990s. The UK has no interest in getting caught up in the dispute over
whether Taiwan is part of China or not. But it does have a strong interest in ensuring that the differences between China and Taiwan do not
result in a military confrontation. In the foreseeable future, China is
unlikely to choose the military option without what it calls 'provoca-
tions' from Taiwan (Tsang 2004a). The UK should make strong diplomatic efforts to encourage the Chinese government not to resort to force
over Taiwan. It will also need to persuade the government in Taiwan to
refrain from any course of action that will trigger China's use of force –
such as changing Taiwan's name officially from 'the Republic of China'
to the 'Republic of Taiwan' as it updates or replaces its existing constitution. The careful balance that the UK must strike in its relations with
China is therefore to support and applaud the deepening of democratization in Taiwan in a manner that will not undermine regional stability.

The UK also has a residual interest and a moral obligation to keep
a watchful eye over developments in the Hong Kong Special
Administrative Region. It might not have left a working democracy in
Hong Kong, but it did leave behind an independent judiciary that
upholds human rights and the rule of law (Tsang 2004b). The UK
should continue to endorse efforts within Hong Kong to protect
human rights and to broaden the electoral basis for choosing the Chief
Executive and the legislature. Progressive developments in Hong
Kong's political system should enable its government to deal more
effectively with unexpected demands in the twenty-first century, as the
highly educated local population increasingly expect to hold their
government democratically accountable. Given how sensitive the

Chinese government is over Hong Kong, it is vital for the UK to remind China that the rest of the world maintains a healthy interest in events within Hong Kong, without giving the impression that there is a plot to sabotage the success of the Chinese takeover, or to use Hong Kong as a 'Trojan horse' to change China politically.

Regarding the issue of human rights within the People's Republic of China itself, the UK government should not treat China differently from other major countries where the protection of rights is an issue. If China is to be encouraged to become a responsible stakeholder in the world, it must be treated in the same way as others in the same position. The UK government should focus on holding the Chinese government to its commitments to uphold its citizens' democratic rights and freedoms, as laid out in Chapter Two of the Chinese Constitution.[4] At the same time, the UK government ought to take the lead in supporting the efforts of UK and other non-governmental organizations (NGOs) to give assistance to Chinese citizens who assert their constitutional rights in Chinese courts. The best way forward for political reform in China is not to subvert Communist Party rule, but to encourage it to transform itself into a political party that upholds the rule of law. The best starting point would be to help Chinese citizens to become familiar with and adhere to the democratic rights and freedoms enshrined in the Chinese Constitution.

The UK government should also take the lead within the European Union (EU) to engage the Chinese in constructive dialogue. This should go beyond the existing 'dialogues', which are largely pro-forma events. What is really needed is for the UK to work with the EU to propose the formation of a new EU–China Human Rights Council that would monitor human rights in both the EU and China. The council should have an equal number of councillors from the EU and from China, and apply the same standards when reviewing human rights conditions in both. When it carries out its duties, its Chinese members must be given, as a matter of course, the same scope as European members to review the conditions of human rights in the EU, and the council should apply the same standards when reviewing conditions in China. It should then be required to carry out annual follow-up reviews in both territories and produce an annual report.

Admittedly, the Chinese are unlikely to find such a proposal appealing, but engaging the Chinese in serious dialogues to create such an institution should in itself be a positive process that will require the Chinese to justify a refusal to accord Chinese citizens the same standard of respect and dignity as EU citizens. To make such an initiative really valuable, the EU must resist allowing it to degenerate into a mere talking shop.

Despite the different approaches taken by the UK and Chinese governments on questions of human rights and democracy, they do share basic strategic interests over Taiwan and Hong Kong. Neither wants to see force being used across the Taiwan Strait, or Hong Kong's continued stability, good order and prosperity being destroyed. The UK's interests in both do not require it to interfere in domestic Chinese affairs. They merely demand that the UK government stay true to the principle of supporting democracy without encroaching on matters that genuinely fall under China's sovereignty.[5] Indeed, China's own national interest should require force not to be used over Taiwan and for Chinese Hong Kong to remain no less successful than under British colonial rule.

Dealing with China's rise

As to the larger question of how the UK should deal with the rise of China, it must be recognized that the basic interests of the UK and the EU, of the wider international community and of China, coincide, at least superficially. It is in everyone's interest for China's rise to be peaceful. To ensure this, the UK and other key governments need to devise a set of clear, realistic, reasonable and consistent principles for dealing with the rise of China, as they would with the rise of any new great power.

A good starting point would be for the UK, the EU and the international community to accept China's policy of 'peaceful development' at face value. In principle, all nations, including China, share the basic interest that a rising power in the twenty-first century should work multilaterally within the UN framework. The UK should therefore work with other states to hold the Chinese government to its articulated policy and stated objectives on issues of governance, democracy and international cooperation.

Taking this approach would send the message that China will not be held to European- or American-imposed standards. Instead, the Chinese would be held to the standards set by themselves in their official policies, which should be supplemented by the international standards at the UN to which the Chinese are signatories. China is one of the founders of the UN, a creator of its Charter, and the holder of one of the five permanent seats at the Security Council.[6] As such, China has long been given the opportunity to function as one of the leading powers and responsible stakeholders in the international system that came into existence at the end of the Second World War.

States may have different interpretations of what is meant by a 'responsible stakeholder', the phrase used by former US Deputy Secretary of State Robert Zoellick when discussing China. The reality is that since the end of the Second World War, a permanent member of the Security Council must, by definition, be a stakeholder in the international order. The only area for controversy is therefore what 'responsible' should mean in such a context. All permanent members of the Security Council should be expected and indeed required to behave responsibly as key stakeholders of the postwar international system. They implicitly agreed to this when they founded the UN at the San Francisco conference of 1945.

Requesting and insisting that China behave like a responsible stakeholder is in line with the basic ideas that underpin China's foreign policies today. How else can a 'harmonious world' be delivered if not by members of the UN and the permanent members of the Security Council in particular, working together through give and take at the UN? Whatever one may think of the efficacy of various UN institutions, there is as yet no alternative to the UN as an instrument to ensure the world is a relatively 'harmonious' one. Indeed, given the discomfort China and a number of UN members have at the tendency of the US administration under President George W. Bush to act unilaterally, it is as much in China's interest as it is in that of the international community that all Security Council members are required to act responsibly as stakeholders.

There are three dimensions to this requirement. The first is for the five permanent members not to abuse their privilege of the veto. The second is for them to contribute their fair share to the improvement of global governance. The third is to help address potential or immediate conflicts around the world in order to prevent their escalation into full-blown military confrontations or humanitarian crises. UK policy towards China should be seen within that context.

If the Chinese government has fallen short as a permanent member of the UN Security Council, it is not in using the privilege of veto excessively – at least not in the actual use of the veto. If a criticism is to be made of China's conduct at the UN Security Council, it is rather that it has not pulled its weight enough. As a permanent member of the Security Council, China has a moral responsibility to help improve global governance in making the UN and its agencies more effective. It should also take an activist stance in world affairs and play a leading role to ease international tension, keep peace and pre-empt humanitarian crises where possible and within its ability. It is reasonable for the international community to expect China to make contributions comparable to those of the other permanent members.

China's record in helping to improve global governance in recent years has in general terms been weak. It is a staunch protector at the UN of some of the world's most irresponsible or repressive regimes, whose abuse of human rights and poor quality of governance impose incredible sufferings on their own people, such as Burma, North Korea, Sudan and Zimbabwe. The Chinese government's insistence on non-interference in individual countries' internal affairs has made it difficult for the UN to work together to compel governments in these countries to reduce abuses. Even in the provision of development loans, which amounted to US$5 billion to African and other developing countries in 2004, the Chinese have been less than responsible. As the China Development Bank adopts a new and aggressive lending policy, it does so regardless of human rights and social and environmental considerations. Having turned itself into one of the six leading creditor nations and thus a significant source of alternative finance in Africa, this Chinese approach undermines the trend of more responsible lending by the World Bank and the International Monetary Fund, and threatens to 'reverse their work of the past decade writing off African countries' official debts and making sure that aid was spent well' (Beattie and Callan 2006).

In this connection it should be highlighted that the expectation that permanent members of the Security Council should play a key part in improving global governance, easing international tension, keeping peace and pre-empting humanitarian crises is not new. These ideas were integral to the founding of the UN. Thus for any UN member to revive and uphold them in the post-Cold War era does not imply accepting a new post-Cold War agenda imposed by the sole remaining superpower. Indeed, given the disparity in military capabilities and other national capacities that the United States enjoys when compared to other nations, it is in the interest of the international community as a whole to ensure that all members of the UN work together through the UN framework to keep international peace. In light of China's complex relations with the United States, it has an interest in strengthening the UN. To do so effectively, China must actively put its own resources at the disposal of the UN as the latter implements its post-Cold War agenda.

China's global role

China is potentially well placed to exert positive influence on some critical international issues. These include North Korea's nuclear weapons programme, the Iranian nuclear programme and the human-itarian crisis in Darfur. One must not, of course, overestimate the diplomatic leverage that China has in these countries. However, is there any permanent member of the Security Council that enjoys greater access and influence than China over the governments of North Korea, Iran and Sudan? For the UK, the foreign policy priority should be encouraging the Chinese to play a constructive role in each of these cases.

China has undoubtedly made a positive contribution in hosting the six-power talks in order to defuse the tension over the North Korean nuclear weapons programme. But whatever efforts China might have made behind the scenes and outside of the six-power talks in engag-ing positively with the North Korean regime, the testing of a nuclear device by North Korea in October 2006 was a huge setback and sug-gests the need for new thinking. Although the international commu-nity responded robustly to North Korea's action, these measures are unlikely to be sufficient to deter Pyongyang from further irresponsi-ble actions. Neither the UN Security Council's strong condemnation of the failed long-range ballistic missile tests by North Korea in July 2006, nor its warning to Pyongyang not to proceed with a nuclear test in early October has so far had the desired effect on North Korea. The UN sanctions, which fell short of requiring all nations to stop sending food and fuel to North Korea, are unlikely to force North Korea to abandon its nuclear weapons programme. Even compre-hensive sanctions involving the full cooperation of pivotal countries like China and South Korea are unlikely to be sufficient to neutralize the new threats that the North Koreans are posing to regional peace and stability.

Given China's interest in preventing the collapse of the North Korean regime, it should use its influence more constructively and proactively. The international community, including the UK and other European states, should encourage it to do so. There are no easy options, but China should be urged to engage in shuttle diplomacy between North Korea, the United States and the UN on a sustained basis, to attempt to break the logjam and work out the basis for a solu-tion. China made moves in this direction when it sent State Councillor and former Foreign Minister Tang Jiaxuan as a personal emissary of Hu Jintao to Washington and then Pyongyang to find a way to reopen the six-power talks after the North Korean test. Tang's success in reopening the talks showed what Chinese diplomacy is capable of achieving.

Over Iran, the United Kingdom, France and Germany have been working hard as part of a European initiative to persuade the Iranians to work with the International Atomic Energy Agency. They, and the wider international community, should encourage China to use its influence to support not undermine these efforts. Given that China is Iran's leading trading partner, and China is heavily dependent on Iran as a source of energy, Beijing has an obvious interest in doing so.

Darfur is another critical issue where the UK, the Europeans and the wider international community should work with the Chinese to encourage them to play a more constructive role. Since 2003, it is estimated that more than 200,000 people have been killed and over 2 million displaced (Majendie 2006). Given its close political and economic relationship with the government of Sudan, China has been very reluctant to criticize Khartoum's policy towards Darfur. However, there is some evidence that the Chinese government has been affected by international criticism of its policy towards Sudan. For example, it endorsed a peacekeeping operation in southern Sudan, against its strong anti-interventionist instincts. In addition, under international criticism, the Chinese did not prevent the UN Security Council from granting the International Criminal Court jurisdiction over gross human rights abuses committed in Darfur. Beijing is concerned about its global image and this creates opportunities to influence Chinese policy.

This does not require outsiders adopting a hectoring tone with China. But it could mean trying to build on positive features of China's policy towards Africa. For example, China currently provides more UN peacekeepers than any other permanent member of the UN Security Council (Blasko 2006: 178). China could dramatically improve its image as a responsible international player if it was prepared to commit Chinese troops to and offer to take over command of a UN force in Darfur. In these circumstances, the Sudanese government might be less resistant to a UN operation.[7]

Taking a lead over Darfur would also enhance China's standing in the international community and strengthen its soft power. China has benefited from the dramatic decline of US soft power under the Bush administration. China is already viewed more favourably than the US by people in various countries (Pew 2006). This is partly because of its economic success. Its export of competitively priced high-quality consumer products has helped to raise living standards elsewhere. Its ability to deliver high levels of economic growth and to maintain stability has also appeared as a model for some developing countries. But China needs to do more to build up its soft power. To do this it must play a leading role in improving global governance, easing global tensions and preventing and resolving global crises within the framework of the UN.

Conclusion

A rising China committed to a policy of 'peaceful development' as a means to build a 'harmonious world' is one that the UK and the wider international community should welcome and embrace. The Chinese government may have a very different long-term ambition about its own position in the world. The international community should be aware of this, but should nonetheless treat China in the same way as any other power on the rise. Even with the best intentions, a rising power not checked and balanced by others cannot but behave like a hegemon when it can do so without having to pay a price. Since China has reassured the world that it has no wish to be a hegemon and is committed to 'peaceful development' within the UN framework, the best way for the UK and the international community to respond is to take the words of the Chinese government at face value and then work closely with it to make sure it adheres to its avowed policy.

Taking the Chinese policy of 'peaceful development' seriously does not mean accepting China's official interpretation of it uncritically. But it should mean that the UK, the Europeans and the wider international community work together with the Chinese to build a greater consensus on these issues and to foster deeper and more constructive global cooperation.

Notes

1 At about US$1 trillion it is about 1¼ to 1½ times the value of China's total imports or equivalent to roughly 45 per cent of economic output in 2005.
2 In reality China was a united country or empire for substantially less than half of its 4,000 years of recorded history, and its pre-eminence was episodic, being true only during part of the Qin, Han, Sui, Tang and Qing dynasties.
3 The People's Republic of China's historical claim over Taiwan is at best dubious but in 1950 its government elevated Taiwan into a 'sacred' territory that must be reunited with mother China, after US President Harry Truman ordered the US navy to prevent a Chinese invasion of Taiwan following the outbreak of the Korean War.
4 The Chinese Constitution (in English) is readily available on the Internet: http://english.people.com.cn/constitution/constitution.html.
5 What appears like an inherent contradiction – that supporting democracy in someone else's country implies a degree of interference in others' domestic affairs – does not need to apply. The UK can support the development of democracy in China, Taiwan and Hong Kong without interfering in their domestic affairs, as the constitutions of China and Taiwan formally uphold democracy, and Hong Kong's Basic Law also commits its government to

develop democracy eventually. For the UK to support democracy in China in accordance with the Chinese Constitution does not require interference in Chinese affairs any more than Chinese support of democracy in the UK requires interference in the British constitutional convention.

6 The highly complex history of China's representation at the UN is irrelevant here. When China was a party to the creation of the UN it was represented by a national government, though that government subsequently lost control of the mainland to the Communist Party of China. The present Chinese government has inherited the rights as well as the obligations of its predecessor – like successor states elsewhere, such as Russia replacing and inheriting the former Soviet Union's seats and legacies at the UN.

7 Chinese troops on UN missions have never taken part in operations to seize alleged war criminals and bring them to trial at the Hague, which should provide reasonable grounds for the Sudanese government to work on the basis that their presence in Darfur would not necessarily result in some members of the Sudanese government being arrested.

References

Beach, M. (2001) 'Water, pollution and public heath in China', *The Lancet*, 358(9283), 1 September, p. 735.

Beattie, A. and Callan, E. (2006) 'China loans create "new wave of Africa debt", *Financial Times*, 7 December; available at: www.ft.com/cms/s/640a5986-863a-11db-86d5-0000779e2340.html.

Blasko, D. J. (2006) *The Chinese Army Today: tradition and transformation for the 21st Century*, London and New York: Routledge.

Browne, A. (2006) 'China's reserves near milestone, underscoring its financial clout', *Wall Street Journal*, 17 October.

de Burgh, H. (ed.) (2006) *China and Britain: the potential impact of China's development*, London: Smith Institute.

The Economist (2004) 'Dragon and the Eagle', 30 September.

Economy, E. (2004) *The River Runs Black: the environmental challenge to China's future*, Ithaca, NY: Cornell University Press.

Elwell, C. K., Lebonte, M. and Morrison, W. M. (2006), *CRS Report for Congress: Is China A Threat to the US?*, Congressional Research Service, CRS-5 and CRS-13.

Lum, T. and Nanto, D. K. (2006) *China's Trade with the US and the World*, Congressional Research Service, CRS-44–45, January; available at: www.fas.org/sgp/crs/row/RL31403.pdf.

Maddison, A. (2001) *The World Economy Volume 1: A Millennial Perspective*, Paris: Organisation for Economic Cooperation and Development.

Majendie, P. (2006) 'Activists around the world focus on Darfur', Reuters, 17 September; available at: http://today.reuters.com/news/articlenews.aspx?type=worldNews&storyID=2006-09-17T184817Z_01_L17479149_RTRUKOC_0_US-SUDAN-DARFUR.xml.

Pew Global Attitudes Project (2006) 'America's image slips, but allies share US concerns over Iran, Hamas'; available at: http://pewglobal.org/reports/display.php?PageID=825.

Shi, T. (2006) '60pc of Yellow River's water unfit to drink', *South China Morning Post*, 14 December; available at: http://china.scmp.com/chitoday/ZZZVAAPVKVE.html.

Tsang, S. (ed.) (2004a) *Peace and Security Across the Taiwan Strait*, Basingstoke: Palgrave Macmillan.

Tsang, S. (2004b) *A Modern History of Hong Kong*, London: I. B. Tauris.

United Nations Conference on Trade and Development (2005), *Trade and Development Report 2005: new features of global interdependence*, Geneva: UNCTAD.

Whallay, J. and Xin, X. (2006) *China's FDI and non-FDI Economies and the Sustainability of Future High Chinese Growth*, Working Paper 12249, Cambridge, Mass.: National Bureau of Economic Research.

Zhuqing, J. (2006) 'Hu calls for a harmonious world at summit', *China Daily*, 19 September; available at: www.chinadaily.com.cn/english/doc/2005-09/16/content_478349.htm.

10

Multilateralism and Global Governance: Accountability and Effectiveness

David Held

This chapter examines multilateralism and global governance arrangements with a view to learning from both their weaknesses and their strengths. The first half of the chapter maps the guiding principles and institutional structures of the multilateral order set down after 1945. Placing these in the context of contemporary globalization, it explores the scope for human development as well as the risks of disruption and destruction that prevail today. The problems and dilemmas of global problem solving are assessed. In the second half of the chapter it is argued that those policies that have largely set the global agenda in recent years – broadly, the Washington security doctrine and the Washington Consensus – are failing, and alternatives are proposed. A human security approach allied to a change of direction in the governance of the world economy would, it is contended, buttress international law and multilateral institutions. It would also be consistent with the universal principles and institutional advances of the post-1945 world. A progressive UK government should champion this approach.

Thinking about the future of a rule-based global order on the basis of the early years of the twenty-first century does not give grounds for optimism. From 9/11 to the 2006 war in the Middle East, terrorism, conflict, territorial struggle and the clash of identities appear to define the moment. The wars in Afghanistan, Iraq, Israel–Lebanon and elsewhere suggest that political violence is an irreducible feature of our age. Perversely, globalization seems to have dramatized the significance of differences between peoples; far from the globalization of communications easing understanding and the translation of ideas, it seems to have highlighted what it is that people do not have in common and find dislikeable about each other. Moreover, the contemporary drivers of political nationalism – self-determination, secure borders, geopolitical and geoeconomic advantage – place an emphasis on the pursuit of the national interest above concerns with what it is that human beings might have in common.

Yet, it is easy to overstate the moment and exaggerate from one set of historical experiences. While each of the elements mentioned poses a challenge to a rule-based global order, it is a profound mistake to forget that the twentieth century established a series of cosmopolitan steps towards the delimitation of the nature and form of political community, sovereignty and 'reasons of state'. These steps were laid down after the First and Second World Wars, which brought humanity to the edge of the abyss – not once, but twice. At a time as difficult as the start of the twenty-first century, it is important to recall why these steps were built and remind ourselves of their significance.

Guiding principles and institutional stepping stones

From the foundation of the United Nations (UN) system to the European Union (EU), from changes in the laws of war to the entrenchment of human rights, from the emergence of international environmental regimes to the establishment of the International Criminal Court (ICC), people have sought to reframe human activity and embed it in law, rights and responsibilities. Many of these developments were initiated against the background of formidable threats to humankind – above all, Nazism, fascism and Stalinism. Those involved in them affirmed the importance of universal principles, human rights and the rule of law in the face of strong temptations simply to pull the shutters closed and defend the position of only some countries and nations. They rejected the view of national and moral particularists that belonging to a given community limits and determines the moral worth of individuals and the nature of their freedom, and they defended the moral status of each and every person. At the centre of such thinking is the cosmopolitan view that human wellbeing is not defined by geographical or cultural locations, that national or ethnic or gendered boundaries should not determine the limits of rights or responsibilities for the satisfaction of basic human needs, and that all human beings require equal moral respect and concern. The principles of equal respect, equal concern, and the priority of the vital needs of all human beings are not principles for some remote utopia; for they are at the centre of significant post-Second World War legal and political developments (Held 2002 and 2004).

These principles set down standards or boundaries which no agent, whether a representative of a global body, state or civil association, should be able to violate. Focused on the claims of each person as an individual, they espouse the idea that human beings are in a fundamental sense equal, and that they deserve equal political treatment: that is, treatment based upon the equal care and consideration of their agency, irrespective of the community in which they were born or brought up. After more than 200 years of nationalism, sustained nation-state formation and seemingly endless conflicts over territory and resources, such principles could be thought of as out of place. But such principles are already enshrined in the law of war, human rights law and the statute of the ICC, among many other international rules and legal arrangements.

Given the weaknesses of the UN in the face of contemporary conflicts (from Darfur to the war in Israel–Lebanon in 2006), its inability to enforce many of its resolutions (on the Israel–Palestine conflict, for example), and its failure to provide a coherent set of policies on such pressing transnational issues as climate change and nuclear proliferation, it can also be forgotten that the multilateral order is effective across a range of problems and issues. A thickening web of multilateral agreements, institutions, regimes and transgovernmental policy networks has evolved over the last six decades, intervening in and regulating many aspects of national and transnational life, from finance to flora and fauna. This evolving complex is, of course, far from a coherent system of global governance, with ultimate legal authority and the means to uphold international law, but it is much more than a system of limited intergovernmental cooperation. With the UN as its institutional core, it comprises a vast range of formal suprastate bodies and regional organizations, as well as regimes and transnational policy networks embracing government officials, technocrats, corporate representatives, pressure groups and non-governmental organizations (NGOs) (see Held and McGrew 2002: ch. 5). Although these bodies and networks lack the kind of centralized, coordinated political programme that is associated with national government, it would be a mistake to overlook the expanding jurisdiction or scope of global policy making, most especially the substantial range of issues it touches on and its growing intrusion into the domestic affairs of states – illustrated, for example, by the rulings of the World Trade Organization's trade dispute panels.

Moreover, global governance today has some of the characteristics of a multilayered, multidimensional and multi-actor system (see Held and McGrew 2002a: 78–84). It is multilayered in so far as the development and implementation of global policies involve a process of political coordination between suprastate, transnational, national and often substate agencies. Attempts to combat HIV/AIDS, for instance, require the coordinated efforts of global, regional, national and local agencies. It is multidimensional in so far as the engagement and configuration of agencies often differs from sector to sector and issue to issue, giving rise to significantly differentiated political patterns. The politics of, for example, global financial regulation is different in many ways from the politics of global trade regulation. Further, many of the agencies of, and participants in, the global governance complex are no longer purely intergovernmental bodies. There is involvement by representatives of transnational civil society, from Greenpeace to the Make Poverty History campaign and an array of NGOs; of the corporate sector, from British Petroleum to the International Chamber of Commerce and other trade or industrial associations; and of mixed public–private organizations, such as the International Organization of Security Commissions (IOSCO). Accordingly, global governance is a multi-actor complex in so far as diverse agencies participate in the development of global public policy. Of course, this broad pluralistic conception of global governance does not presume that all states or interests have an equal voice in, let alone an equal influence over, its agenda or programmes.

Another important feature of the formulation and implementation of global public policy is that it occurs within an expanding array of different kinds of network – transgovernmental networks (such as the Financial Action Task Force (FATF)), trisectoral networks involving public, corporate and NGO groups (such as the World Commission on Dams Forum), and transnational networks (such as the International Accounting Standards Board (IASB)) (McGrew 2002; Slaughter 2004). These networks – which can be ad hoc or institutional – have become increasingly important in coordinating the work of experts and administrators within governments, international organizations and the corporate and NGO sectors. They function to set policy agendas, disseminate information, formulate rules and establish and implement policy programmes – from the money-laundering measures of the FATF to global initiatives to counter AIDS. While many of these networks have a clear policy and administrative function, they have also become mechanisms through which civil society and corporate interests can become embedded in the global policy process (examples are the Global Water Partnership and the Global Alliance for Vaccines and

Immunization). In part, the growth of these networks is a response to the overload and politicization of multilateral bodies, but it is also an outcome of the growing technical complexity of global policy issues and the communications revolution.

To this complex pattern of global governance and rule making can be added the new configurations of regional governance. The EU has taken Europe from the edge of catastrophe in two world wars to a world in which sovereignty is pooled across a growing number of areas of common concern. For all its flaws, it is, judged in the context of the history of states, a remarkable political formation. In addition, there has been a significant acceleration in regional relations beyond Europe: in the Americas, in Asia-Pacific and, to a lesser degree, in Africa. While the form taken by this type of regionalism is very different from the model of the EU, it has nonetheless had significant consequences for political power, particularly in Asia-Pacific, which has seen the formation of the Association of South East Asian Nations (ASEAN), Asia-Pacific Economic Cooperation (APEC), the ASEAN Regional Forum (ARF), the Pacific Basin Economic Council (PBEC) and many other groupings (see Payne 2003). Furthermore, as regionalism has deepened, and as old and new regional groups have sought to consolidate their relations with each other, so interregional diplomacy has intensified. In this respect, regionalism has not been a barrier to globalization; it has been a building block for it (see Hettne 1997).

At the core of all these developments is the reconfiguration of aspects of political power since 1945. While many states retain the ultimate legal claim to effective supremacy over what occurs within their own territories, this claim has to be understood in relation to the expanding jurisdiction of institutions of global and regional governance and the constraints of, as well as the obligations derived from, new and changing forms of international regulation. This is especially evident in the EU, but it is also evident in the operation of intergovernmental organizations (IGOs) such as the World Trade Organization (WTO) (Moore 2003). Moreover, even where sovereignty still seems intact, states by no means retain sole command of what transpires within their own territorial boundaries. Complex global systems, from the financial to the ecological, connect the fate of communities in one locale to the fate of communities in distant regions of the world. There has, in other words, been a transformation or an 'unbundling' of the relationship between sovereignty, territoriality and political outcomes (see Ruggie 1993).

This unbundling involves a plurality of actors, a variety of political processes and diverse levels of coordination and operation. Specifically, it includes:

- different forms of intergovernmental arrangements embodying various levels of legalization, types of instrument utilized and responsiveness to stakeholders;
- an increasing number of public agencies, such as central bankers, maintaining links with similar agencies in other countries and, thus, forming transgovernmental networks for the management of various global issues;
- diverse business actors – that is, firms, their associations and organizations such as international chambers of commerce – establishing their own transnational regulatory mechanisms to manage issues of common concern;
- NGOs and transnational advocacy networks – that is, leading actors in global civil society – playing a role in various domains of global governance and at various stages of the global public policy-making process; and
- public bodies, business actors and NGOs collaborating in many issue areas in order to provide novel approaches to social problems through multistakeholder networks.

There is nothing inevitable, it should be stressed, about these trends and developments. While they are highly significant to understanding the nature and form of global politics, they are contingent upon many factors, and could be halted or even reversed by protracted global conflicts or cataclysmic events.

Political opportunity and vulnerability

The growing interconnectedness of countries – or the process of 'globalization' as it is often called – can readily be measured by mapping the ways in which trade, finance, communication, pollutants and violence, among many other factors, flow across borders and lock the well-being of countries into common patterns (see Held et al. 1999). The deep drivers of this process are likely to be operative for the foreseeable future, irrespective of the exact political form that globalization takes. Among these drivers are:

- the changing infrastructure of global communications linked to the information technology revolution;
- the development of global markets in goods and services, connected to the new worldwide distribution of information;

- the pressure of migration and the movement of peoples, linked to shifts in patterns of economic demand, in demography and in environmental degradation;
- the end of the Cold War and the diffusion of democratic and consumer values across many of the world's regions, alongside some marked reactions to this; and
- the emergence of a new type and form of global civil society, with the crystallization of elements of a global public opinion.

Despite the fractures and conflicts of our age, societies are becoming more interconnected and interdependent. As a result, developments at the local level – whether economic, political or social – can acquire almost instantaneous global consequences and vice versa (Held 2004: chs 4–6; Giddens 1990: ch. 2). Link to this the advances in science across many fields, often now instantly diffused through global communication networks, and the global arena becomes an extraordinary potential space both for human development and for disruption and destruction by individuals, groups or states (cf. Rees 2003).

The serious challenges faced at the global level fit into three broad categories – those concerned with sharing our planet (global warming, biodiversity and ecosystem losses, water deficits), sustaining our humanity (poverty, conflict prevention, global infectious diseases) and our rulebook (nuclear proliferation, toxic waste disposal, intellectual property rights, genetic research rules, trade rules, finance and tax rules) (see Rischard 2002: 66). In our increasingly interconnected world, these global problems cannot be solved by any one nation state acting alone. They call for collective and collaborative action – something that the nations of the world need to be much better at if these pressing issues are to be tackled. Is there appropriate governance capacity to resolve these challenges? If not, can it be put in place?

Among the spectrum of international organizations are those whose primary concerns are technical: the Universal Postal Union, the International Civil Aviation Organization, and the World Meteorological Organization, for example. These agencies have tended to work effectively, often providing extensions to the services offered by individual nation states (Burnheim 1985: 222). To the extent that their tasks have been sharply focused, they have usually been politically uncontroversial. At the opposite pole lie organizations like the World Bank, the International Monetary Fund (IMF), the UN Educational, Scientific and Cultural Organization (UNESCO) and, of course, the UN itself. Preoccupied with central questions of war and peace, and of resource allocation, these bodies have been highly politicized and controversial. Unlike the smaller, technically based agencies, these organizations are at the centre of continual conflict over aspects of their nature and form, and over the policy that they generate or fail to develop.

The difficulties faced by these more contested agencies and organizations stem from many sources, including the tension between universal values and state sovereignty built into them from their beginning. In the first instance, many global political and legal developments since 1945 do not just curtail sovereignty, but in fact support it in many ways. From the UN Charter to the Rio Declaration on the environment, international agreements often serve to entrench the international power structure. The division of the globe into powerful nation states, with distinctive sets of geopolitical interests, was embedded in the articles and statutes of leading IGOs (see Held 1995: chs 5 and 6). Thus, the sovereign rights of states are frequently affirmed alongside more cosmopolitan principles. Moreover, while the case can be made that cosmopolitan principles are part of 'the working creed' of officials in some UN agencies, such as the United Nations Children's Fund (UNICEF), UNESCO and the World Health Organization (WHO), and NGOs such as Amnesty International, Save the Children and Oxfam, they can scarcely be said to be constitutive of the conceptual world and working practices of many politicians, democratic or otherwise (Barry 1998: 34–5).

Secondly, the cosmopolitan reach of contemporary regional and global law, referred to at the outset, rarely comes with a commitment to establish institutions with the resources and clout to make declared cosmopolitan values and objectives effective. The susceptibility of the UN to the agendas of the most powerful states, the partiality of many of its enforcement operations (or complete lack of them), the underfunding of its organizations, the continued dependency of its programmes on financial support from a few major states, and the weaknesses of the policing of many environmental regimes (regional and global) are all indicative of the disjuncture between cosmopolitan principles (and aspirations) and their partial and one-sided application.

Problems and dilemmas of global problem solving

Problem-solving capacities at the global and regional level are weakened by a number of structural difficulties, which compound the problems of generating and implementing urgent policy with respect to global goods and bads. These difficulties are rooted in the postwar settlement and the subsequent development of the multilateral order. Four deep-rooted problems need highlighting (see Held 2004: ch. 6).

A first set of problems emerges as a result of the development of globalization, which generates public policy challenges that span the 'domestic' and the 'foreign', and the interstate order with its clear political boundaries and lines of responsibility. A growing number of issues can be characterized as intermestic – that is, issues which cross the *inter*national and do*mestic* (Rosenau 2002). These are often insufficiently understood or acted upon. There is a fundamental lack of ownership of many problems at the global level. It is far from clear which global public issues – such as global warming or the loss of biodiversity – are the responsibilities of which international agencies, and which issues ought to be addressed by which particular agencies. The institutional fragmentation and competition leads not just to the problem of overlapping jurisdictions among agencies, but also to the problem of issues falling between agencies. This latter problem is also manifest between the global level and national governments.

A second set of difficulties relates to the inertia found in the system of international agencies, or the inability of these agencies to mount collective problem-solving solutions when faced with uncertainty about lines of responsibility and frequent disagreement over objectives, means and costs. This often leads to the situation where the cost of inaction is greater than the cost of taking action. Bill Gates recently referred to the developed world's efforts in tackling malaria as 'a disgrace'; malaria causes an estimated 500 million bouts of illness a year, kills an African child every thirty seconds, and costs an estimated $12 billion a year in lost income, and, yet, investment in insecticide-treated bed nets and other forms of protective treatment would be a fraction of this (Meikle 2005: 22). The failure to act decisively in the face of urgent global problems not only compounds the costs of dealing with these problems in the long run, but can also reinforce a widespread perception that these agencies are not just ineffective but unaccountable and unjust.

A third set of problems arises because there is no clear division of labour among the myriad of international governmental agencies; functions often overlap, mandates frequently conflict, and aims and objectives too often get blurred. There are a number of competing and overlapping organizations and institutions, all of which have some stake in shaping different sectors of global public policy. This is true, for example, in the area of health and social policy where the World Bank, the IMF and the WHO often have different or competing priorities (Deacon 2003); or, more specifically, in the area of AIDS/HIV treatment, where the WHO, Global Fund, the Joint UN Programme on HIV/AIDS (UNAIDS) and many other interests vie to shape reproductive health care and sexual practices.

A fourth set of difficulties relates to an accountability deficit, itself linked to two interconnected problems: the power imbalances among states as well as those between state and non-state actors in the shaping and making of global public policy. Multilateral bodies need to be fully representative of the states involved in them, and they rarely are. The main problem can be qualitative, 'how well various stakeholders are represented' (Kaul et al. 2003: 30). Having a seat at the negotiating table in a major IGO or at a major conference does not ensure effective representation. For even if there is parity of formal representation (a condition often lacking), it is generally the case that developed countries have large delegations equipped with extensive negotiating and technical expertise, while poorer developing countries frequently depend on one-person delegations, or have even to rely on the sharing of a delegate. In addition, there should be dialogue and consultation between state and non-state actors, and these conditions are only partially met in many multilateral decision-making bodies.

Underlying these institutional difficulties is the breakdown of symmetry and congruence between decision-makers and decision-takers (see Held 1995: part I). The point has been well articulated recently by Kaul and her associates in their work on global public goods. They speak about the forgotten *equivalence* principle (see Kaul et al. 2003: 27–8). At its simplest, the principle suggests that those who are significantly affected by a global good or bad should have a say in its provision or regulation: that is, the span of a good's benefits and costs should be matched with the span of the jurisdiction in which decisions are taken about that good (see Held 2004: 97–101). Yet, all too often, there is a breakdown of 'equivalence' between decision-makers and decision-takers, between decision-makers and stakeholders, and between the inputs and outputs of the decision-making process. To take some topical examples: a decision to permit the 'harvesting' of rainforests (which releases carbon dioxide into the atmosphere) may contribute to ecological damage far beyond the borders which formally limit the responsibility of a given set of decision-makers. A decision to build nuclear plants near the frontiers of a neighbouring country is a decision likely to be taken without consulting those in the nearby country (or countries), despite the many risks for them. Accordingly, the challenge is to find ways to align the circles of those to be involved in decision making with the spillover range of the good under negotiation; to create organizational mechanisms for policy innovation across borders; and to find new ways of financing urgent global public goods.

There are many organizational questions that need addressing, and the time has come, to say the least, to address them. Surprisingly perhaps, it is an opportune moment to pursue this project. With the resurgence of nationalism and unilateralism in US foreign policy, uncertainty over the future of Europe after the 'no' votes to an EU constitution in France and Holland in 2005, the crisis of global trade talks and development strategies, the growing confidence of China, India and Brazil in world economic fora (especially in relation to world trade negotiations), and the unsettled relations between Islam and the West, the political tectonic plates appear to be shifting. It is highly unlikely that the multilateral order can survive for very much longer – a decade or two perhaps – in its current form.

Moreover, the policies of what can be called the 'old order' have not fulfilled expectations. The dominant policy packages of the last several years in economics and security – that is, those policies which have largely set the global agenda – are failing. The Washington Consensus and Washington security doctrines – or market fundamentalism and unilateralism – have dug their own graves (Held 2004; Barnett et al. 2005). The fastest-developing countries in the world (China, India, Vietnam, Uganda, among them) are successful because they have not followed the Washington Consensus agenda (see Rodrik 2005), and the conflicts that have most successfully been defused (the Balkans, Sierra Leone, Liberia, Sri Lanka, among others) are ones that have benefited from concentrated multilateral support and a human security agenda (see the Human Security Centre 2005). Here are obvious clues as to how to proceed, and to build alternatives to both the Washington Consensus and the Washington security doctrines. We need to follow these clues and learn from the mistakes of the past if the rule of law, human rights and the multilateral order are to be advanced.

9/11, the war in Iraq and human security

If 9/11 was not a defining moment in human history, it was for today's generations. The terrorist attack on the World Trade Center and the Pentagon was an atrocity of immense proportions. Yet after 9/11, the US and its allies could have decided that the most important things to do were to strengthen international law in the face of global terrorist threats, and to enhance the role of multilateral institutions. They could have decided it was important that no single power or group should act as judge, jury and executioner. They could have decided that global hotspots like the Middle East which help feed global terrorism should be the main centre of international attention. They could have decided to be tough on terrorism and tough on the conditions which lead people to imagine (falsely) that al-Qaeda and similar groups are agents of justice in the modern world. But they have systematically failed to pursue this agenda. In general, the world after 9/11 has become more polarized, international law weaker, and multilateral institutions more vulnerable.

The wars in Afghanistan in 2002 and Iraq in 2003 gave priority to a narrow security agenda which is at the heart of the Bush administration's foreign policy doctrine. This doctrine contradicts many of the core tenets of international politics and international agreements since 1945 (Ikenberry 2002). It sets out a policy which is essentially hegemonic, which seeks order through dominance, which pursues the pre-emptive and preventive use of force, which relies on a conception of leadership based on a coalition of the willing and which aims to make the world safe for freedom and democracy – by globalizing American rules and conceptions of justice. The doctrine was enacted as the 'war on terror'. The language of inter-state warfare was preserved intact and projected on to a new enemy. As a result, the terrorists of 9/11 were dignified as soldiers and war prosecuted against them. But this strategy was a distortion and simplification of reality and a predictable failure. In pursuing dominance through force, the 'war on terror' killed more innocent civilians in Iraq than the terrorists on 9/11, humiliated and tortured many Iraqis, and acted as a spur to terrorist recruitment (see Soros 2006). It showed little, if any, understanding of the dignity, pride and fears of others, and of the way the fate and fortune of all peoples are increasingly tied together in our global age. And it unleashed an orgy of sectarian killing among the Sunni and Shia in Iraq, and the displacement of over 300,000 people. Instead of seeking to extend the rule of law, seeking dialogue with the Muslim world, strengthening the multilateral order and developing the means to deal with the criminals of 9/11, the US and its allies (notably the UK) pursued old-war techniques and have made nearly everyone less secure.

The new doctrine has many serious implications (Hoffmann 2003, 2006). Among these is the return to an old realist understanding of international relations as a sphere in which states rightly pursue their national interests unencumbered by attempts to establish internationally recognized limits (self-defence, collective security) on their ambitions. Yet if this 'freedom' is granted to the US, why not also to Russia, China, India, Pakistan, Israel, Iran and so on? It cannot be consistently argued that all states bar one should accept limits on their self-defined goals. The flaws of international law and the UN Charter can either be addressed, or taken as an excuse for further weakening international institutions and legal arrangements.

Today, the attempt to develop international law and to enhance the capacity of international institutions for peacekeeping and peacemaking is threatened not just by the dangers posed by extensive terrorist networks, but also by the deeply misguided responses to them. There are a number of very pressing issues which need to be addressed if we are to salvage the achievements of the post-1945 world and build on them in a manner that provides not just security in the narrowest sense – protection from the immediate threat of coercive power and violence – but security in the broadest sense – protection for all those whose lives are vulnerable for whatever reason: economic, political or environmental. The way forward involves almost the opposite of what has been promulgated: that is to say, the development of a human security agenda that is based on multilateralism and common rules, which seeks order through law and social justice, which seeks to relink security and the human rights agenda, which seeks to strengthen global governance, and which aims to make the world safe for humanity, with global justice and impartial rules.

A human security agenda requires three things of governments and international institutions – all currently missing (Held and Kaldor 2001). First, there must be a commitment to the rule of law and the development of multilateral institutions – not the prosecution of war as the first response. Civilians of all faiths and nationalities need protection. Terrorists and all those who systematically violate the sanctity of life and human rights must be brought before an international criminal court that commands cross-national support. This does not preclude internationally sanctioned military action to arrest suspects, dismantle terrorist networks and deal with aggressive rogue states – far from it (see Hoffmann 2004). But such action should always be understood as a robust form of international law enforcement; above all, as a way, as Mary Kaldor (1999) has most clearly put it, of protecting civilians and bringing suspects to trial. In short, if justice is to be dispensed impartially, no power can arrogate to itself the global role of setting standards, weighing risks and meting out justice. What is needed is momentum towards global, not American or Russian or Chinese or British or French, justice. We must act together to sustain and strengthen a world based on common principles and rules (Solana 2003).

Secondly, a sustained effort has to be undertaken to generate new forms of global political legitimacy for international institutions involved in security and peacemaking. This must include the condemnation of systematic human rights violations wherever they occur, and the establishment of new forms of political and economic accountability. This cannot be equated with an occasional or one-off effort to create a new momentum for peace and the protection of human rights, as is all too typical.

And, finally, there must be a head-on acknowledgement that the global polarization of wealth, income and power cannot be left to markets to resolve alone. Those who are poorest and most vulnerable, linked into geopolitical situations where their economic and political claims have been neglected for generations, may provide fertile ground for terrorist recruiters. The project of economic globalization has to be connected to manifest principles of social justice; the latter need to frame global market activity (see below).

Of course, terrorist crimes of the kind witnessed on 9/11 and on many occasions since (in Chechnya, Saudi Arabia, Pakistan, Morocco, Spain, the UK and elsewhere) may often be the work of the simply deranged and the fanatic, and so there can be no guarantee that a more just and institutionally stable world will be a more peaceful one in all respects. But if we turn our back on this project, there is no hope of ameliorating the social basis of disadvantage often experienced in the poorest and most dislocated countries. Gross injustices, linked to a sense of hopelessness born of generations of neglect, feed anger and hostility. Popular support against terrorism depends upon convincing people that there is a legal and peaceful way of addressing their grievances. Without this sense of confidence in public institutions and processes, the defeat of terrorism becomes a hugely difficult task.

Elsewhere, I have sought to set this agenda out at length (Held 2004; Barnett et al. 2005). Here I will simply list some of the steps which could be taken to help implement a human security agenda at the heart of discussion in many parts of the world today ('old Europe', Latin America, Africa and Asia). These include:

- relinking the security and human rights agenda in international law – the two sides of international humanitarian law which, together, specify grave and systematic abuse of human security and well-being, and the minimum conditions required for the development of human agency;
- reforming UN Security Council procedures to improve the specification of, and legitimacy of, credible reasons for, credible threshold tests for, and credible promises in relation to, armed intervention in the affairs of a state – the objective being to link these directly to a set of conditions which would constitute a severe threat to peace, and/or a threat to the minimum conditions

for the well-being of human agency, sufficient to justify the use of force, and which would lock the deployment of force into a clear framework of international humanitarian law;

- recognizing the necessity to dislodge and amend the now out-moded 1945 geopolitical settlement as the basis of decision making in the Security Council, and to extend representation to all regions on a fair and equal footing;
- expanding the remit of the Security Council, or creating a parallel Social and Economic Security Council, to examine and, where necessary, intervene in the full gambit of human crises – physical, social, biological, environmental – which can threaten human agency; and
- founding a World Environmental Organization to promote the implementation of existing environmental agreements and treaties, and whose main mission would be to ensure that the development of world trading and financial systems is compatible with the sustainable use of the world's resources.

In order to reconnect the security and human rights agendas and to bring them together into a coherent framework of law, it would be necessary to hold an international or global legal convention. Rather than set out a blueprint of what the results of such a convention should be, it is important to stress the significance of a legitimate process that reviews the security and human rights sides of international law and seeks to reconnect them in a global legal framework. For too long, security and development, and the security and human rights agendas, have been treated as separate intellectual and foreign policy domains, but they should not have been, and they cannot be any longer.

If the developed world wants rapid progress towards the establish-ment of global legal codes and mechanisms to enhance security and ensure action against the threats of terrorism, then it needs to be part of a wider process of reform that addresses the insecurity of life expe-rienced in developing societies. Across the developing or majority world, issues of justice with respect to government and terrorism are not widely regarded as a priority on their own, and are rarely per-ceived as legitimate unless they are connected with fundamental humanitarian issues rooted in social and economic well-being, such as education, clean water and threats to public health.

To address these problems requires a shift not just in how security is conceived and pursued, but also in how economic development is elaborated and managed. The narrow liberal economic agenda domi-nant in recent years needs to be recast and economic strategy linked to a larger socioeconomic framework of global economic governance, setting fundamental standards for all human life and rethinking the economic tools available to global economic policy. A broader human security agenda needs to be matched by a broader programme of economic development.

The contested nature of global economic governance

For the last two to three decades, the agenda of economic liberaliza-tion and global market integration known as the Washington Consensus has been the mantra of many leading economic powers and international financial institutions. This view of economic develop-ment has maintained that the path to economic and social well-being is economic liberalization and international market integration. As Martin Wolf put it, 'all else is commentary' (2004: 144). But is this true? There are strong grounds for doubting that the standard liberal economic approach delivers on promised goods and that global market integration is the indispensable condition of development. Moreover, their forceful implementation by the World Bank, the IMF and the leading economic powers has often led to counterproductive results.

Countries that have benefited most from globalization are those that have not played by the rules of the standard liberal market approach, including China, India and Vietnam (Rodrik 2005). In addition, those that have – for example, the Latin American and the Caribbean countries – have done worse judged by the standards of East Asia and their own past. In other words, the link between growth, economic openness and liberalization is weaker than the standard liberal argument suggests. The widespread shift among developing countries to greater openness has coincided with a slowdown in the rate of world economic growth compared to earlier in the postwar period, from 2.7 per cent during 1960–78 to 1.5 per cent during 1979–2000 (Milanovic 2005).

The link between growth and poverty reduction is also not as close as the liberal argument would predict. Accounts of this type generally assume a catch-up or convergence story whereby poorer countries, by opening their markets and liberalizing, are expected to grow richer at a faster rate, so that income differentials narrow over time. However, the evidence to support this is controversial, at best. In the first instance, outside the phenomenal development of China and to some extent India, the reported number of people living below the World Bank poverty line of $1 a day has actually risen in the two decades since 1981 (see Wade 2006). There is also a near-perfect correlation between a group's relative standing at the beginning of the 1990s and its real cumulative income gains in the years that followed (see Pogge 2006). The evidence shows that gains at the bottom of the global income hierarchy were minimal or even negative, as the first – that is to say, bottom – percentile lost 7.3 per cent and the second gained only 1 per cent. Moreover, the World Bank's measure of absolute poverty, based on $1 a day, is to a large extent arbitrary. If you take the figure of $2 a day, you can actually show the reverse trend (see Held and Kaya 2006).

Examining and evaluating trends in income inequality between countries, it is clear that much depends again on how China's economic success and subsequent reduction in poverty is treated. If China is excluded from consideration, inequality between countries can be shown to have increased since 1980. This is an important date because it is often claimed to be the moment when income inequality between countries reached its peak. Of course, there is much to be said for including China in the account, but then it has to be borne in mind that China's success has depended significantly on a host of factors, not all of which fit neatly into the liberal argument. For example, China has staggered and regulated its entry into the global market; tariffs have been cut, but after economic take-off, particularly heavily in the last ten to twelve years; capital movements have remained tightly regulated; and foreign direct investment is locked into partnerships often with significant political controls.

None of this is to argue that trade and international capital flows do not provide important potential gains to many countries. The question is rather: under what conditions are trade and capital flows (and what kinds of trade and capital flow) introduced to maximize benefit? Thinking of globalization as either an inextricably positive force or the opposite is likely to miss the core conditions for successful development and political change. The choice is not between globalization in its liberal free market form and no globalization. Instead, what is at issue is the proper form that globalization should take.

This critical issue cannot be resolved within the terms of the Washington Consensus because its thrust is to enhance economic liberalization and to adapt public policy and the public domain to market-leading institutions and processes. It thus bears a heavy burden of responsibility for the common political resistance or unwillingness to address significant areas of market failure, including:

- the problem of externalities, such as the environmental degradation exacerbated by current forms of economic growth;

- the inadequate development of *non*-market social factors, which alone can provide an effective balance between 'competition' and 'cooperation', and thus ensure an adequate supply of essential public goods such as education, effective transportation and sound health; and
- the under-employment of productive resources in the context of the demonstrable existence of urgent and unmet need.

The Washington Consensus has weakened confidence in public authority and in that authority's ability – locally, nationally and globally – to govern and provide urgent public goods. Economic freedom is championed at the expense of social justice and environmental sustainability, with damage to both. It has, moreover, confused economic freedom and economic effectiveness. The question is (and it is, of course, a big question): how can markets, democratic choices about public goods and a concern with basic universal standards, such as human rights and environmental protection, be pursued systematically and simultaneously? What follows constitutes some first steps in addressing this question.

To begin with, bridges have to be built between international economic law and human rights law, between commercial law and environmental law, between state sovereignty and transnational law (Chinkin 1998). It is as if all these things refer to separate domains and do not speak to each other, with the consequence that entrenched interests trump social and environmental considerations, among other urgent matters. What is required is not only the firm enactment of existing human rights and environmental agreements, and the clear linking of these with the ethical codes of particular industries, but also the introduction of new terms of reference into the ground rules or basic laws of the free market and trade system. Helpful precedents exist in the social chapter of the Maastricht agreement and in the attempt to attach labour and environmental conditions to the North American Free Trade Agreement (NAFTA) regime.

At stake, ultimately, are three interrelated transformations. The first would involve engaging companies in the promotion of core universal principles, as the UN's Global Compact does at present. This would be a significant step forward if it led to the entrenchment of human rights and environmental standards in corporate practices. But if these principles are to be anything other than voluntary, then they will need to be elaborated in due course into a set of more codified and mandatory rules. Thus the second set of transformations would involve the entrenchment of revised rules and codes on health, child labour, trade union activity, environmental protection, stakeholder consultation and corporate governance in the articles of association of economic organizations and trading agencies. The key groups and associations of the economic domain would have to adopt in their very modus operandi a structure of rules and procedures compatible with universal social requirements, if these requirements were to prevail. Of course, it can be countered that poorly designed regulatory structures can harm employment levels, but Scandinavian countries show that it is possible to be both business-friendly and welfare-orientated.

There are several possible objections to the scheme set out. However, most of these are misplaced. The framework of human rights and environmental values is sound because it is concerned with the equal liberty and equal development possibilities of all human beings, and is consistent with the universal principles enshrined in the post-1945 multilateral order. But it has to be conceded that without a third set of changes the advocacy of such standards descends into high-mindedness because it fails to pursue the socioeconomic changes that are a necessary part of such a commitment. At a minimum, this means that development policies must be linked to:

- promoting the development space necessary for national trade and industrial incentives, including infant industry protection;
- building robust public sectors nurturing political and legal reform;
- developing transparent, accountable political institutions;
- ensuring long-term investment in health care, human capital and physical infrastructure;
- challenging the asymmetries of access to the global market, which are often hypocritical and indefensible;
- ensuring the sequencing of global market integration into a framework of fair rules for trade and finance; and
- eliminating unsustainable debt, and creating new finance facilities for development purposes.

In addition, if such measures were combined with a Tobin tax on the turnover of financial markets, and/or a consumption tax on fossil fuels, and/or a shift of priorities from military expenditure, now running at $900 billion per annum globally, towards the alleviation of severe need, this would have a major impact on reducing poverty and underdevelopment.

The UN budget is $1.2 billion per annum plus peacekeeping, but the US and Europe each spend vastly more annually on chocolate and bubble gum, alcohol, cars, pet food and so on. The expenditure on each of these items dwarfs the amounts available for direct poverty alleviation and for dealing with urgent diseases. The US and its allies went to war after 9/11; 9/11 was a serious matter, a crime against the United States and a crime against humanity. But every day ten times as many people die as were lost on 9/11 of poverty, malnutrition and poverty-related diseases. However, there is no war or, better still, decisive social change in relation to these life and death issues. The resources are available, but the question is political will and choice.

In conclusion

The postwar multilateral order is in trouble. Clear, effective and accountable decision making is needed across a range of urgent global challenges; and, yet, the collective capacity for addressing these matters is in doubt. Nonetheless, this is an opportune moment to rethink foreign policy goals and objectives; given shifts in political and economic power across the world, it is highly unlikely that the multilateral order in its present shape and form will endure unchallenged in the years ahead. The dominant policy packages of the last several years in economics and security have not delivered the goods and a learning opportunity beckons. We need to build on the cosmopolitan steps of the twentieth century and deepen the institutional hold of this agenda. Further steps in this direction remain within our grasp, however bleak the first few years of the twenty-first century have been. A human security approach allied to a change of direction in the governance of the world economy would both buttress international law and multilateral institutions and ensure that the wisdom embedded in the universal principles and institutional advances of the post-1945 era is safe-guarded, nurtured and advanced for future generations.

References

Barnett, A., Held, D. and Henderson, C. (eds) (2005) *Debating Globalization*, Cambridge: Polity.

Barry, B. (1998) 'International society from a cosmopolitan perspective', in D. Mapel and T. Nardin (eds), *International Society: diverse ethical perspectives*, Princeton, NJ: Princeton University Press.

Burnheim, J. (1985) *Is Democracy Possible?*, Cambridge: Polity.

Chinkin, C. (1998) 'International law and human rights', in T. Evans (ed.), *Human Rights Fifty Years On: a reappraisal*, Manchester: Manchester University Press.

Deacon, B. (2003) 'Global social governance reform: from institutions and policies to networks, projects and partnerships', in B. Deacon, E. Ollida,

M. Koivusalo and P. Stubbs (eds), *Global Social Governance*, Helsinki: Hakapaino Oy.

Giddens, A. (1990) *The Consequences of Modernity*, Cambridge: Polity.

Held, D. (1995) *Democracy and the Global Order: from the modern state to cosmopolitan governance*, Cambridge: Polity.

Held, D. (2002) 'Globalization, corporate practice and cosmopolitan social standards', *Contemporary Political Theory*, 1(1), pp. 59–78.

Held, D. (2004) *Global Covenant*, Cambridge: Polity.

Held, D. and Kaldor, M. (2001) *What Hope for the Future?*; available at www.lse.ac.uk/depts/global/maryheld.htm.

Held, D. and Kaya, A. (eds) (2006) *Global Inequality: patterns and explanations*, Cambridge: Polity.

Held, D. and McGrew, A. (2002a) *Globalization/Anti-Globalization*, Cambridge: Polity.

Held, D. and McGrew, A. (eds) (2002b) *Governing Globalization: power, authority and global governance*, Cambridge: Polity.

Held, D. McGrew, A. Goldblatt, D. and Perraton, J. (1999) *Global Transformations: politics, economics and culture*, Cambridge: Polity.

Hettne, B. (1997) 'The double movement: global market versus regionalism' in R. W. Cox (ed.), *The New Realism: perspectives on multilateralism and world order*, Tokyo: United Nations University Press.

Hoffmann, S. (2003) 'America goes backward', *New York Review of Books*, 50(10), 12 June, pp. 74–80.

Hoffmann, S. (2004) *Gulliver Unbound: the imperial temptation and the war in Iraq*, Lanham, Md.: Rowman and Littlefield.

Hoffmann, S. (2006) 'The foreign policy the US needs', *New York Review of Books*, 53(13), 10 August, pp. 60–4.

Human Security Centre (2005) *Human Security Report 2005: war and peace in the 21st century*; available at http://www.humansecurityreport. info.

Ikenberry, G. J. (2002) 'America's imperial ambition', *Foreign Affairs*, 81(5), pp. 44–60.

Kaldor, M. (1999) *New and Old Wars*, Cambridge: Polity.

Kaul, I., Conceição, P., Le Goulven, K. and Mendoza, R. U. (eds) (2003) *Providing Global Public Goods*, Oxford: Oxford University Press.

McGrew, A. (2002) 'Between two worlds: europe in a globalizing era', *Government and Opposition*, 37(3), Summer, pp. 343–58.

Meikle, J. (2005) 'Bill Gates gives $258m to world battle against malaria', *Guardian*, 31 October.

Milanovic, B. (2005) *Worlds Apart: measuring international and global inequality*, Princeton, NJ: Princeton University Press.

Moore, M. (2003) *A World Without Walls: freedom, development, free trade and global governance*, Cambridge: Cambridge University Press.

Murphy, C. (2000) 'Global governance: poorly done and poorly understood', *International Affairs*, 76(4), pp. 789–803.

Payne, A. (2003) 'Globalization and modes of regionalist governance', in D. Held and A. McGrew (eds), *The Global Transformations Reader*, Cambridge: Polity.

Pogge, T. (2006) 'Why inequality matters', in D. Held and A. Kaya (eds), *Global Inequality: patterns and explanations*, Cambridge: Polity.

Rees, M. (2003) *Our Final Century*, New York: Arrow.

Rischard, J.-F. (2002) *High Noon*, New York: Basic Books.

Rodrik, D. (2005) 'Making globalization work for development', Ralph Miliband Public Lecture, London School of Economics, 18 November.

Rosenau, J. N. (2002) 'Governance in a new global order', in D. Held and A. McGrew (eds), *Governing Globalization: power, authority and global governance*, Cambridge: Polity.

Ruggie, J. G. (1993) 'Territoriality and beyond: problematizing modernity in international relations', *International Organization*, 47(1), Winter, pp. 139–74.

Slaughter, A.-M. (2004) *A New World Order*, Princeton, NJ: Princeton University Press.

Solana, J. (2003) 'The future of transatlantic relations', *Progressive Politics*, 2(2), pp. 61–66.

Soros, G. (2006) *The Age of Fallibility: consequences of the war on terror*, New York: Public Affairs.

Wade, R. (2006) 'Should we worry about income inequality?', in D. Held and A. Kaya (eds), *Global Inequality: patterns and explanations*, Cambridge: Polity.

Wolf, M. (2004) *Why Globalization Works*, New Haven: Yale University Press.

11

Global Economic Governance: A Programme for Reform

Ngaire Woods

A progressive UK foreign policy should seek to make the institutions of global economic governance much more effective in meeting common global problems. In a world that is ever more interdependent and interconnected, strong global institutions are not merely desirable but essential for addressing a broad range of global issues, from development to human rights, climate change to global economic stability. Over the last decade, the UK has made a significant contribution to the debate about the reform of the United Nations (UN), the international financial institutions (IFIs) and, to a lesser extent, the World Trade Organization (WTO). And in recent years there has been some progress on reform in respect of each of these institutions, with moves towards more openness and transparency and better systems for evaluating the impacts of their policies.

Does this mean that these international organizations are now fit for purpose: structured and equipped to meet the diverse demands made of them? In this chapter, I argue that this is not the case. Existing global economic institutions are still failing to fulfil their potential.

Part of the problem is a lack of coordination and cooperation between the major institutions. The institutions we have operate very separately from one another – the International Monetary Fund (IMF) in one city, directed by one set of ministries, the WTO in another, directed by a different set of ministries. This locks the goals and policies of international institutions into silos where special interests dominate. The efficacy of the institutions is also weakened by structural constraints. The WTO, the World Bank and the IMF are all inadequately representative, failing in particular to represent the interests, voices and priorities of developing countries. In recent years there have been various initiatives to 'open up' and make these institutions more participatory and democratic. Yet the trend has been towards ad hoc consultations such as a town hall meeting in a poor community or a special summit with leaders of developing countries. These are a very poor substitute for substantive representation in forums which make decisions. Inviting African leaders to a Group of Eight (G8) lunch confers no rights and creates no responsibilities. The new participatory trend is well intentioned but cannot substitute for genuine participation through representation in formal decision-making structures.

In this chapter I put forward some concrete policy recommendations – reform proposals that a progressive UK government ought to be pressing for. My particular focus is on the WTO, the IMF and the World Bank. In broad terms, what should be expected of each institution is threefold. Firstly, as *public* (not private or for-profit) institutions they should offer governments a forum within which shared public purposes can take centre-stage. International institutions will inevitably reflect the interests of their most powerful member states. The key is: which interests from within those powerful states? Protected importers? The aid lobby? Churches and civil society groups? Multilateral institutions should offer a forum for states to share broader public purposes as opposed to narrower mercantilist interests.

Secondly, global public institutions have a regulatory function. They must ensure that markets work effectively and equitably: for example, by setting basic standards and preventing the collapse of markets into monopolies. They also exist to limit negative externalities and ensure an adequate supply of global public goods, such as preventing a global economic depression, reducing unnecessary global pollution and managing common resources.

Thirdly, institutions have a crucial role (and progressives should attach particular importance to this) in enhancing the opportunities of poorer countries and marginalized people, those who are exploited or otherwise fail to benefit from global markets. They can do this through aid transfers to alleviate poverty or through a range of other policy interventions which help to reduce global political and economic inequalities. But what kind of specific reforms should a progressive UK government be pressing for?

Governing trade

In relation to the World Trade Organization and the rules of international trade, progressives should be advocating reform in three areas. First, they should seek to limit the scope of trade talks, resisting pressures from mercantilist interests to push into new areas, and ensuring progress on the issues of most concern to developing countries.

The rules we associate with the WTO were negotiated in the Uruguay Round in the late 1980s. With hindsight, it is clear that these negotiations were dominated by large industrialized countries that stand accused of railroading poorer countries into hard and enforceable commitments, in return for vaguer promises to liberalize agriculture and 'do the right thing' (in other words, liberalize) on other issues (Jawara and Kwa 2004). The most recent trade talks – the ongoing Doha Round of multilateral trade negotiations which began in 2001 – have not redressed this perception or changed this much in substantive terms.

Wealthy countries are still refusing to open their markets in agriculture. This matters to developing countries because it covers so much of what they produce. In the European Union (EU) barriers are used to keep other countries' agricultural products out. In the US a massive farm programme is deployed to subsidize farmers, making it difficult for any other country to compete. Instead of being able to rely upon open markets, poor countries must rely on special discretionary deals or bilateral agreements that Europe and the US control and can use to divide and rule.

While agriculture is not liberalized, huge negotiating resources and time are being put into widening the scope of WTO rule in other areas. In part this was a strategy adopted in the Uruguay Round when the US and Europe pushed for a 'single undertaking', which meant that member countries had to accept everything or nothing. This laid the path for forcing through an expanded trade agenda, including a range of issues to which developing countries had in the past objected, such as intellectual property protection (see chapter 4 in this volume).

Secondly, progressives should expose western double standards on trade. Rich industrialized countries have negotiated binding rules in the WTO that 'kick away the ladder' that they themselves used to get to the top. These rules proscribe the rich array of tariffs and industrial policies that the UK, Germany, the US, Canada and Japan each used to ensure that their economies produced more and more valuable exports (Lall and Teubal 1998; Wade 1990; Chang 2002). South Korea, Taiwan, China and Vietnam – the fast ladder-climbers of today – each used combinations of industrial policies and tariffs to protect new basic industries, along with new and better technologies, access to markets, and other forms of national support for potential export successes. These mixtures of policies enabled them to industrialize and to export higher-value-added goods. Obviously, not all the countries that used these policies succeeded. However, it is hard to think of a single successful globalizer that has not. And yet, these kinds of state intervention are now mostly outlawed by WTO rules.

As a consequence of WTO rules, developing countries are also being asked to achieve what no other country did: to industrialize without industrial policy or to develop rapidly without industrialization. The latter is impossible while rich countries' markets in agriculture are protected. Meanwhile, industrialization is being made much more difficult (DiCaprio and Gallagher 2006). Sharp limits on access to technology have been imposed by new stringent intellectual property rules, which economists argue will increase dependence and lower welfare in developing countries (Hanns 2004; Chin and Grossman 1991; Markusen 1998).

Industrialization is also made more difficult by new barriers erected by rich countries. For example, by alleging that other countries are 'dumping' products (which means selling them at a price lower than the price normally charged on their own home market), rich countries erect barriers to imports. In 2003, the US alleged that six countries were selling shrimps too cheaply in the US and, on this basis, levied extra duties on Brazil, China, Ecuador, India, Thailand and Vietnam. On top of this, poor countries are expected to divert significant resources into compliance with detailed and complicated rules already agreed within the WTO.

Progressives should advocate trade rules that take account of countries' different starting points and levels of development. They should also permit less developed countries to use the kinds of policy that rich countries used to get to the top and to give them breathing space.

Thirdly, a commitment to global equity should involve fairer enforcement of international trade rules. In theory, the creation of the WTO in 1994 offered a revolution to developing countries – a robust rule-based system that would be enforced by a less politicized body than ever before. Until 1994, the enforcement of trade rules had been highly political. A consensus of the Council of the General Agreement on Tariffs and Trade (GATT) would have to agree with a decision that a member had broken the rules, in order for that decision to be upheld. This gave all countries in the system a veto on the enforcement of any rule. In the WTO the consensus is reversed. Rulings are made by panels of experts. These rulings hold unless there is consensus against them. But does this work to the advantage of developing countries?

Developing countries face serious barriers when bringing a case to a panel (let alone to the appellate body) against a large trading partner that is breaking the rules. Any country dependent on a large trading partner will be likely to exercise restraint for fear either of losing discretionary trade access, or of jeopardizing aid, military assistance or other foreign policy advantages (Bown and Hoekman 2005). It is worth noting, for example, that no aid-dependent country has ever brought a case to the dispute settlement process. An equally important barrier exists because of the way enforcement actions begin. In the US and EU they rely on wealthy private firms and industry associations developing the litigation agenda and pursuing and defending issues before the WTO. The pre-litigation work is costly and time consuming and governments do not do it themselves (Shaffer 2003). Subsequently, the costs of litigation in bringing a typical case have been estimated at US$500,000 (Advisory Centre on WTO Law 2004). After that there are vital post-litigation expenses required for public relations and political lobbying to generate compliance.

In theory, all countries can enforce trade rules. In practice, it takes strong and well-funded business associations to find possible cases and persuade their governments to bring them to the WTO. Once rulings are made, enforcement depends equally upon strong and well-organized interests lobbying a government to push for compliance by trading partners or even to take (or threaten) retaliatory actions against the country in breach.

One small effort to bolster the capacity of developing countries to use the dispute settlement process is the Advisory Centre on WTO Law (ACWL), which was established in Geneva in 2001. It provides subsidized legal advice on WTO law and support in settlement proceedings of WTO disputes, as well as some training. But two obvious limitations affect the ACWL. First, its budget is partly funded by rich countries and several see a direct conflict of interest in funding a centre that helps to prepare cases against them (the US, France, Germany and Japan do not contribute). Furthermore, the centre does not do pre-litigation work to find practices that are potentially in breach of WTO law and that could be amenable to a challenge. Nor does the centre do the technical work, such as economic analysis, required to support cases (Bown and Hoekman 2005).

A progressive UK government should press for a number of changes to make the enforcement of WTO trade rules fairer and more robust. Better information should be made available to all countries about who is breaking the rules. The WTO could play a much stronger role in pooling and disseminating this information, not just from official government sources but from others. This information could allow countries to group together more often in taking cases, not only to share direct costs but to spread the political pressures against taking action. More robust enforcement, such as the direct application of fines or sanctions by the WTO, is also required if the interests of smaller countries are to be upheld.

Governing global money

Effective governance of global money is an absolutely essential global public good. Without cooperation on exchange rates and public finances, the world economy is capable of crashing as it did in the 1930s. So how should a progressive UK government encourage better governance in this area? There are three specific priorities.

First, some important reforms are required to the work of the International Monetary Fund. Voting power and shares in the organization have long been based on an outdated model of economic power. In theory, each member enjoys power proportionate to their economic weight in the world economy. In practice, the determinations are much more political. Small revisions have recently been made. But marginal voting increments do not redress the core problem of a lack of confidence on the part of many developing countries. Indeed, even discussions about how to reform the institution have been hived off to a group created by the Group of Seven in the wake of the East Asian financial crisis – the Group of Twenty.

Ideologically, the IMF is struggling to operate in a world where its carefully honed tools are aimed at macroeconomic stabilization and structural adjustment. However, it is failing to address what its members now expect of it – standard setting, institution building and poverty reduction, and effectiveness in aiding its poorest borrowing members. The institution needs to be closer to its borrowing members, producing less lofty and more practical solutions for them. IMF research also needs to be closer to the ground and structured to provide policy-makers with practical insights drawn from the experiences of other IMF members.

When it comes to the IMF's wider surveillance function, it should be pooling information and analysis from a wide range of sources and networks. That information should be presented to members not as a lengthy series of bureaucratic reports but to highlight problems needing collective action and offering clear collective strategies for overcoming them.

Governance affects both what the IMF does and how it does it. The IMF is governed by a small executive board, which might be described as semi-representative, semi-technocratic and semi-efficient. It neither makes countries feel represented, nor acts independently of them. Countries do not feel represented because most countries are bundled into groups and represented by a technocrat they do not know and cannot hold to account (Woods and Lombardi 2006).

An immediate reform would be to require every member of the IMF's board to represent a group of countries. There should be no division – as there is at present – between countries that have their 'own' immediately accountable executive director, and all the other countries, which have been grouped together and have little means by which they can hold their director to account. By better arranging constituencies, and requiring more direct consultation, reporting and accountability, the board members could have much more immediate incentives to be directly engaged and accountable (Woods and Lombardi 2006).

Another key reform would be to require every decision to command a majority of voting power (the most powerful shareholders' support) as well as a majority of countries (giving a direct incentive to the powerful to consult large groups of small, poor countries). This proposal for 'double majority voting' is elaborated fully in *The Globalizers* (Woods 2006).

Finally, although the board is supposed to oversee the management of the organization – ensuring that member countries hold the organization to account – in fact it is chaired and run by the Managing Director. This tradition must change. At present the board is locked into a pattern of approval or veto which flies in the face of modern norms of corporate governance. Although a full transcript of board debates and discussions is kept, it is not made public. At the very least, the board should have its own chair appointed from among its own ranks, rather than being chaired by the Managing Director whose work the board is supposed to oversee.

More radically, the Governor of the Bank of England recently proposed getting rid of the resident IMF board and replacing it with a non-resident group of policy-makers meeting periodically. This could well solve some problems. It would put 'heavyweights' on the board, who could give strategic direction to the organization and ensure more effective oversight of the management and staff of the organization. More direct and high-level representation might also make countries feel better represented.

What the non-resident board idea misses is the elephant in the room. Privately, policy-makers across the developing world concede that, to them, the IMF is a US institution. It is located in Washington DC, very close to the US Treasury. By convention its First Deputy Managing Director and Chief Economist are chosen by the US, which is also the only country that can single-handedly veto significant decisions in the organization. The thin veneer that separates the US from the IMF is in essence the board of the organization, which sits in Washington DC, manfully attempting to hold up a semblance of multilateralism and accountability to the membership (Woods 2006).

A second critical area for reform would be to get the IMF to help countries cope better with economic shocks. The most important role the IMF can perform for most of its members is to help them – through advice, lending and cooperation – to deal with the 'excesses' of global markets. Global capital markets can send different kinds of shock through small economies. Exchange rates can suddenly shift, in the absence of the coordination depicted above. Commodity prices can shift, too, devastating small and poor commodity-producing countries. A crisis in another part of the world can cause short-term capital suddenly to leave the country. The result can be a triple crisis of devastating proportions. So how can countries insure against this? And how can the IMF help?

Currently what the IMF does in an exchange rate crisis is a combination of lending or emergency support and conditionality. This marries two of the IMF's original roles: maintaining stable exchange rates and helping countries to resolve their short-term balance of payments crises. This marriage is deeply problematic.

The IMF was created to offer short-term loans to countries with a balance of payments problem, in a world of controlled (not mobile) capital. But today, as trillions of dollars slosh around the globe, a country's balance of payments crisis becomes rapidly inseparable from its exchange rate and banking system. The IMF finds itself trying to deal with an exchange rate crisis, a current account crisis and a banking sector crisis with one rather crude instrument – conditional lending. Meanwhile, short-term investors flee and the institution is castigated for bailing out reckless investors.

Missing from the IMF toolkit have been tried and trusted measures which fall short of the pure economic 'ideal'. For example, countries can use prudent measures to buffer shocks from global capital markets in the event of a crisis. Such measures helped countries such as Malaysia, Singapore, India and South Africa to mitigate the effects of the 1997 Asian financial crisis, which each weathered much better than its neighbours (see *Global Governance* 2006). Each had liberalized carefully, leaving in place measures that permitted them some control over incoming and outflowing capital. Yet the IMF does not give practical advice to countries on how they might use capital controls.

For a long time the IMF pushed capital account liberalization in a fairly undifferentiated way on all its borrowing members (IMF Independent Evaluation Office 2004). This reflected the preferences of powerful members with strong financial systems and an attachment to a particular kind of theorizing about economics. Subsequently, research within the organization highlighted vulnerabilities and problems with the policy (Prasad et al. 2003).

What the organization now needs to do is to evaluate seriously what kinds of capital controls or precautionary measures can work, and to weave this into its advice to members (see Joshi 2003). At present it is only halfway towards this goal, not least because its most powerful members continue to push for capital account liberalization. What many of the IMF's members need is practical advice on how to use capital controls, not a blanket prescription not to.

The IMF is already having to listen more closely to emerging economies. In part this is because in 2006 some were given more voting power (China, Korea, Mexico and Turkey: see www.imf.org for full details). In part it is because the organization's day-to-day finances rely on its fee-paying clients taking loans from the organization and repaying with interest. As the IMF's big borrowers (such as Brazil and Argentina) walk away from the institution, it is left with no big borrowers to pay its bills. For these reasons, the IMF has a strong incentive to tailor its work better to its borrowers.

A third vital area for IMF reform concerns international monetary cooperation. The most difficult role for the IMF is perhaps its most important – helping to ensure stable exchange rates. Exchange rates are like traffic signals on the highways of the global economy. They manage and signal the intersections between economies. Ideally, exchange rates shift in a stable, predictable way, because unstable exchange rates cause havoc in economies by affecting exports, imports and external borrowings. Originally, the IMF oversaw a fixed exchange rate system but that changed in the 1970s, and since 1978 exchange rates have been a free-for-all with some floating, some managed and some fixed.

In the free-for-all system of global exchange rates, the IMF attempts to promote stability by 'surveillance' and by reporting on individual countries and the global economy as a whole. However, IMF surveillance has little, if any, effect on members' policies (Lombardi and

Woods 2007). Wealthy, powerful members of the IMF whose exchange rate arrangements have the largest impact on all other countries in the global economy remain fairly immune to judgements on their policies made by the IMF.

The alternative to the free-for-all system is a multilateral system of coordination. This requires a forum within which countries could agree and an institutional back-up to monitor and report on compliance. The goal could be one of two things: a free-floating system in which all major currencies agree freely to float their exchange rates, letting market transactions determine values, or a targeted band system where governments coordinate and each commits to keeping its exchange rate within the targeted 'band' (Joshi 2006).

At present, countries cannot individually fix their exchange rates without risking speculative attack, such as occurred after 1997 in Thailand, Russia and Argentina. At the same time, governments that try more subtly to manage exchange rates require a huge amount of dollars taken out of their economy to keep in reserve so that they can buy and sell their own currency when the need arises. The result is a massive outflow of capital from developing and emerging economies to buy dollar-liquid forms of reserves such as US Treasury bills from the rich industrialized countries.

To address this problem, Joseph Stiglitz has recently proposed an international currency or unit of account for reserves (Stiglitz 2006). The Stiglitz plan would involve countries forgoing their own holdings of reserves in favour of the new fiat currency held by (and only convertible through) a global reserve system. This would save countries from having to amass their own reserves so as credibly to deter others from speculating against their currencies, relying instead upon a form of collective monetary security.

There are two serious problems with this. First, countries do not stockpile reserves just for a rainy day. Rather, China and other Asian economies are sustaining their rapid export-led growth by intervening to keep their exchange rates low.[1] This is an important part of the reason why they end up buying such large quantities of US Treasury bills. No system of pooled reserves will resolve the underlying trade issues. For a solution to this problem, we must shift our attention to the global trading system (as above) and ask what alternative means are left for developing and emerging economies to move up the ladder of export-led industrialization.

Secondly, a global reserve system would need an institution at its core. The obvious contender is the IMF. However, for the IMF to operate as a pooled system of reserves, its members would need confidence that the institution was as much 'theirs' as their own reserves are. But officials from the Asian countries, which are currently building up massive reserves, speak in private of the IMF as too much of a US institution. The kind of IMF that would command their confidence would have to be restructured to overcome this perception. An alternative to the Stiglitz proposal would be to build on alternative arrangements already emerging among Asian countries. The Association of South East Asian Nations (ASEAN) plus China, Japan and South Korea have swap arrangements among themselves. This means they can rely on loans from one another to bolster their reserves in a time of need and, at the same time, make use of IMF conditionality as a backstop or agency of external restraint.

The IMF is supposed to be a forum for multilateral cooperation. However, in practice the IMF is not used by its members as a forum in which exchange rate arrangements are candidly discussed. Moreover, many of its newer members lack confidence in the institution as an even-handed monitor and enforcer of agreements.

In recent history, powerful countries in the IMF have used the organization to exhort smaller, borrowing members to comply with standards and rules. They have moved away from using the organization as a place where they commit themselves to self-restraint or the pursuit of shared global goals or goods. But exchange rate stability can be achieved only by cooperation among the powerful. To reinvigorate monetary cooperation, the governments of powerful countries must commit to a radically reformed IMF.

Governing development assistance

The World Bank sits at the heart of the global development assistance system and support for it should be central to a progressive approach to UK foreign policy. The logic for this is impeccable. A multilateral aid agency permits countries to pool their aid efforts. In theory, this should mean more effective, better-informed development assistance with fewer transaction costs. The World Bank should permit rich countries to facilitate growth and human development in poor countries more effectively than through individual national aid agencies. But securing these outcomes requires further changes to the work of the Bank.

There is a key role for the Bank in providing pragmatic and trusted policy advice. However, since the 1980s much of the World Bank's advice has been anchored in a model of liberalization and deregulation as the route to economic growth. This can be seen even in the

World Bank's special branch for lending to the world's poorest countries: the International Development Association (IDA). This decides how good a country's policies are using a Country Performance and Institutional Assessment (CPIA), which assesses economic management, structural policies, policies for social inclusion and equity, and public sector management and institutions. For seven years these ratings were kept secret within the Bank. Since 2005 they have been published and open to public scrutiny (Kanbur 2005).

A country wanting a top score in the CPIA needs first to show that it has liberalized and deregulated its economy. It needs to have reduced its tariffs on imports to less than 7 per cent of their value. It needs a strong financial sector and functioning capital markets, public spending that does not crowd out private investment, public debt in a low ratio to GDP, and employment laws that allow workers to be hired and fired at low cost. These criteria reflect one particular model of development (Kanbur 2005).

Rooted in the structural adjustment of the 1980s, the Bank's general recipe has been to deregulate, liberalize and wait for growth. It has invested a lot in models and research which are said to reinforce its case for liberalization and deregulation. One of the most widely cited World Bank studies uses a cross-country analysis of data to argue that liberalization leads to growth and poverty reduction (Dollar and Kraay 2000). The study provoked vigorous debate both within and outside the Bank, with several leading scholars highlighting flaws in the work (Milanovic 2003; Easterly et al. 2003; Rodrik and Rodríguez 1999).

Dollar and Kraay define 'globalizers' as countries that experience increases in trade and foreign direct investment – as opposed to countries that have made 'liberalizing' policy decisions. Critics point out that growth may well have driven openness. Indeed, in China, India and Vietnam, all countries that have outperformed their peers in terms of growth in recent years, domestic economic reform was undertaken behind a screen of capital and trade controls before any serious attempts were made to globalize (Galbraith 2002).

Politically, the Dollar and Kraay findings have been very influential, being used by the US's trade negotiators and others to make the case for liberalization. Yet politically, poor countries have been ill-served by the Bank. When 'good performers' arrive at the WTO to negotiate a trade deal, they quickly find that the World Bank has inadvertently persuaded them to give away all their trump cards – unilaterally to disarm in the face of powerful countries, which do not do the same. The currency of trade negotiations is access to markets. Countries that drop their tariffs unilaterally often have little bargaining power in the first place. But having dropped their trade barriers before negotiations even begin, they soon find that they have even less to bargain with.

Economically, the case for liberalization depends (much more than the Bank has ever admitted) on careful planning and sequencing (Rodrik 1992; Rodrik and Rodríguez 1999). The social and distributional effects of liberalization are also highly disputed. The Dollar and Kraay work cited above has led to a sharp debate about whether globalization increases inequality within and among countries (Wade 2004). Dollar and Kraay argue that globalization is a 'powerful force for equality', reducing inequality between countries and having a neutral effect on inequality within countries (Dollar and Kraay 2002). One of their World Bank colleagues, however, argues that increased openness (measured by trade as a percentage of national income) does not have a neutral effect. Rather it reduces the income share of the bottom six deciles, thus increasing national inequality (Milanovic 2004).[2]

More generally, efforts to get the Bank to consider an alternative set of principles have failed. One example was Japan's push to conduct a study on the East Asian model of development. The result was a report which did little to redress the core emphasis on what used to be called the Washington Consensus (Rodrik 1994). Subsequently, although a lively variety of research is reported across the Bank's web pages, the conditions imposed by the Bank when it makes loans continue to focus on a traditional liberalization and deregulation paradigm. This has to change.

There is also an important potential role for the Bank in coordinating aid. The World Bank is at the centre of an international development assistance regime that is notoriously fragmented, duplicative and cluttered with a large number of different donors. In theory, the World Bank, by pooling information and resources, should vastly reduce transaction costs on both sides of the aid relationship. But the major donors, such as the United States, Japan and the United Kingdom, do not rely on the World Bank in this way. Instead they sustain and expand their own separate aid agencies and processes. The result is that already overstretched government officials in very poor countries are forced to spend most of their time strengthening and maintaining external relations with donors rather than addressing the pressing development needs of their people.

More perversely, even when national donors use the World Bank, they encumber it with special demands, special funds and additional procedures. This practice can be traced back to the increasing use of 'trust funds' in the World Bank. These are funds given to the Bank for a particular use – often supplementary to the institution's core work.

As described by a former UK government aid official, 'we construct an elaborate mechanism for setting priorities and discipline in the Bank, and then as donors we bypass this mechanism by setting up separate financial incentives to try to get the Bank to do what we want' (Ahmed 2006: 90).

At the highest level, donors have engaged in a discussion about how they might better coordinate, harmonize and align their aid efforts (Organisation for Economic Cooperation and Development 1996, 2005). That said, the rate of progress on the ground has been glacial. For example, one area in which donors have agreed to streamline their efforts is public financial accountability. But a 2004 joint assessment, completed by the World Bank, the European Commission and the UK Department for International Development (DFID) reports that:

- Too many different audits have been taking place in each country in the area of public expenditure and financial accountability (their role is important but limited in enhancing capacity or fiduciary assurance).[3]
- Existing tools pay too little attention to other institutions (the legislature, civil society, institutional and governance factors, and asset management) and what a government can realistically achieve.
- Existing instruments have been too short term and inadequately linked into key in-country planning instruments such as the Country Assistance Strategy and the Poverty Reduction Strategy Papers (PRSP).
- Heavy transaction costs have been imposed in-country, which are related to the inadequate sharing of information among international development partners (Allen et al. 2004).

These findings highlight the yawning gap between the talk about coordination and ownership, and actual donor practices, which are neither coordinated nor linked to instruments or institutions within aid-receiving countries.

One concrete result of donors' commitments to coordination and ownership has been the unleashing of competition among aid agencies as to who should 'lead' on coordination and ownership. The Development Assistance Committee of the Organisation for Economic Cooperation and Development won out as the forum for the debate. From a practical point of view, however, the World Bank is well placed to take the lead, having led on the PRSP and developed its role from there. Snapping at its heels, the UNDP is keen to lead in preparing national development strategies and formal mechanisms for dialogue. The result is a somewhat complicated situation in which officials from

DFID, the World Bank, the IMF, the UNDP and other bilateral donors seem to be arguing over who should have the lead role in supporting 'country-led' strategies. Meanwhile, in Paris, donors create elaborate concordats for high-level cooperation and coordination among themselves. Squashed out is a genuine space for developing countries to lead in formulating their own development solutions.

The World Bank has the potential to be a good multilateral forum on development assistance. However, this will require the Bank first to command the confidence of both donors and aid recipients. Donors will cling to their own programmes if they see in the Bank's programme the political vision of individual shareholders, such as the United States. Indeed, to guard against this the Bank was born with constitutional guarantees against political interference both in its funding and in its governance structure. Those guarantees were rapidly pushed aside when the Bank was headquartered in Washington DC and it became clear that the US Executive Director's approval would be a *sine qua non* for any loan (Woods 2006: ch. 1).

Going forward, and to gain greater confidence from donors and aid recipients, the presidency of the Bank should be opened up to an international field, and an appointment made on a meritocratic basis (the President is currently de facto a US appointment). Like the IMF, the board of the World Bank will need reform to give formal power to borrowers. Only once these basic steps are made to shift the accountability of the organization towards its full membership will the Bank earn the trust of those whose cooperation it requires.

Conclusion

The WTO, the IMF and the World Bank each needs substantial reform. The argument against reforming these institutions is often expressed as a trade-off between effectiveness and legitimacy. Effective institutions get things done. This is because they enjoy 'hard power' and can make rules, but also enforce them with pressure and even coercion where required. By contrast, legitimate institutions are talking shops. They spend time and effort ensuring representation and participation, but get little done (the United Nations General Assembly is often cited). Opening up the WTO, the IMF and the World Bank, it is said, will render them ineffectual. But this is false reasoning. Different institutions derive their legitimacy from different sources. A central bank's legitimacy may derive from its fulfilment of inflation targets, while a parliament's legitimacy derives from its representativeness, not its impact on inflation. In the case of the WTO, the World Bank and the IMF, there are very strong grounds for believing that the exclusion and alienation of many developing countries from formal power is a barrier to their effectiveness, and that more openness, accountability and representativeness will enhance their performance.

To meet the challenges of the coming decade, the world needs stronger global economic institutions that are well led and properly resourced, representative and equipped to provide a diverse set of global public goods. As a leading player in international development and with a record of sound economic management, the UK is well placed to contribute to this debate and to help influence international thinking. A progressive UK government should be a powerful advocate for far-reaching reform to the structures of global economic governance.

Notes

1 I am particularly grateful to Vijay Joshi for his clear exposition of this.
2 Milanovic notes that since Dollar and Kraay use purchasing power parity (PPP)-adjusted income figures, the importance of traded prices to the economy is massively reduced; when he removes this PPP adjustment, the result changes.
3 The Bank subsequently integrated its own assessments (for example, in the Philippines, Bosnia and Herzegovina, Turkey and Zambia).

References

Advisory Centre on WTO Law (2004) 'Advisory Centre on WTO Law Decision 2004/3', 26 March; available at: www.acwl.ch/e/pdf/time_budget_e.pdf.
Ahmed, M. (2006) 'Votes and voice: reforming governance at the World Bank', in N. Birdsall (ed.), *Rescuing the World Bank: a CGD Working Group report and selected essays,* Washington, DC: Center for Global Development.
Allen, R., Schiavo-Campo, S. and Columkill-Garrity, T. (2004) *Assessing and Reforming Public Financial Management: a new approach*, Washington, DC: World Bank.
Bown, C. and Hoekman, B. (2005) 'The WTO dispute settlement and the missing developing country cases: engaging the private sector', *Journal of International Economic Law*, 8(4), pp. 861–90.
Chang, H. (2002) *Kicking Away the Ladder: development strategy in historical perspective*, London: Anthem Press.
Chin, J. and Grossman, G. (1991) *Intellectual Property Rights and North–South Trade*, National Bureau of Economic Research Working Paper no. 2769, Cambridge, Mass.: NBER.

DiCaprio, A. and Gallagher, K. (2006) 'The WTO and the shrinking of development space: how big is the bite?', *Journal of World Investment and Trade*, 7(5), pp. 781–804.

Dollar, D. and Kraay, A. (2000) *Trade, Growth and Poverty*, World Bank Policy Research Working Paper no. 2615, Washington, DC: World Bank.

Dollar, D. and Kraay, A. (2002) 'Growth is good for the poor', *Journal of Economic Growth*, 7(3), pp. 195–225.

Easterly, W., Levine, R. and Roodman, D. (2003) *New Data, New Doubts: revisiting aid, policies and growth*, Working Paper no. 26, Washington, DC: Center for Global Development.

Galbraith, J. (2002) 'By the numbers, response to Dollar and Kraay', *Foreign Affairs*, 81(4), pp. 178–9.

Global Governance (2006) 'Special Issue: Understanding the pathways through financial crises and the impact of the IMF', *Global Governance*, 12(4), October–December.

Hanns, U. (2004) 'Expansionist intellectual property protection and reductionist competition rules: a TRIPS perspective', *Journal of International Economic Law*, 7(2), pp. 401–30.

IMF Independent Evaluation Office (2004) *Evaluation of the IMF's Approach to Capital Account Liberalization*, Washington, DC: International Monetary Fund.

Jawara, F. and Kwa, A. (2004) *Behind the Scenes at the WTO: the real world of international trade negotiations*, London: Zed.

Joshi, V. (2003) 'India and the impossible trinity', *World Economics*, 26(4), pp. 555–83.

Joshi, V. (2006) 'Global exchange rate arrangements are not fit for purpose', manuscript, Oxford University.

Kanbur, R. (2005) *Reforming the Formula: a modest proposal for introducing development outcomes in IDA allocation procedures*, Ithaca, NY: Cornell University.

Lall, S. and Teubal, M. (1998) 'Market-stimulating technology policies in developing countries: a framework with examples from East Asia', *World Development*, 26(8), pp. 1369–85.

Lombardi, D. and Woods, N. (2007) 'The political economy of surveillance', manuscript, Oxford.

Markusen, J. (1998) *Contracts, Intellectual Property Rights, and Multinational Investment in Developing Countries*, National Bureau of Economic Research Working Paper no. 6448, Cambridge, Mass.: NBER.

Milanovic, B. (2003) 'The two faces of globalization: against globalization as we know it', *World Development*, 4(4), pp. 667–83.

Milanovic, B. (2004) 'Can we discern the effects of globalization on income distribution? Evidence from household surveys', *World Bank Economic Review*, 19(1), pp. 21–44.

Organisation for Economic Cooperation and Development (1996) *Shaping the 21st Century: the contribution of development cooperation*, Paris: OECD.

Organisation for Economic Cooperation and Development (2005) 'Paris declaration on aid effectiveness', 'Aid harmonisation and alignment: summary of initiatives', *Harmonisation, Alignment, Results: report on progress, challenges and opportunities*. Background paper for the High-Level Forum on Aid Effectiveness, Paris, 28 February–2 March, Paris: OECD.

Prasad, E., Rogoff, K., Wei, S. and Kose, M. (2003) *Effects of Financial Globalization on Developing Countries: some empirical evidence*, Washington, DC: International Monetary Fund.

Rodrik, D. (1992) 'The limits of trade policy reform in developing countries', *Journal of Economic Perspectives*, 6(1), pp. 87–105.

Rodrik, D. (1994) *King Kong meets Godzilla: the World Bank and the East Asian miracle*, CEPR Discussion Paper no. 944, London: Centre for Economic Policy Research.

Rodrik, D. and Rodríguez, F. (1999) *Trade Policy and Economic Growth: a skeptic's guide to the cross-national evidence*, National Bureau of Economic Research Working Paper no. 7081, Cambridge, Mass.: NBER.

Shaffer, G. (2003) *Defending Interests: public–private partnerships in WTO litigation*, Washington, DC: Brookings Institution Press.

Stiglitz, J. (2006) *Making Globalization Work*, London: Allen Lane.

Wade, R. (1990) *Governing the Market: economic theory and the role of government in East Asian industrialization*, Princeton, NJ: Princeton University Press.

Wade, R. H. (2004) 'Is globalisation reducing poverty and inequality?', *World Development*, 32(4), pp. 567–89.

Woods, N. (2006) *The Globalizers: the IMF, the World Bank, and their borrowers*, Ithaca, NY: Cornell University Press.

Woods, N. and Lombardi, D. (2006) 'Uneven patterns of governance: how developing countries are represented in the IMF', *Review of International Political Economy*, 13(3), pp. 480–515.

12

Redesigning UK Foreign Policy

Leni Wild and Paul D. Williams

How can the machinery of the UK state be changed to help put progressive principles into practice, and how can the individuals who make
UK foreign policy be encouraged to pursue more progressive options?
In this chapter we address these questions. We explore the UK Labour
government's record on foreign policy since it took office in May 1997
and we propose a framework that might guide progressive foreign
policy making in the UK. Here we align ourselves with the approach to
defining 'progressive' set out by the editors in the introduction to this
volume.

By 'policy' we mean the 'formulation of desired outcomes which are
intended (or expected) to be consequent upon decisions adopted (or
"made") by those who have the authority (or ability) to commit the
machinery of state and a significant fraction of national resources to
that end' (Vital 1968: 11). Policy making thus involves discernment of
what a desirable world might look like and how state representatives
may bring it about through conscious action. By 'foreign policy' we
mean the sum of official attempts to formulate desired outcomes for
issues that lie beyond the territory of the UK state. Foreign policy is
therefore about choices. This chapter is concerned with setting out
what might count as progressive political choices and how they might
be effectively operationalized.

It is also important to be clear about whether our focus is redesign-
ing a single UK foreign policy or lots of different UK foreign policies.
Here we take our cue from David Vital's conclusion that 'there is no
such animal' as 'British foreign policy in general . . . Instead, there
are . . . a great many policies on a great many matters, coexisting,

often uncomfortably and uncertainly, at various levels of definition, priority and recognition' (Vital 1968: 10). It therefore seems sensible to draw a distinction between grand strategy – that is, attempts to steer a coordinated path for the UK's external affairs – and specific foreign policies.

Since it assumed office in 1997, the Labour government has set out its desired outcomes in a variety of key statements and publications (see Williams 2005). These were summarized by the then Foreign Secretary Jack Straw in the Foreign and Commonwealth Office (FCO) White Paper of March 2006. 'At the heart of any foreign policy', Straw wrote,

> must lie a set of fundamental values. For this Government, the values that we promote abroad are those that guide our actions at home. We seek a world in which freedom, justice and opportunity thrive, in which governments are accountable to the people, protect their rights and guarantee their security and basic needs. We do so because these are the values we believe to be right. And because such a world is the best guarantee of the security and prosperity of the people of the United Kingdom. (Foreign and Commonwealth Office 2006: 4)

The bumper-sticker version of these principles is that the FCO's aim for the next decade or so is a safe, just and prosperous world to be achieved through the realization of ten core objectives (see the appendix). Few would disagree with such goals. The controversy lies in how these concepts are defined and implemented within particular contexts. A new orientation in the formulation and implementation of foreign policies could help them cohere around these 'fundamental values', as well as setting them within a progressive, but realistic, framework.

We suggest that any reorientation should ensure that future progressive foreign policies:

- involve a broad definition of UK interests;
- secure domestic legitimacy;
- are devised through accountable and transparent structures;
- show a respect for international law;
- are consistent and coherent; and
- are designed on the basis of a realistic appraisal of the available resources.

The rest of this chapter sets out these six dimensions and analyses the UK Labour government's record in each of them.

Broadening interests

Whose interests should be served by UK foreign policies? For progressives, the foreign policy-making machinery has moved beyond traditional, narrow definitions of the UK's national interest, which emphasized the accumulation of power in order to balance potential rivals. Today, an exclusively national conception of security is neither politically nor morally tenable for a power in the UK's position. Global interdependence has blurred the distinction between national and international security. More than ever before, 'our' security now depends on achieving greater security for others (Wild 2006). Consequently, we suggest that UK interests should include broader global security challenges and an enhanced emphasis on global social and economic justice.

Reframing traditional definitions of the UK's core national interests would involve a recognition that progressive states should not pursue foreign policies that ignore the needs of foreigners. Instead, as E. H. Carr put it nearly seventy years ago, a progressive 'British policy must take into account the welfare of Lille or Düsseldorf or Lodz as well as the welfare of Oldham or Jarrow' (Carr 1939: 239). Today places beyond Europe such as Bunia, Dili, El-Fashir, Freetown, Grozny and Harare should be added to Carr's list.

Broadening our conception of the national interest has both ethical and strategic imperatives. For progressives, a commitment to tackling global issues like climate change, poverty, underdevelopment, large-scale human rights abuses and major health challenges like polio and HIV/AIDs should necessarily be part of a commitment to global social justice. But strategically too, the UK's interests are largely manifested within the global economy and within regional and international institutions. Ensuring greater international stability by tackling conflict, poverty or climate change should therefore be seen as part of 'our' national interest.

To a certain extent, Blair's government has made significant progress in defining the UK's interests in a way that takes account of common global issues such as climate change, world poverty and international peace and security, as well as more specific agendas like the Millennium Development Goals and prioritizing development in Africa. But some of its policies, for example towards Iraq, have contributed to global instability. They may have also impacted directly on the UK's 'narrow' national interest – for example, by increasing the likelihood of terrorist attacks.

Progressive policies are not defined solely by their content. The process by which they are formulated is also important. A broad understanding of the UK's interests should also involve changes to the policy-making process, to ensure that (a) there is a broad understanding of the long-term trends and drivers which may impact on those interests; and (b) there is much greater interrogation of policy decisions throughout the policy-making process.

First, one practical way in which the process of decision making could be coordinated around a progressive agenda is to develop a more systematic appreciation of long-term trends and drivers of sociopolitical change. Too often the UK may have overlooked events or developments (from terrorism to climate change) which impact on UK security because of insufficient mapping of these trends in the first place. Currently this kind of evaluation is primarily carried out by the Ministry of Defence (MOD), although the FCO also produces longer-term analysis on an ad hoc basis (Yiu and Mabey 2005). Several other departments also engage in long-term strategic planning, including the Department for International Development (DFID), the Department of Trade and Industry (DTI), the Department of Environment, Food and Rural Affairs (DEFRA) and the Treasury. However, there is little sharing of data and analysis across departments. One suggestion put forward by the Prime Minister's Strategy Unit in 2005 was for the Cabinet Office to play a greater role in long-term trend analysis, with a bigger team devoted to modelling and analysis that could pull together the relevant data from each government department (Prime Minister's Strategy Unit 2005). At its core, such a team should operate within a 'progressive framework' informed by a broad definition of UK interests.

Secondly, there are surprisingly few mechanisms which ensure that policies are interrogated and challenged throughout the policy-making process, from inception to development to implementation (Lodge and Kalitowski 2007). When making foreign policy, numerous unforeseen challenges to policy evaluation and learning may emerge. In such politically charged and time-sensitive environments, an exhaustive bureaucratic process of evaluation would make little sense. But the necessity of engaging in crisis management should not stop policy-makers asking whether particular policies worked or what might be learnt for the future. Instead, 'Systematic appraisal and evaluation needs to be institutionalised and should not just take place "after-the-event" but needs to be an iterative process, ensuring the deliverability of policy is challenged throughout' (Lodge and Kalitowski 2006: 30).

In essence, progressives should encourage UK foreign policy-makers to go beyond lowest common denominator standards on issues of global concern, and to open up the process by which UK foreign policies are developed and formulated. The aim of this exercise should be to bring the government's understanding of what is progressive and what is realistic closer together.

Domestic legitimacy

Since progressive foreign policies should be conducted in the name of the British people, those policies need to be perceived as legitimate by them. In practice, UK foreign policies need to resonate with the self-images of three key constituencies:

- The government: do policies conform to the UK's self-image as a member of the European Union (EU), a permanent member of the United Nations (UN) Security Council and a liberal democracy?
- The political party elected to power: do policies conform to the party's manifesto commitments?
- The public: do policies enjoy a broad degree of support in measures of public opinion?

The last of these constituencies is clearly the most nebulous, but the difficulties involved in measuring or responding to public opinion should not serve as an excuse to ignore the importance of seeking domestic legitimacy for foreign policies. Although diminishing turnout at recent elections suggests that the British public is increasingly turned off by politics in Westminster, public awareness of and interest in international issues has grown significantly in recent years, with events such as 9/11, campaigns centred on international debt relief and 'making poverty history', and opposition to the Iraq war serving as particular focal points.

Yet widespread public interest in foreign policies remains erratic, with issues related to the Middle East and the 'war on terror' dominating the public agenda. New Labour's years in power have also witnessed a significant rise in domestic advocacy groups where certain constituencies lobby the government extensively on a few specific foreign policy issues. Examples are the South Asian diaspora advocating policies on the conflict in Kashmir, Muslim groups raising concerns about the UK's role in the US-led 'war on terror' and environmental activists pressing the government to tackle global climate change.

Involving the general public in foreign policy is both operationally difficult and may not improve the policy-making process if participants are not well informed. As Christopher Hill puts it, foreign policy is 'a serious business – too serious . . . to risk it falling into inexpert hands' (Hill 2003a: 234).

One way to enhance domestic legitimacy could be to ensure that policy formulation draws more effectively on those individuals and groups with relevant expertise. This would not guarantee greater public support for a given foreign policy, but it would open up the foreign policy-making process and could encourage a greater element of contestation and discussion regarding policy making. To date, Blair's government has made a more concerted effort than its predecessors to involve outside parties in the policy-making process. It has done so both by hiring greater numbers of staff from relevant non-governmental organizations (NGOs) and the business sector to work within government and by engaging in a variety of public consultation exercises. Yet the Strategic Defence Review, arguably the most significant of these exercises for foreign policy, appears to have been rather unwilling to take heterodox views into account (Croft 2001).

The current civil service structure also often works against hiring those with real expertise, except at a limited number of entry points. For example, the FCO has only one main entry point for 'high flyers' (the Fast Track scheme). Creating more of a 'revolving door' culture in which specialists could be brought in on fixed-term contracts to work on specific projects might enable the utilization of a greater spectrum of expertise and a wider basis for comparing alternative policy options. Such initiatives would have to be carefully managed to avoid them contributing to a loss of cohesion within the diplomatic profession and civil service. Nevertheless, the arguments for not engaging more thoroughly with outside sources of expertise are no longer persuasive.

More broadly, the concept of 'contestability' has become increasingly popular within domestic public service delivery, but it has yet to be applied to the policy process (Lodge and Kalitowski 2006). This is particularly true in relation to foreign policy. As a result, the civil service has not fully exploited the range of expertise and knowledge available. This may point to the need to redefine the role of the civil service in the policy-making process. For example, ippr research has revealed a trend towards remodelling the role of senior civil servants, from providing policy advice to acting as policy coordinators: building networks and policy communities with experts on the outside and facilitating feedback and learning (Lodge and Rogers 2006). This recasting of the role of senior civil servants would require new skills and training, as well as attitudinal shifts within departments involved in making foreign policies.

Accountability and transparency

During Blair's period in office the most pressing foreign policy decisions were formulated within an unusually small core executive – the so-called 'denocracy' (Seldon 2004) – and through various forms of (often informal) bilateralism between No. 10 and the relevant ministry (Heffernan 2006). In a sense, this was neither completely novel nor surprising: the most significant foreign policies have traditionally been decided by the top levels of the decision-making hierarchy (the Prime Minister, their advisers and various Cabinet committees), whereas routine matters of lesser significance have been left to ministers and officials lower down the pecking order. Yet particularly after the invasion of Iraq, most public criticism of UK foreign policy focused on two issues that flowed directly from Blair's style of government: the secretive manner in which key foreign policy decisions appear to have been taken (Kettell 2006) and the increased potential for 'groupthink' to occur when decision-makers did not subject their views to rigorous critical scrutiny from sceptical parties (Butler 2004). Progressive foreign policies must therefore ensure that greater levels of transparency, accountability and critical reflection are built into the decision-making system. This should also help build support for policies within domestic society.

In the UK case, two key areas of concern in terms of accountability revolve around the powers bestowed under the royal prerogative and the inability of the current system of select committees effectively to hold the executive to account.

The historical evolution of the royal prerogative has enabled the government to declare war and sign treaties without first having to secure permission from Parliament. Like its predecessors, Blair's government justified the use of the royal prerogative by highlighting that ministers are still held to account in Parliament through the doctrines of collective and individual responsibility. Yet the current system of ministerial accountability to Parliament is widely acknowledged to be too broad, retrospective and vulnerable to executive power to be an effective check on the Prime Minister's use of the prerogative (Burall et al. 2006). In one sense, the Iraq war represented a departure from normal practice in that Parliament actually voted on a substantive motion to deploy armed forces abroad before fighting had begun. Yet the vote was not necessary for the Prime Minister to authorize the invasion, and Parliament had to rely on the government to provide sufficient information and allow for debate.

These concerns were echoed in a 2005 report by the House of Lords Constitution Committee, which concluded that 'the exercise of the

Royal prerogative by the Government to deploy armed force overseas is outdated and should not be allowed to continue as the basis for legitimate war-making in our 21st century democracy' (House of Lords 2005: 41). The report recommended the creation of 'a parliamentary convention determining the role Parliament should play in making decisions to deploy force or forces outside the United Kingdom to war, intervention in an existing conflict or to environments where there is a risk that the forces will be engaged in conflict' (House of Lords 2005: 42).

If adopted, this recommendation would involve scrutinizing a wide variety of operations in which British troops participate and where the likelihood of them engaging in violent conflict is high. In the last decade, this would have included operations assembled by the UN, the EU, the North Atlantic Treaty Organization (NATO) and coalitions of the willing such as the Australian-led INTERFET force in East Timor (1999) or the International Security Assistance Force in Afghanistan (2001). It might also raise questions about the deployment of troops in more traditional peacekeeping environments such as UNFICYP in Cyprus or UNMIK in Kosovo.

Previous attempts to find a statutory solution have proved unsuccessful and unworkable, as seen by the failures of various Private Member's Bills. For some, however, the Iraq war vote can be seen as playing a precedent-setting function for such a convention. For instance, Chancellor of the Exchequer Gordon Brown highlighted his commitment to this idea in his speech to the Labour Party conference in September 2006: 'while there must be scope for emergency action, it is in my view right that in future, Parliament, not the executive, makes the final decisions on matters as important as peace and war' (Brown 2006).

A challenging issue is: which deployments of UK forces would count as those requiring parliamentary scrutiny? For example, in June 2003, just months after the invasion of Iraq, approximately 100 British troops were deployed to the Democratic Republic of the Congo (DRC) as part of a French-led Interim Emergency Force that was expected to engage in violent conflict. Codenamed Operation Artemis, this force was granted a Chapter 7 mandate by the UN Security Council and was intended to act as a fire-fighting force to help beleaguered UN forces in the eastern DRC province of Ituri. The decision to deploy these British troops was not put to Parliament. On its own, therefore, and at least in deployments authorized by the UN Security Council, the Iraq vote was not enough to generate the kind of procedural sea-change that both Brown and the House of Lords report discussed. It may, however, have set a progressive precedent for the next occasion when the government wishes to deploy troops without clear UN Security Council authorization.

The House of Lords committee argued that if such a convention did become the norm, Parliament would be empowered to scrutinize any government proposal to deploy troops on the basis of a range of evidence and information provided by government. It would also need to be kept informed of the progress of such deployments. Subject to some specified exceptions, prior parliamentary approval would be required to authorize deployment. In exceptional cases, for reasons of emergency or security, retroactive ratification could be permitted (House of Lords 2005). These recommendations provide the starting point for designing a practical solution to the democratic deficit inherent in the royal prerogative powers. In an era when troop deployment is likely to be both frequent and controversial, reform is badly needed.

The royal prerogative powers also cover the signing of treaties, concluding international agreements and conducting trade negotiations. The UK government currently enters into approximately fifty treaties a year through the use of these powers. These treaties cover a huge range of topics, from security issues to vital economic matters with profound effects on the UK and the world, including agreements between the UK and organizations like the World Trade Organization and the International Monetary Fund (House of Commons 2003).

The lack of parliamentary scrutiny of these major decisions represents a further obstacle to accountability in foreign policy making. Despite their importance, there is no publicly available single list of all the UK's treaty obligations: the FCO estimates that the UK is party to 14,712 treaties but does not know for certain how many of these are still in force (Burall et al. 2006). There is no need for parliamentary approval or ratification if a treaty can be implemented without new legislation. While governments clearly need to retain some flexibility when engaging in international negotiations, other liberal democracies, including the US, do allow for parliamentary ratification of their treaty commitments. Burall et al. (2006) thus recommend that before any major negotiations, there should be dialogue between government and the relevant select committee to ensure parliamentary input at the formative stages. This is a sensible suggestion which would give ministers a 'soft mandate' from Parliament while still allowing for some flexibility.

Any increases in parliamentary oversight will need to be accompanied by an increase in the resources, staffing and status accorded to the select committees. Here the differences between the UK's select committees and the American congressional committees are significant. While allowing for the differences between US and UK political systems, the UK could do worse than embodying some elements of the US committee system, especially since some UK select committees often fail to fulfil even their basic scrutiny roles. As Anthony Sampson notes, on the crucial issue of the Iraq war, the relevant select committees lacked 'the proper legal resources, and they did not discover anything of importance about the goings-on before the Iraq war to compare with the mine of information that Lord Hutton produced' (Sampson 2004b). In comparison, congressional committees are able to employ 'teams of lawyers and researchers who amass volumes of evidence and who can conduct hearings like major trials, attracting both publicity and respect' (Sampson 2004a: 14). Short of fundamentally altering the UK's political structures, there is no simple solution to this problem. For example, granting the select committees more resources will not alter the fact that the political party in power has a majority on all of them. But as a first step, the committees require more funding so that they can recruit expert staff in order better to carry out their basic functions.

Whilst improving accountability is crucial, and some possible reforms have been highlighted above, another important area is transparency and scrutiny. During Blair's government there were several examples of murky decision making. Key among them was the UK's decision in June 2004 to renew the 1958 US–UK Mutual Defence Agreement. This was done with almost no public debate despite the fact that the agreement may well be in breach of the UK's commitment to disarm its nuclear arsenal under Article VI of the Nuclear Non-Proliferation Treaty (NPT) (Singh and Chinkin 2004).

Similar issues of transparency could be raised about the debate on whether to replace the Trident nuclear system, the decision to build two new 65,000-ton *Queen Elizabeth* class aircraft carriers and the decision to support the US system of missile defence. For instance, the government's secretive behaviour on the last of these decisions prompted the Commons Defence Committee to accuse then Defence Secretary Geoff Hoon of displaying a 'lack of respect' for those opposed to the government's decision and acting 'in a way that has effectively curtailed [public] discussions'. The committee concluded that the MOD had handled 'the public debate' on the issue in a 'deplorable' manner (Defence Committee 2003).

One area where issues of public scrutiny have been particularly contentious is the use of the UK's intelligence services. The Butler inquiry shed considerable light on the way the UK's £1.5 billion p.a. intelligence services had been used by the Labour government. But such ad hoc inquiries, with terms of reference set by the executive, are no substitute for institutionalized parliamentary oversight of security intelligence (Gill and Phythian 2006).

The UK's Intelligence and Security Committee should theoretically provide this oversight, but it has a limited mandate (mainly focusing on finance and administration of policy) and it reports to the Prime Minister rather than to Parliament. This has prompted calls for a joint parliamentary committee that would assume strategic oversight of international defence and foreign policy interests (Burall et al. 2006). However, this would duplicate much of the work conducted by the existing House of Commons Defence and Foreign Affairs Select Committees. A more practical proposal would be for these two committees to receive increased resources and staff to allow more coordinated oversight of these issues (as recommended in House of Lords 2005).

Legality

Progressive foreign policies should be formulated with respect for international law and should encourage other states to do likewise. First and foremost this means that progressive policies should live up to the UK's international legal obligations (in public international law, human rights law and international humanitarian law). They should also be sensitive to the commitments the UK has entered into through its membership of approximately 120 international organizations. This is particularly important with regard to the multilevel governance structures in which the UK participates as a member of the EU.

Although the vast majority of New Labour's foreign policies clearly operated with respect for international law, critics have pointed to some high-profile cases that call into question the depth of the government's commitment in this regard. These include:

- the so-called 'Arms-to-Africa' affair where the FCO turned a blind eye to a UK private military firm providing weapons to the government of Sierra Leone in breach of a UN arms embargo;
- the persistent aerial bombing of Iraq in order to protect the no-fly zones in the north and south of the country;
- UK participation in NATO's bombardment of Kosovo/Serbia in 1999;
- the renewal of the US–UK Mutual Defence Agreement (2004) that was arguably in breach of Article VI of the NPT; and
- the invasion of Iraq in March 2003.

Of course, since international law is not static, progressive policies should also be formulated to make the case for changing certain international legal conventions. Such proposals, however, should resonate with customary practice and *opinio juris*.

In this regard, it is the Blair government's position on the legality of unilateral humanitarian intervention (i.e. intervention without UN Security Council authorization) that has been most widely debated (Williams 2005). A controversial case was NATO's use of humanitarian arguments to justify its intervention in Kosovo/Serbia in 1999. The government's legal position was summarized by Defence Secretary George Robertson in the following terms:

> We are in no doubt that NATO is acting within international law. Our legal justification rests upon the accepted principle that force may be used in extreme circumstances to avert a humanitarian catastrophe. These circumstances clearly exist in Kosovo. The use of force . . . can be justified as an exceptional measure in support of the purposes laid down by the UN Security Council, but without the Council's express authorisation when that is the only means to avert an immediate and overwhelming humanitarian catastrophe. (Robertson 1999)

The UK's argument thus hinged on its claim that states had a limited right to enforce existing UN Security Council resolutions authorized under Chapter 7 of the UN Charter in cases where the use of force was necessary to avert an imminent humanitarian catastrophe. Most international lawyers took a different view and condemned NATO's actions as illegal. After the bombings, however, the Independent International Commission on Kosovo concluded that the intervention was 'illegal but legitimate' (Independent International Commission on Kosovo 2000).

As the Kosovo case demonstrates, progressives may sometimes need to devise trade-offs between their commitment to international law and their commitment to act to prevent gross human rights abuses. Such scenarios are likely to occur because the UN Security Council has never authorized a humanitarian intervention against the wishes of a functioning state government, even though many states persistently fail to live up to their responsibility to protect their citizens. But where possible, a progressive government should remain within the boundaries of international law and maintain a commitment to push legal conventions to develop in progressive directions. The Iraq invasion was particularly damaging to Blair's government in this respect, not least because it has reduced the likelihood of creating an international consensus about the circumstances in which unilateral humanitarian intervention might be considered legitimate (Evans 2004).

A less controversial example of changing international law in a progressive direction is the way in which the Labour government, unlike its Conservative predecessor, decided to join the so-called Like Minded Group of states during the preparatory negotiations to create an International Criminal Court. This was designed to complement the work of national courts in trying individuals charged with genocide, crimes against humanity and war crimes.

Consistency and coherence

Progressive policies should be logically consistent with one another and strive to avoid double standards and contradictions across different issue areas. This does not mean ignoring the unique circumstances of specific cases and adopting a uniform or principled response regardless of all other considerations. For instance, it is unhelpful and unrealistic to argue that because the government was able to use military force in defence of human rights in Sierra Leone, it is automatically obliged to do so in other desperate situations such as Chechnya, Zimbabwe and Myanmar (Brown 2003).

Rather, it implies that declared policy goals should be consistent with one another and that the means that are most likely to bring about those ends in the long term should be adopted. The means/ends issue has been the source of much controversy since the UK declared its support for the US-led 'war on terror'. As the debates over the Prevention of Terrorism Act 2005 highlight, a key issue has been the methods called for by the government to combat terrorism, and the alleged trade-offs between human rights and security considerations (see chapter 3 in this volume).

The Labour government's foreign policies have also suffered from a variety of contradictions and double standards at the level of grand strategy (Dunne 2004, Williams 2005). For example, an important tension emerged between the UK's commitment to stand 'shoulder to shoulder' with the US in its 'war on terror' and its goal to promote multilateralism, especially within the EU (see chapter 6 in this volume).

There have also been tensions between the government's declared support for development and its desire to sell British military systems and arms abroad. For example, the FCO's 2005 Human Rights Report identified twenty 'major countries of concern' but failed to acknowledge that, in 2004, UK arms export licences were approved to thirteen of these (Campaign Against the Arms Trade 2006). Equally, arguments surfaced between DFID and the Treasury on the one hand and the MOD, DTI and No. 10 on the other over the licensing of a £28 million, BAE-built military air-traffic control system to Tanzania in December 2001. The latter group won out, and the air-traffic control system was sold to Tanzania despite the fact that this breached the government's own guidelines on sustainable development (see Stavrianakis 2005).

Strategies are therefore needed that will encourage greater policy coherence where departmental priorities conflict and will provide incentives for those individuals and/or departments articulating progressive policies. Some important lessons might be learned from the experience of Sweden, which in 2003 instituted a government-wide policy of 'coherence' to ensure that all departmental policies are consistent with each other and with the Swedish government's commitment to development (Swedish Government Communication 2005). Overall, coherence is likely to be enhanced if the policy-making process is more transparent and there is greater coordination across departments.

Better coordination would help reduce the likelihood of conflicting priorities arising in the first place. 'Joined-up government' has been something of a mantra for New Labour but it has proved difficult to achieve in practice. To take just one example, the Africa All Party Parliamentary Group concluded in 2005 that effective implementation of the recommendations set out in Blair's Commission for Africa would require new and coordinated action from the Attorney General, the Office of the Leader of the House of Commons and nine UK government departments. Yet in practice, some departments have been working at cross-purposes. For example, UK attempts to recruit African doctors and nurses to work in the National Health Service have contributed to the African 'brain-drain', which depletes some of the continent's poorest states of significant numbers of their health professionals (although a Code of Practice on International Recruitment has sought to address this issue).

This is exacerbated by the fact that over the last decade, departments traditionally seen as 'domestic' have become increasingly concerned with foreign policy. The domestic–foreign divide is arguably most blurred in the EU context where, for example, the Home Office has been heavily involved in negotiations on Romanian and Bulgarian EU accession due to the links with immigration issues. If progressive foreign policies are to be pursued effectively, it will be necessary to develop a more holistic approach to foreign policy making that embraces all relevant departments.

A positive attempt to join up departments emerged in 2001 with the establishment of the Conflict Prevention Pools (one for Africa and one for the rest of the globe). The pools are jointly run by the FCO, MOD and DFID, and aim to enhance the UK's contribution to conflict prevention and management. Although credited as a worthy venture, they lack sufficient resources and are often hard-pressed to find common ground on which to agree (Austin Brusset et al. 2003). It is too early to say whether the Post-Conflict Reconstruction Unit (established at the end of 2004) will surmount these barriers more effectively. But while more cross-departmental initiatives like this would be useful, they alone do not provide a solution.

Another proposal for improving 'joined-up' foreign policies would be to strengthen links between, but not re-merge, the FCO and DFID. In line with the Labour Party's tradition (started in 1964) of having a separate department for international development, Blair's government established DFID instead of retaining the Conservative approach of administering overseas aid from within the FCO. This was an important indication of Labour's ongoing commitment to international development.

Since 1997, DFID has grown in international status to become a leading player in the development community. But the FCO and DFID are now perhaps too separate, with different cultures, processes and priorities. In terms of priorities, for instance, the FCO leads on the 'high politics' of diplomatic relations whereas DFID focuses on the implementation of the UK's aid programmes and its support for the provision of key services and capacity building. But in practice, diplomatic relations should also take account of development needs and impacts. Similarly, development projects need to take greater account of the broader political context in which they operate. To some extent such a synthesis is taking place (e.g. Department for International Development 2006), but real benefits may result from further linking up the analyses of both departments.

Greater sharing of analysis and trend-spotting could only strengthen the work of both the FCO and DFID. One way of improving coherence between the two departments would be to develop joint DFID/FCO analysts, perhaps through the creation of a joint DFID/FCO Strategy Unit. This could improve the strategic analysis of both departments as well as ensuring that both departments work from the same assessment of a given situation. Indeed, there is some evidence of this approach in practice. In 2002, for instance, DFID and the FCO established an integrated unit to coordinate their policies on Sudan. At country level too, housing DFID offices within British embassies would also ensure that staff in the two departments are operationally integrated. This would both cut the costs of operation and facilitate more cross-departmental initiatives in a given country.

Resources

Finally, progressive foreign policies must be realistic. This does not, however, mean following the 'might is right' doctrine of *realpolitik*. Rather it means that foreign policies should be formulated in light of the resources, capabilities and instruments available (see Hill 2003b). It is of little use, except perhaps to the government's critics, to create unrealistic expectations about what UK foreign policies can achieve. A progressive grand strategy needs to recognize the limits of UK power while also attempting to promote change for the better through specific foreign policies. Defining what is realistic today will require a reappraisal of the UK's available resources and ensuring that they are used as wisely as possible.

This raises two related questions: what are the key instruments that the UK has at its disposal, and in what circumstances and parts of the world can these instruments be used most effectively to promote progressive outcomes?

The UK has a number of foreign policy instruments to wield. Here we will mention just four. First, the UK's armed forces could play important roles in certain circumstances. Given their experience in extraterritorial policing and their emphasis on expeditionary campaigns, they are well suited to conducting peace operations and, potentially, humanitarian interventions. As of 31 October 2006, however, the UK provides only 275 troops to three UN peacekeeping operations (in Cyprus 269, Liberia 3 and Sudan 3) and it is ranked thirty-seventh in the UN's list of contributors to peace operations, just above Togo.

Secondly, the UK's strong economy is an important asset when it comes to backing progressive policies with resources as well as words. The UK has an impressive record on development so far, but could afford to give even more support to campaigns of global importance such as those that combat HIV/AIDS. It could also act more decisively to lower carbon emissions; something that the Stern Review on the Economics of Climate Change has suggested is in everyone's long-term interests. Ultimately, decisions will have to be taken about the allocation of national resources, which in foreign policy terms at least remain heavily weighted in favour of the MOD. In comparison, the FCO and DFID are forced to operate on a financial shoestring.

The UK also possesses a significant degree of 'soft power', defined as 'the ability to get what you want through attraction' in circumstances where 'our policies are seen as legitimate in the eyes of others' (Nye 2004: x). The UK can generate soft power by developing its reputation for progressive action to the extent that other actors accord it some degree of authority on the issue(s) in question. This would allow the UK to attract other actors to its foreign policy agenda. Under the Labour government, this type of leadership was evident in several areas, such as debt relief for heavily indebted poor states and bringing attention to Africa's challenges. However, particularly after 9/11, it has become crucial for the UK to enhance its soft power in relation to the Islamic world, and more needs to be done here to offset the negative effects of the Iraq war and the failure to implement the Road Map for peace in the Middle East.

Finally, the importance of the English language abroad should not be underestimated. In this sense, both the British Council and the British Broadcasting Corporation (BBC) are potentially very important vehicles for disseminating information and engaging in public diplomacy. At times, such institutions may help explain UK policies to sceptical, confused, ignorant or even hostile audiences. However, accurate reporting of events can also play an important role in conflict management by dampening ethnic tensions and offering counter-narratives to outlets of ethnic hatred. The BBC World Service's planned Arabic news channel, as well as its planned Farsi language channel, are important developments in this respect (BBC News 2006).

The UK has a significant opportunity to wield all these instruments, not least because of its unique position of being a permanent member of the UN Security Council, as well as a member of the Group of Seven, the EU and the Commonwealth. It should use its prominent position in these organizations to shift the global agenda in progressive directions.

Conclusions

We have offered six principles that should underpin progressive UK foreign policies:

- a broad definition of UK interests;
- the importance of domestic legitimacy;
- the need for accountable and transparent structures;
- respect for international law;
- consistency and coherence across all departments; and
- a realistic appraisal of the available resources.

A key future goal should be to close the gap between what is considered realistic and what is considered progressive. In this vein, we have sought to demonstrate that a commitment to progressive values *can* deliver both ethical and strategic imperatives. At the same time, it is important to acknowledge that these principles may at times pull in different directions on specific issues. The challenge for policy-makers is to devise ways of mediating such conflicts when they do occur.

However, we have also suggested that progressive policies are not defined solely by their content; the process by which they are formulated is also important. Any future government with a commitment to progressive foreign policies must take steps to improve accountability and transparency in foreign policy making. This means: improving Parliament's ability to scrutinize government policy and actions; designing policy-making structures and government departments that offer incentives for the individuals within them to articulate and defend progressive choices; and allowing a space for an informed public debate on grand strategies and choices for UK foreign policy.

Blair's government has a mixed record on these issues. Although it may not be fashionable for any future government or leader to discuss foreign policy implementation, its importance should not be overlooked. Establishing a convention on Parliament's role in decisions to deploy troops or ensuring much greater parliamentary oversight overall, for example, would increase the likelihood that progressive values are put into practice. Policy implementation should be brought in from the cold and placed at the heart of discussions about progressive UK foreign policy.

Appendix: The UK's international priorities (as of September 2006)

- Making the world safer from global terrorism and weapons of mass destruction.
- Reducing the harm to the UK from international crime, including drug trafficking, people smuggling and money laundering.
- Preventing and resolving conflict through a strong international system.
- Building an effective and globally competitive EU in a secure neighbourhood.
- Supporting the UK economy and business through an open and expanding global economy, science and innovation, and secure energy supplies.
- Achieving climate security by promoting a faster transition to a sustainable, low-carbon global economy.
- Promoting sustainable development and poverty reduction underpinned by human rights, democracy, good governance and protection of the environment.

- Managing migration and combating illegal immigration.
- Delivering high-quality support for British nationals abroad, in normal times and in crises.
- Ensuring the security and good governance of the UK's Overseas Territories.

Note

For their helpful comments on earlier drafts of this chapter, thanks go to Simon Caney, Alex Glennie, Alan Hunt, Guy Lodge, David Mepham, Steve Tsang and Ian Taylor.

References

Africa All Party Parliamentary Group (2005) *The UK Government and Africa in 2005: how joined up is Whitehall?*, House of Commons, March.

Austin Brusset, E., Chalmers, M. and Pierce, J. (2003) *Evaluation of the Conflict Prevention Pools: synthesis report*, commissioned by DFID; available at: www.dfid.gov.uk/aboutDFID/performance/files/ev647synthesis.pdf.

BBC News (2006) 'BBC to launch TV channel for Iran', *BBC News Online*; available at: http://news.bbc.co.uk/1/hi/entertainment/6037832.stm.

Brown, C. (2003) 'Selective humanitarianism: in defence of inconsistency', in D. K. Chatterjee and D. E. Scheid (eds), *Ethics and Foreign Intervention*, Cambridge: Cambridge University Press.

Brown, G. (2006) 'We will always strive to be on your side', speech to the Labour Party Conference, 25 September; available at: www.labour.org.uk/index.php?id=news2005&ux_news[id]=onyourside&cHash=dde8057373.

Burall, S., Donnelly, B. and Weir, S. (2006) *Not in Our Name: democracy and foreign policy in the UK*, London: Politico's.

Butler, F. E., Lord (2004) *Review of Intelligence on Weapons of Mass Destruction* (Butler Report), London: The Stationery Office, HC 898.

Campaign Against the Arms Trade (CAAT) (2006) *An Introduction to the Arms Trade*; available at: www.caat.org/publications/intro-briefing-2006.pdf.

Carr, E. H. (1939) *The Twenty Years' Crisis: an introduction to the study of international relations*, London: Macmillan.

Croft, S. (2001) 'Britain's nuclear weapons discourse', in S. Croft, P. Dorman, W. Rees and M. Uttley, *Britain and Defence, 1945–2000*, Harlow: Longman.

Defence Committee (2003) *Missile Defence: first report, 2002–03*, London: The Stationery Office, HC290-I.

Department for International Development (2006) *Eliminating World Poverty: making governance work for the poor* (Government White Paper); available at: www.dfid.gov.uk/wp2006/default.asp.

Dunne, T. (2004) ' "When the shooting starts": Atlanticism in British security strategy', *International Affairs*, 80(5), pp. 893–909.

Evans, G. (2004) 'When is it right to fight?', *Survival*, 46(3), pp. 59–81.

Foreign and Commonwealth Office (2006) *Active Diplomacy for a Changing World: the UK's international priorities*, FCO, Cm 6762.

Gill, P. and Phythian, M. (2006) *Intelligence in an Insecure World*, Cambridge: Polity.

Heffernan, R. (2006) 'The Blair style of central government', in P. Dunleavy, R. Heffernan, P. Cowley and C. Hay (eds), *Developments in British Politics 8*, Basingstoke: Palgrave Macmillan, pp. 17–35.

Hill, C. (2003a) 'What is to be done? Foreign policy as a site of political action', *International Affairs*, 79(2), pp. 233–55.

Hill, C. (2003b) *The Changing Politics of Foreign Policy*, Basingstoke: Palgrave Macmillan.

House of Commons (2003) *Taming the Prerogative: strengthening ministerial accountability to Parliament*, 4th report of session 2003–04, Select Committee on Public Administration.

House of Lords (2005) *Waging War: Parliament's role and responsibility*, 15th report of session 2005–06, Select Committee on the Constitution.

Independent International Commission on Kosovo (2000) *The Kosovo Report: conflict, international response, lessons learned*, Oxford: Oxford University Press.

Kettell, S. (2006) *Dirty Politics? New Labour, British democracy and the invasion of Iraq*, London: Zed.

Lee, D. (2004) 'The growing influence of business in UK diplomacy', *International Studies Perspectives*, 5(1), pp. 50–4.

Lodge, G. and Kalitowski, S. (2007) *Civil Service Reform: international comparisons*, London: Institute for Public Policy Research.

Lodge, G. and Rogers, B. (2006) *Whitehall's Black Box*, London: Institute for Public Policy Research.

Nye, J. S. (2004) *Soft Power: the means to success in world politics*, New York: Public Affairs.

Prime Minister's Strategy Unit (2005) *Investing in Prevention: an international strategy to manage risks of instability and improve crisis response*, Cabinet Office: PMSU.

Robertson, G. (1999) *Hansard* (Commons), 25 March, cols 616–17.

Sampson, A. (2004a) *Who Runs This Place? An anatomy of Britain in the 21st century*, London: John Murray.

Sampson, A. (2004b) RSA Lecture, Edinburgh International Book Festival, 15 August; available at: www.rsa.org.uk/acrobat/anthony_sampson_lecture.pdf.

Seldon, A. (2004) *Blair*, London: Free Press.

Singh, R., QC, and Chinkin, C. (2004) Legal Opinion, Matrix, 20 July; available at: www.basicint.org/nuclear/MDAlegal.htm.

Stavrianakis, A. (2005) '(Big) business as usual: sustainable development, NGOs and UK arms export policy', *Conflict, Security and Development*, 5(1), pp. 45–67.

Swedish Government Communication (2005) *Sweden's Global Development Policy* (Communication 06:204); available at: www.sweden.gov.se/content/1/c6/07/01/68/3e990ee4.pdf.

Vital, D. (1968) *The Making of British Foreign Policy*, London: George Allen and Unwin.

Wild, L. (2006) 'Rules of engagement', *Progress Magazine*, 28 February.

Williams, P. D. (2005) *British Foreign Policy under New Labour, 1997–2005*, Basingstoke: Palgrave Macmillan.

Yiu, C. and Mabey, N. (2005) *Countries at Risk of Instability: practical risk assessment, early warning and knowledge management*, PMSU Background Paper, February, Cabinet Office: Prime Minister's Strategy Unit.

Index